Reunion

REUNION

The Girls We Used to Be,

the Women We Became

ELIZABETH FISHEL

RANDOM HOUSE

NEW YORK

RANDOM HOUSE and colophon are registered trademarks of Random House, Inc.

Library of Congress Cataloging-in-Publication Data
Fishel, Elizabeth.
Reunion : the girls we used to be, the women we became / Elizabeth Fishel. — 1st ed.
p. cm.
ISBN 0-679-44983-3 (alk. paper)
1. Brearley School. Class of 1968.   2. Brearley School—Alumni and alumnae Biography.
I. Title.
LD7501.N494F575   2000
373.747'1—dc21   99-15801

Random House website address: www.atrandom.com
Printed in the United States of America on acid-free paper
2 4 6 8 9 7 5 3
First Edition
Book design by Victoria Wong

To
Franny Taliaferro
and
the Class of '68

The events of childhood do not pass
but repeat themselves like seasons of the year.

—ELEANOR FARJEON

Acknowledgments

Above all my heartfelt thanks and appreciation to my Brearley classmates of 1968 for sharing their lives with me and for their openness and honesty about the years since graduation, the dark times as well as the light. Although I have told their stories as accurately as possible, I have changed their names to protect their privacy.

A special thank-you to Barbara Kohn Katz, my lifelong friend, classmate, and confidante, for sharing her memories and insights, and to the many schoolmates in other classes, faculty, and staff who also contributed valuable observations.

My editor, Kate Medina, and assistant editor, Meaghan Rady, helped shape this manuscript at every stage, and I am greatly indebted to their thoughtful questions and wise suggestions. My appreciation as well to my agent, Joy Harris, and her assistant, Kassandra Duane, who supported and shepherded this project through four years from idea to completion.

Many people gave me welcome advice and encouragement and read the manuscript at various stages. I am especially grateful to my sister, Anne Fishel, also a Brearly alumna as well as an accomplished psychologist and writer, who generously shared her wisdom from all three realms. Special thanks also to my brother-in-law, Christopher Daly, for his journalistic expertise and to consultants and friends

Eileen Pearlman, Ph.D., Michael Thompson, Ph.D., Leah Fisher, Mona Halaby, Josie Gerst, Dusky Pierce, Nancy Pietrefesa, and Merry Selk.

Finally, my deepest gratitude for the love and encouragement of my parents, Edith and James Fishel, who gave me the gift of a Brearley education; my husband, Robert Houghteling, who is my first and most painstaking reader, always supportive both as editor and life mate; and my sons, Nate and Will, whose humor and energy help keep everything in perspective.

Contents

REUNION

Twenty-fifth Reunion

W hen the announcement of my twenty-fifth high school reunion arrived, this book was barely a glint in my eye, a
glimmer just below consciousness. So I circled around the prospect
warily. Was the invitation a gift or a mail bomb? I had spent thirteen
years at the Brearley School, one of New York City's most presti-
gious girls' schools, from kindergarten innocence to senior year
pseudosophistication. Now I wondered how twenty-five years of
history had written on the class of '68 and how my classmates had
written their own histories. One minute affection drew me back
toward the sisterlike closeness I once shared with these women, for
there were only twenty-five who graduated together, one of Brearley's smallest classes ever. The next minute I balked, wanting to
keep my distance from a closeness that, after all those years of school
together, had became cloying.

Something powerful still drew this group back together, even
though most had kept in touch with only a few others after graduation. Many hadn't made a contribution to the school or sent in an
alumnae note to its quarterly for years. When the school held its annual alumnae luncheon, other classes' tables were crowded with
smartly dress-and-jacketed women, buzzing with school spirit and
conviviality. But the class of '68 was always represented spottily.

Even after all this time, my classmates were still not joiners. They were still enough the daughters of iconoclastic times to be wary of institutions, uncomfortable saluting the status quo.

But nonetheless, many classmates showed up at the evening reunion party, even some who had left the school long before graduating, to go to boarding school or to move to another town. Some, blessed with what Cambridge, Massachusetts, psychologist Michael Thompson calls "school brains"—minds that could readily process learning as it was taught in the fifties and sixties—had grateful memories of the place where their talents were first recognized, their gifts first nurtured. Others remembered the school with thorny ambivalence but had let their grudges be softened somewhat by the intervening years. And still others recalled the school almost literally as an alma mater, a kindly mother. For girls whose home lives were unpredictable, the school provided a welcome haven. Its structure, stability, and consistently lofty expectations offered an oasis of civility and dependability in an uncertain childhood landscape.

"We're Brearley born and Brearley bred and when we die, we'll be Brearley dead," schoolmates used to sing. At one time the class was so close the girls knew every detail of one another's lives. If a classmate's essay was found on the floor, others could recognize her handwriting instantly. But as the class graduated, the culture convulsed, and the tight band of girls scattered to different colleges, new and mind-boggling ideologies, and newfound friends who knew them as the fully sculpted characters they'd become, not the shapeless lumps of clay they once were. Old friendships grew awkward, a possible source of embarrassment, like a tactless old relative who remembers you before you stopped sucking your thumb or changed your hair color, and might mention it loudly to a crowd.

But suddenly at forty, old classmates woke up to realize they had more in common with one another than with many others on earth. Once they had dwelt on their differences (the jocks versus the bohemians, the girls who flirted with boys versus the ones who hardly knew the other sex existed). Now they acknowledged their bonds (uniforms, posture pictures, memories of prune whip in the cafeteria and the poems of John Donne). Like old army buddies, they'd been through the wars together and could now grudgingly admit, as my father does about World War II, that it was one of the more colorful and psyche-shaping times of their lives.

So there was an instant, if wary, camaraderie twenty-five years later, when twenty-one classmates gathered for dinner in Simone's showplace Park Avenue apartment. One of the class's handful of late-to-the-altar brides, Simone had just recently married a man whose wealthy parents had recently died, leaving this apartment to him. Everything was done in peaches and cream, with so many plump pillows on the couches that there was no room to sit down. So the long-lost friends all ate sitting cross-legged on the floor, balancing plates on laps, as if back at someone's third-grade birthday party. Along with the peaches-and-cream apartment, Simone's in-laws had also bequeathed a stunning art collection, so classmates nibbled their catered cold salmon, their radicchio salad, and white chocolate cake surrounded by Calder and Nevelson and Niki de Saint-Phalle (coincidentally, class of '49). There was a feeling of "let's pretend," as if furtive daughters were sneaking this party in while parents were away for the weekend. At any minute the older generation could surprise the younger faking it as adults, dressed in their parents' clothes, eating cavalierly off their parents' best china. Behind the gloss of worldly wisdom, the grown women saw each other as little girls walking around in adult-size bodies, crumpled kneesocks and failed spelling tests poking out beneath the designer clothes.

After the coffee was served, the gossip shared, the affectionate sizing-up completed, there was still one surprise that no one could have anticipated. Alexa had come all the way from California for this reunion. Although she had not been in the class since third grade (when she defected to another girls' school, where the academic pressure was less intense), she had come tonight on a special mission. Once she had been best friends with the class's most troubled soul, a twin named Lily. As a young girl, Lily had been eccentric and artistically gifted; while others chuckled over *Peanuts,* she idolized the sinister and sophisticated *New Yorker* cartoonist Edward Gorey. Classmates would huddle around her chair while she drew, almost shamanlike, horses, unicorns, scary but mesmerizing creatures. Her twin sister, Alice, was not as strikingly gifted but was also not as shaky; she was the designated coper in their uneasy symbiosis.

Now, almost three decades after Alexa had last seen her friend, she opened a nondescript folder and spread a sheaf of drawings out across the plush carpet. They were Lily's drawings, and Alexa had saved them since 1960, the year the two girls were ten. They were elaborately detailed drawings of animals and armor, minutely rendered drawings of geometric patterns and shapes. They would have been impressive for an artist of any age. For a girl of ten, they were extraordinary.

Alexa cried softly as she showed them first to Alice, then to the rest of the group, and Alice wept too, for she had not seen any of her sister's artwork in twenty-five years. Lily had burned every other trace of it before she died at eighteen.

The room fell silent as all eyes focused on the pictures and Lily's presence filled the room. The ghost of all that unfulfilled promise, all that talent gone awry, hung heavy, like a shroud.

But it was not just Lily's ghost that haunted the gathering that evening. The room was dense with other unfulfilled promises, other expectations never met. The entire group quaked a little, staring at the gap between schoolgirl dreams, passionate but undefined, and midlife realities. Everyone blushed to survey the distance between what had actually been accomplished and what parents had imagined for their daughters—expectations all the more inflated by postwar fervor, memories of Depression deprivations, and, for mothers especially, frustration over talents unexpressed, potential unexplored. And the group also wondered, perhaps more in private than together, whether this class had disappointed its school.

Brearley girls had always been told they were special. They were told they were lucky to be at the finest girls' school in the biggest city in the most powerful country in the world. But this privilege was both a blessing and a curse. Being special provided a benchmark to live up to, but it was also a long shadow clouding their path. And when the elusive mantle of specialness was combined with the idealism and antimaterialism of the sixties counterculture and the feminism of the seventies women's movement, the double and triple messages could be paralyzing as well as empowering.

Only occasionally did this multiply threaded legacy drive girls to the brink, create internal pressure so overwhelming that it completely stalled forward momentum. Indeed, even tonight there were several old classmates too fragile to show up, too conscious of their vulnerabilities, too fearful of being judged. Some were too hobbled by emotional pain to touch base with the rest of the class; they were still struggling for equilibrium, in and out of treatment, which had never been entirely effective. The others spoke of these classmates kindly, in hushed, protective voices, understanding their pain.

For by forty-three, everyone who turned up at the reunion had reaped the benefits of her education, her privileged milieu, her historical moment, but had also paid the price. The shared culture that the group celebrated that reunion night was marked just as surely by disappointment as by success, by regret as much as by expectations fulfilled.

"There was a feeling that we had to be great—this was our destiny" was the way one classmate, Sophia, articulated for the rest of the group the pressures they had all experienced turning the corner from youth to middle age. The definition of "great" could be different for every member of the class, as indeed for every member of this opportunity-laden, sky's-the-limit generation. Change the world, believed one; amass great wealth and power, dreamed another; write a bestseller, hoped a third; find a cure for cancer, imagined still another. And the early forties came to feel like a time of last-ditch effort, a time, as Sophia put it, of a "last desperate wish for the perfection and greatness we hoped to achieve." When greatness did not come—at least not on the scale or in the shape the girls had once fantasized—"it was a tremendous shock."

So the classmate who had taught part-time so she could raise three children and support her husband when his job assignments bumped them from state to state worried that her interrupted career would seem inconsequential. And the classmate who taught full-time, but taught privileged suburban kids rather than needy inner-city youth, agonized that she had sold out her sixties ideals and betrayed her legacy. The women who "just" stayed home with their kids, satisfied as they might be in private, wondered if others scorned them for underemploying their brains. And the many who didn't have kids at all peeked surreptitiously at the ones showing off family photos and worried that they had missed out on one of life's sweetest pleasures.

Like so many in this choice-rich generation, the class of '68, twenty-five years out of school, was now reaping the consequences of its choices. Once emboldened by seemingly limitless possibilities, now, at midlife, each woman was calculating the distance between the choices she'd made and the ones she'd left untouched. There was satisfaction in this calculus, but also dismay.

"There's a lot of sadness in this room," Alice murmured to a friend, casting her eyes around the group of women, chattering and sipping white wine. Partly she was whispering about herself, dressed head to toe in black. She was just back from years of self-imposed exile in France, with an ended marriage behind her, and she was moving into a new chapter in her life. But many others seemed rudderless and disappointed too. When one friend asked another, "What do you do when you wake up in the morning?" (meaning "What gives direction to your life? What work do you do?"), the response was chillingly literal. "I drink a cup of coffee," she answered. "I eat a bagel. I smoke a cigarette. I make a list of what I hope to accomplish that day." Did she go anywhere or do anything? She didn't say. Like the jaded heroines of the Françoise Sagan novels she loved as a brilliant, curious adolescent, she seemed world-weary. Along with several others, she seemed to be drifting through her life, not shaping it. Were they overwhelmed by too many choices and not able to put passion behind any particular one?

It was from my curiosity about this gap between childhood dreams and midlife realities, between youthful promise and womanly fulfill-ment, that the idea for this book was conceived. Raised to believe they were among their generation's best and brightest, my class can be seen as a bellwether for a generation caught without a compass on the cutting edge of uncharted territory. After graduation they faced an explosion of choices unimaginable when they were school-girls. Each graduate, willing or no, prepared or not, would become a pioneer trying to discover her path on roads that were not yet on anybody's map. Their choices energized and empowered some, stymied or sidelined others. I began this book to find out why.

One Flounders,
the Other Thrives

The day I graduated from Brearley was the day after Robert Kennedy was shot. "He would have wanted your graduation to go on today," the headmistress announced confidently. With her billowing black academic robe, her close-cropped hair, and her Scottish brogue, she was Olympian. Who could doubt her? That noblesse oblige, that expectation of a pipeline from the seat of power to the Brearley girls, was as much a part of the school's philosophy as its academic excellence, its intellectual rigor, its bluestocking eccentricity, its beaver mascot, its motto, "By Truth and Toil."

The school trained the daughters of Rockefellers and Rothschilds, Roosevelts and Kennedys. (The Nixon girls went to Brearley's rival, Chapin, across the street. They were not missed.) Brearley drew its student population from the rich and the nouveaux riches, but mostly from the old rich; many of their daughters never realized their nannies, their East Side brownstones, and their second homes in Amagansett or Bar Harbor were anything out of the ordinary. So when a new girl who entered in high school tried to flaunt "the terraces" of her parents' Fifth Avenue duplex—that *s* was her undoing—she was laughed at behind her back. No one had to advertise her family's wealth. The others took it for granted. But privilege, though it insulated our early lives, would not protect my classmates or me from the shock waves massing beyond the school's walls.

Brearley provided a classical education built on a seventy-five-year tradition, yet it was educating girls for a world that was fast becoming obsolete. They learned Latin and French, read a Shakespeare play every year, from *Julius Caesar* in seventh grade to *Hamlet* senior year, brooded over Charlotte Brontë and Virginia Woolf, and studied the Old Testament as well as the New, debating the ethics of the Book of Job. They were trained to think for themselves but to act like ladies ("Ladies do not sit with their legs apart, talk with their mouths full, or chew gum"). In public speaking, they had the "you knows," "ums," and "ers" removed from their presentations. They were taught to grapple with complex texts and primary sources and analyze them to frame a persuasive essay. They were led to believe that mustering the right evidence would point to an indisputable conclusion.

My classmates were told they could be anything they dreamed of—or at least marry it. But above all, they were expected to take their God-given place in the ruling class, maneuver to the center of the web, use their brains, and make their mark.

Tradition Collides with the Future

Samuel Brearley founded the school in 1884, in a decade that also witnessed the dedication of the Washington Monument, the completion of the Brooklyn Bridge, and the installation of Cleopatra's Needle near the Metropolitan Museum. It was an era of landmarks, and although Brearley was not quite the first New York City girls' school, it would become one of the most venerable and enduring. Mr. Brearley, a Harvard- and Oxford-educated private tutor who had been bypassed as headmaster of Phillips Exeter Academy, made it his mission to offer New York City girls a private-school education of the quality that their brothers took for granted. He struck a rich vein in the upper crust. The first year he had fifty students; the next year one hundred and fifteen; the year after that (which would be his last before his untimely death at thirty-six), there were more students eager for his school's education than he could accept.

From the beginning the school attracted the daughters of both New York City's wealthy Wasp elite and the German-Jewish, Our Crowd aristocracy, who were unwelcome at most other private schools. The roster of parents often read like a Who's Who in the arts, politics, and science. Over the years the daughters and granddaughters of such notables as Eugene O'Neill, Margaret Mead, Henri Matisse, and Leonard Bernstein attended Brearley. In my class alone were offspring of Oscar Hammerstein, Walter Cronkite, the financier Huntington Hartford, and Presidents Franklin Delano Roosevelt and William Howard Taft. Although the school tried to keep its famous families in low profile, at times the telltale signs were as unavoidable as Caroline Kennedy's bodyguards, stationed outside her classroom the year she attended eighth grade, seven years after my class did.

Even after the uptight fifties had given way to the hang-loose sixties, my classmates and I still had one foot firmly planted in the Victorian world, more the descendants of Henry James than the would-be inheritors of Henry Miller. Childhood role models were classic storybook heroines like the Little Princess and Anne of Green Gables. Certain older brothers called their fathers "sir," and most of my schoolmates curtsied when greeting and saying goodbye to one another's parents. One girl remembers curtsying on the receiving line at a seventh-grade dance and being gently corrected: "Now we just extend our hand and nod." She refers to that episode wryly as "the last curtsy in New York." My classmates' lives were full of such anachronisms.

My class's graduation year, 1968, was also the year that *Time* magazine would say "shaped a generation." In 1968 society was upended, and everything the school stood for was suddenly called into question—its staid traditions, its academic single-mindedness, its dedication to good manners, its identification with the power elite, its almost century-old history and continuity. Bracketing my classmates' transition from the sheltered cove of school into the wider, rougher, realer world, crisis and protest rocked the country—events that would come to define the sixties. The year of my commencement was also the year of the barricades, when anti-establishment uprisings, often instigated and led by students, disrupted New York City, this country, the world.

In January of 1968 North Vietnam mounted its Tet offensive, and in its wake the antiwar movement intensified. In April, Martin Luther King's assassination in Memphis provoked nationwide shock and unrest, and nineteen days later, the student occupation of Columbia University buildings brought the student movement only a few miles away from Brearley. In May, student riots at the Sorbonne shut down Paris and riveted worldwide attention. In June, Robert Kennedy's assassination the night he clinched the California primary (only a day before our graduation day) further sobered an assassination-saturated public. And in August, the head-bashing clash between students and police at Chicago's Democratic National Convention stunned my peers yet again with its violence, its senselessness.

On the impressionable brink of independence, my classmates were caught between the old world they had been educated to enter and the new world that was springing up faster than the daisies that hippies incongruously tucked in National Guardsmen's rifles. Seismic shock waves rattled the culture; as Dylan sang, the old order was rapidly changing. Everyone of my generation felt these shock waves, but for my classmates, who came from a rarefied, cushioned world, the jolt was all the more startling. Their disorientation reflects and underscores the unmooring of an entire generation.

Breaking away from Brearley's cloistered, well-mannered, navy-blue-uniformed domain, my classmates were faced with violent upheaval for which Virginia Woolf and the Book of Job left them sorely unprepared. Campus unrest. Sexual revolution. Antiwar politics. Women's liberation. Black power. Psychedelic counterculture. They had been taught to play by one set of rules, but those rules no longer applied. They were practiced in the lessons of the intellect—literature, history, science—but they were neophytes from the neck down. They were privileged but emotionally and sexually naïve. Their innocence, I now see, was colossal. They were wallflowers at the orgy, white-gloved, well-heeled ladies at the revolution.

Between Two Worlds

The class of '68 came of age caught between the contradictions of two colliding cultures. Behind was the old, safe, traditional, middle-class and upper-class model, silver-spoon-fed to them by mothers and by the school. It was a world of pearls and cashmere and Pappagallo shoes, *The Nutcracker Suite* every Christmas, and hot chocolate at Rumpelmayer's. Ahead, beckoning seductively, were the exotic, dangerous, and new—love beads and tie-dye and Spartacus sandals that laced up the leg, acid-rock and marijuana brownies. Behind them, girdles, garter belts, and stockings; ahead, unshaved legs, hairy armpits. Behind, *Tiffany's Table Manners for Teenagers;* ahead, *The Joy of Sex.* Behind was the ambition of marrying well, husband, hearth, home, and family, possibly a little part-time work to pay for extras when the kids were in school. But luring my classmates onward was the tantalizing promise of experimenting, not settling down, free love and a string of partners, taking care of themselves, work that defined them, or maybe no work at all. And in this new version of the future, of course, marriage and babies were options, not givens.

Crunched between two worlds, two sets of assumptions, two prospects, they were shaken by the dramatic explosion of choices. Secure or free, traditional or liberated, ambitious or experimental, solo or linked? My classmates and I hit the crossroads between school and college in the middle of a revolution, a scary experiment of uncertain outcome. Take the old path, deeply inbred, and they'd meet old expectations, please parents, vindicate teachers; follow the new and they'd be on their own and impress their peers. How to please themselves would take decades to figure out. Yes, they could decipher Shakespeare, but could they discover the truth of their own feelings? Yes, they had material comforts, but did they have the ultimate security of self-esteem? For the class of '68, as for others of their generation, growing up and growing into themselves meant trying to secure their shaky inner worlds, to close the gap between their overtended minds and the underexplored, subterranean world of their emotions.

By midlife, if satisfaction can be measured on the scales of love and work, few of this group had found it easy to balance the two; many had found satisfaction in neither. Many entered their forties divorced or never married; many have not had children or found the life-defining focus and fulfillment of meaningful work. Only a handful have had the chance—or is it the impetus?—to make that contribution to society for which their education prepared them.

In contrast, at the twentieth reunion for my sister's Brearley class, the class that graduated just five years after mine, in 1973, the room was filled with doctors and lawyers, psychologists and professors, bouncing their 2.5 children on their knees. The five years that separated my class from hers were the equivalent of at least a generation, almost a lifetime. Even by 1969, only a year after my class graduated, "a great wave washed over the school and it was a different place," according to Evelyn Halpert, a historian, alumna, and the school's headmistress from 1975 to 1997. There was, she recalled, a "semipermeable membrane between the life of students in a school like Brearley and the life of students on campuses like Columbia."

After Columbia students, the school's uptown neighbors, challenged their administration in 1968, Brearley students gradually realized that they too might shake up the status quo. Four years after my class was gone, my sister led a sit-in in the headmistress's office to protest the daily uniform requirement. She emerged victorious, the Bernadine Dohrn of gabardine; after that demonstration, uniforms were required for gym only.

The clash of cultures that broke over my classmates in 1968 could be assimilated much more gradually by my sister and her peers during their teens in the early seventies. The class of '73 absorbed the aftershocks while they were still safely sheltered by school. But for my class, there was a brand-new language in the air, and it caught my classmates up short. My sister's class could learn the new vocabulary more slowly, and practice the lingo before it counted too much. In tenth grade in 1971, my sister and her friends were baring their souls in a consciousness-raising group, talking feminist talk, becoming liberated women. By the time they graduated in 1973, the old model—feminine mystique and all—had been trashed. When they graduated, they surged forth with gusto, energized by the emerging women's movement; their dreams were already being translated into ambitions. The women of '73 confidently and single-mindedly owned their plans for the future; by contrast, the dreams of '68 were vague and confused, ambitions muted and ambivalent.

Today these younger women of my sister's class are masters of the juggling act. The daughter of Supreme Court Justice Ruth Bader Ginsburg is among them; she's a Columbia Law School professor and mother of two, like her mother. But in my class, surely the match of my sister's class in brains and talent, many of the dreams have gone unfulfilled. There is a sense of women who did not shape their lives as they might have if born a little later, who meandered through their lives instead of taking charge of them.

Looking back, I see a group of women lurching toward the barricades of 1968 with the innocent frenzy of mice in *The Nutcracker Suite*, flailing cardboard swords against toy soldiers. Some girls lost their balance, yet found a way to regain it; several went belly-up; a few were forever lost, falling between the cracks.

Portrait of a Generation

This book is a portrait of my generation—that post–World War II, Eisenhower- and Kennedy-led, fifties-bred and sixties-sped baby-boom generation—as reflected and epitomized by the Brearley class of '68. Granted this group was more cocooned and cosseted than many. But even with the benefits and pressures of this privilege, the class of '68 sheds light on a wider circle of age-mates—the cohort who were educated in the shadow of Sputnik, came to maturity in the shadow of the Vietnam War, and are raising their own children in the shadow of AIDS. Touching base with my Brearley class after twenty-five years also gave me a vantage point from which to assess what happened to a generation of women caught in the middle on a fault line in American society, caught between old traditions and new liberations, between a known, familiar language and a heady new vocabulary, between well-worn patterns and ground-breaking new paths.

This book explores what enabled some women to cope with these nonstop, head-spinning changes, adapt, and thrive, and what prevented others from coping, what overwhelmed them and caused them to flounder. What helped some women synthesize the old world they inherited and the new, unfolding, yet-to-be-defined world, while others stumbled blindly into the chasm created between the two clashing cultures? This book examines how my class-mates and their generation navigated the intersection between personal and social history, between what they brought to adult-hood from home and family, school and social milieu, and what the tempo and texture of the times layered over them. This book sets out to untangle the complicated web of factors that brought success to some and setbacks to others, ambition realized for some, and for others, self-defeat, and to see what qualities inspired fulfillment and what undermined it.

During my four years of work on this book, I spoke with fifty Brearley schoolmates. To encourage honest self-revelation and protect my classmates' privacy, I have changed all of their names.

I traced my classmates to the four corners of the country and points in between—from New York to San Francisco, from Boston and Putney to Aspen and Los Angeles. My phone calls to arrange an interview often catapulted me into the middle of schoolmates' lives that were light-years away from the ones we were raised to lead. In the mid-sixties schooldays, a phone call would interrupt an evening of homework and sitcoms. In the nineties I found one classmate taking her fifteen-year-old daughter to a weekly AA meeting; another just returning from the funeral of a friend who'd died of AIDS. Settling into midlife, the class of '68 has found the world both more dangerous and more dazzling than they ever dreamed it could be.

Generational Changes

Placing my class against the dramatic backdrop of social changes in order to understand and illuminate its context, I find it represents the Janus-headed, in-between generation, neither as traditional nor as radical as the generations that buttress it.

My classmates are vastly more experimental than their parents but less cutting-edge than their younger sisters. They're more ambitious and freer of constraining gender stereotypes than their mothers, but less professionally successful than their younger sisters. They're more deft at juggling multiple commitments than their mothers were as younger women, but are clumsier at the juggling act than younger sisters. While my classmates sit more comfortably with their liberation than their mothers ever dreamed of doing, their younger sisters have adapted to new definitions of womanhood so completely that they seem to take their new identities for granted. But just as confronting the restlessness and dissatisfactions of their mothers' lives mobilized my generation to rethink their roles, so, too, my classmates' early, tentative forays into liberation helped pave the way for my sister's generation to own their new choices with greater ease and confidence.

More Liberated Than Their Mothers

Compared with their mothers, my classmates consider themselves new and liberated women, primed to take advantage of the past decades' social and emotional transformations. During the fifties and early sixties, for instance, only a few of the class's mothers worked professionally outside the home. Although some had held good jobs before having children (several had worked for the Department of Defense during the war), motherhood generally nipped their budding careers. Once they had children, their talents and ambitions were either played out on the stage of their children's lives or translated into volunteerism. That mothers would be unemployed, flexible, and available was so taken for granted that all school functions that parents might want to attend took place during the day, and every Friday school ended at 1:00. A mother who challenged these mores was a lone voice in the wilderness or, worse, was patronized for "having to work."

Unlike their mothers, almost all of my classmates have worked at least part-time. They've worked primarily in careers traditionally open to women—many as teachers, several as artists; a handful have chosen occupations more accessible now than in their mothers' generation—business, medicine. Several classmates have entered the working class, either by design—the politically correct thing to do—or by default: they needed the dough. One dropped out of college to organize cannery workers in the late sixties heyday of the Worker-Student Alliance; another worked as a baker and then a grave digger; another did road construction and worked her way up the chain of command until she was supervising men twice her size. By contrast, their mothers' alliance with the working class would be, at best, bonding with a housekeeper or their apartment building's handyman.

Of the married women in my class, more than 60 percent have kept their own names and faced the world as Ms. not Mrs. (among their mothers, only one, a writer, continued using her own name). *Ms.* magazine appeared for the first time in the year of our college graduation, and my classmates rode the first wave of the title's popularity (their younger sisters did not surpass them in this one liberated act—only 55 percent of the class of '73 kept their names after marriage; five years after the trend began, it was already starting slightly to wane).

As married women, my classmates have rarely been able to rely on husbands for sole financial support the way their mothers had. As wives, most have contributed to the family income, either by choice or by necessity. The average weekly earnings of American workers—on the rise since 1950, the year my classmates and I were born—peaked in 1972 and 1973, and then started a steady decline, which has yet to bounce back, as Stephanie Coontz reported in *The Way We Really Are*. Since the 1970s, according to economists Gordon Berlin and Andrew Sum, American families have kept their standard of living up by means of four responses: postponing marriage, having both spouses work, having fewer children, and going into debt. My classmates reflect all four strategies, plus another—benefiting from inherited family money.

Like a sizable slice of their generation, many of the class of '68 have found themselves downwardly mobile compared with their families of origin. At times they've had to comfort themselves with what filmmaker and social observer Whit Stillman shrewdly calls "the memory of money," rather than with the benefits of money itself. But some classmates have also continued to take advantage of the comforts provided by family money, passed along as gifts or trust funds, while maintaining a lifestyle whose values stayed more countercultural than ruling class.

Only a quarter of the class have put down roots as adults in New York City, a trend which in some cases reflects the downward mobility of their family incomes (no one wants to limp along financially in a town where they used to live like swells). The diaspora suggests that others in this rarefied group just needed to break free of its cocoon. Marriage, work, or the need for self-definition propelled others beyond the Big Apple. (Interestingly, exactly a quarter of my sister's class has also remained in Manhattan, and the rest have likewise scattered.)

Still, whether or not their new family income matches their parents', all but three classmates have had the wherewithal, and made it a priority, to send their own children to private school. Precious few of these have chosen single-sex schools for their children, suggesting that while they valued and wanted to recapture for their kids the academic excellence private school could offer, they did not necessarily want to shelter their own kids from half the human race, as they had been cloistered as schoolgirls. Indeed, only one classmate is sending her own daughter to Brearley.

Almost half my classmates have juggled work and marriage and raising children, although many have scaled back ambitions for more family time, or dropped out of the workforce when kids were young and reentered later, following a generational trend of sequencing commitments rather than trying to meet them all at once. Several married for the first time in their forties, and three have never married at all. Still, the expectation of marriage was so universally held that even the two who ultimately defined themselves as gay married first before realizing they preferred female life partners to husbands.

My classmates divorced twice as often as their parents did, a pattern also reflecting wider social changes. Only slightly more than one in four marriages ended in divorce in the fifties, whereas by the eighties half of all marriages came undone. Eleven women out of the extended group of sixty-four (including all the classmates who didn't graduate with the class) believed so passionately in the dream of marriage that they've married twice; one has married three times. Whether their parents' longer-lasting marriages were actually happier than my classmates' interrupted and reconfigured ones is a judgment call, happiness being an elusive quality to measure. The stigma attached to divorce has clearly softened, liberating my classmates to enter and exit their marriages more readily than their mothers did. One classmate ended her vows at her first marriage ceremony with the ambivalent, open-ended promise "as long as we both shall dig it." The marriage broke up when they no longer "dug it"; now she's more happily married for a second time, and the mother of two sons.

Nevertheless, the daughters of divorce in this class all spoke of the splitting of their families as psyche-shattering disruptions which sent them reeling as children, disoriented them as young adults, and haunted them again when they became wives and mothers themselves. And several whose parents divorced have, not surprisingly, ended up divorced themselves.

Divorcing twice as often, my classmates also married out of their faiths twice as often as their parents did; Jewish girls married non-Jews, Protestant girls married Jews or Catholics. In choosing life partners, my class, like the rest of its generation, took advantage of the multicultural stewpot of the times. Their parents married in a climate of post–World War II clannishness and suspicion of outsiders and were far likelier to stick to their own religious kind when pairing up. Three decades later, when my classmates married, they benefited from the cultural mellowing that had taken place, in particular from the easing of anti-Semitism and general de-Wasping of America. Still, where my classmates may have married outside of their faiths more often than their parents, not one crossed racial barriers when choosing a life mate.

The class's patterns of procreation reflect the shifting definitions of womanhood in the intervening decades more than almost any other factor. Their mothers defined themselves as mothers first and foremost, equating their worth, in part, with their family's health and size. Becoming mothers themselves, the class of '68, like the rest of its generation, felt motherhood was a vital piece of their identity but not the be-all and end-all. That internal shift, plus a trend toward marrying and having children later, plus increased social awareness about the negative fallout of the population explosion have all combined to produce a striking decrease in generativity.

Family size has shrunk dramatically. My classmates have produced fewer than half as many children as their mothers did; the twenty-five women of the class of '68 mothered only thirty children, whereas their mothers begat a whopping sixty-six (all right, one classmate's mother had ten!).

Only three classmates have three-child families; nine of their mothers had at least three children—or many more. And seven of my generation have had only one child, whereas only one classmate was an only child herself. Marrying late, infertility problems, financial concerns, or the desire for increased lifestyle freedoms have all made the choice to have just one child the favored option for many in this group.

Less Purposeful Than Their Younger Sisters

Still, if the class of '68 has reaped the benefits of the past three decades' social changes, they have not absorbed these changes as easily as their younger sisters have. Facing many major life decisions—work, marriage, children, and the arithmetic of combining all three—they've typically been more conservative or ambivalent or fraught with doubts and second guesses than their younger sisters. One of the most noteworthy changes is illustrated by the two groups' differing choices about postgraduate education, professional training, and career paths. In 1972, when my classmates graduated from college and faced these worklife decisions, women were just starting to crack the barriers of predominantly male bastions like law, medicine, and business. Just five years later when my sister's class came to this crossroads, the demographics of admissions to graduate and professional schools had changed significantly, and women were entering these fields in far greater numbers. In 1972, for example, when my classmates might have applied to law school, only 15 percent of Harvard Law School's freshman class were women; by 1977, when my sister's class applied to law school, Harvard Law's admissions for women had jumped to 27 percent (by 1998, 43 percent of the entering class were women, almost on a par with men).

Among my classmates when barriers to opportunities were still formidable, only a quarter attained advanced degrees. Five years later, in my sister's class, almost half received Ph.D.s or degrees in law, medicine, or business.

The two groups' contrasting professional choices reflect not only the widening opportunities for women but the way my sister's class, five years farther along in the sexual revolution, felt more empowered to take advantage of them. My class, for instance, generated two lawyers, neither of whom was practicing by midlife. Both signed on for law school in the first wave of opportunity. Both practiced briefly, then fled the law when they found the aggressive nature of the work, the colleagues, and the lifestyle (especially combined with motherhood) incompatible with their goals and personalities. One became an academic dean, the other a mother and painter.

By contrast, nine of my sister's classmates chose law and have remained in law, making it the most frequently chosen profession among them. (There are seven psychologists in my sister's class as well, including my sister, in comparison with only one in my class.) At midlife the lawyers are distinguishing themselves in private practice and also as an assistant attorney general and an assistant U.S. attorney; all but one are also combining motherhood with the law.

This is in keeping with another difference between my class and our five-years-younger sisters. Fewer than half of the women of '68 are now, at midlife, comfortably balancing marriage, work, and family, while a full three-fifths of my sister's class have successfully accomplished this juggling act. For the next younger half-generation, liberating social changes provided more opportunities, social support, and role models, and therefore more confidence to make a balancing act possible and satisfying.

One more disturbing difference between the two groups: Although as a student I was largely unaware of emotional land mines, I found decades later, exploring my classmates' lives for this book, a surprising and troubling amount of emotional instability in the class of '68—suicide attempts, hospitalizations, ongoing mental distress—and significantly less emotional distress among my sister's classmates. More than any other factor, this difference suggests how radically the ground was shifting beneath my classmates, both creating and exacerbating shaky internal fault lines. Just five years later when my sister's classmates came of age, social convulsions had diminished considerably, and her classmates' greater equanimity reflects the wider culture's settling down.

Ten Portraits / Four Styles

When the class of '68 graduated, Brearley's headmistress, Jean Fair Mitchell, described them in her good-bye remarks as a lively mix of "dreamers and doers; outgoing students, reserved students; reflective minds, restless, inquiring minds; leaders and followers; calm, responsive-to-suggestion students, boisterous and mischievous ones." Out of this larger pool—a mix without being heterogeneous, for we were all from the same lily-white, upwardly mobile, upper-middle-class nest—I have chosen to focus on ten women who seem to me to best illustrate the way women in the class of '68 have adapted to life, or failed to do so. Over the course of several years I've spoken with each of these women at least three or four times in widely ranging, emotionally charged, and intensely personal interviews. Weaving these stories into a larger group portrait has allowed me to explore how a privileged group of bright women traveled the territory between resilience and despair, between coping and caving in, between contentment and uncertainty, between the old America and the new.

My mix includes athletes and brains, artists and intellectuals, hot-shot students who thrived at the school and girls whose talents were nonacademic and who struggled to keep pace. My sample includes girls from rock-solid families and, more often, girls from troubled or fractured ones, girls of vast wealth as well as girls who were less financially secure. I have also chosen not only girls who graduated with my class but also girls who ultimately graduated from other schools.

For my class, as for my generation, 1968 and its upheavals was a defining year with repercussions reverberating far into adulthood. How my classmates handled the tumultuous changes of the sixties, whether they slouched or soared through them, is the fulcrum on which many later life events turned. Some lost their balance in the sixties but later came up the stronger for it. Others skirted the sixties' countercultural messages, and still others found a way to integrate them into adult lives—to balance personal growth and attachment to family and community, sex and love, experimentation and steadiness. Others—in my class and my subculture—were blindsided by that haywire time and are still, thirty years later, trying to find their way.

I begin my inquiry with the 1968 graduation, that pivotal juncture between the old world and the new. Then I trace my classmates' adult choices in love and work as they're played out in four distinct styles I've discovered against the background of sixties upheavals—the untraditional traditionalist, the unconventional career-tracker, the seeker, and the juggler. The untraditional traditionalist craves security but can find it only after a far-out experimental phase; the unconventional career-tracker, her opposite, wants professional glory but often attains it through unconventional routes; the seeker longs for awareness and spiritual transformation and shuns conventional paths altogether; and the juggler is striving for balance among marriage, family, and career, and between traditional options and brand-new directions.

These four styles describe four adaptive patterns I've identified among my classmates, but they're also characteristic of the baby-boom generation that this group belongs to—a generation cross-hatched by contradictions. It's threading through these contradictions that distinguishes my generation from the ones just before and just after. A generation earlier, the traditionalists would have dominated, unworried by the untraditional traditionalist's ambivalences; a generation later, the career-trackers would be launched onward and upward, not lured or derailed by unconvention. Later, as well, the seekers would become an anomaly, a distinctive artifact of post-sixties counterculture, and the jugglers more commonplace, less conflicted. Trailing these contradictions, their resolutions and open-ended questions, gives my search its framework.

Sink or Swim?

The class's troubled twin, Lily, had been hanging by a thread all through high school. In tenth grade when her sister, Alice, left for boarding school, Lily, struggling with paralyzing depression, was hospitalized, at first in the adolescent unit at Columbia Presbyterian Hospital. After two years there, when her illness had not improved but she could no longer qualify as an adolescent, she was moved to a state hospital whose hellish conditions exacerbated her fragile condition.

By then I had graduated from Brearley and was a freshman at Radcliffe. I was lured by the bigger stage and thrilled by my wider domain. But I could not shake the image of Lily, disturbed and isolated, playing out another script in an institution not entirely of her own choice.

Twenty-five years later the same questions still haunt me. Why does one person cope and another flail, one reach for solid ground and the other sink into despair? What curious alchemy of temperament and family history, school and culture, friendships, opportunity—and sheer dumb luck—creates resilience in one child and desperation in another? What enabled only a small handful of the girls I went to school with to make a mark in the world or deliver on the heady promise of their youth, and what sent so many floundering? I noticed many still struggling at midlife to balance their lives and wondered whether they were still in recovery from sixties shock, from that disorienting time when, as Joan Didion wrote (adapting Yeats), "the center did not hold."

Was it that expectations for women changed, but after theirs were fixed? Was the benchmark set by families and school, or their own internal benchmark, too high? Did expectations overreach preparation and support? I saw many in this group get caught in the crossfire and then the fallout of the counterculture, led astray by the beguiling promises of the sixties—sex, drugs, rock and roll, and revolution—without the training to cope, because these seductions clashed so sharply with the mores of the protected ruling class these girls were groomed to join. I saw them struggling to make sense of contradictory messages—achieve and drop out, be good and act up, keep secrets and speak out. Was it their fate to be caught between two worlds, not comfortable embracing either one?

By midlife, some have made their peace with these contradictions and some have not. Some have assimilated the changes of the past decades, and others either have turned their backs on them or are still reeling, still searching for solid ground. Some find their lives in balance, and others are satisfied in one sphere but not another, fulfilled in work, but not in love or happy in love but not in work. Some still dream of being settled somewhere in the distant future, and even nearing fifty, several still wonder who they'll be when they grow up.

Interviewing my classmates over the past four years and studying the arc of their lives from five to fifty, I've tried to understand what traits have helped some flower and thrive, while, lacking them, others have stumbled. What has generated resilience and what undermined it? Having the privilege of a long shared history with these girls-become-women, I've been able to explore firsthand the way childhood drafts a script that adulthood revises and to search out the moments of transformation as well as the stuck places on this journey. I've looked both from a distance and up close— dispassionately, as a reporter, examining the way the class of '68 intersects with and reflects the larger story of its generation's complicated and colorful times, and compassionately, as a classmate, friend, and peer, searching the varied lives of '68, their triumphs and heartaches, for clues to help me better understand and shape my own.

There is also, I admit, a voyeuristic rush that comes from meeting up again as adults and asking all those nosy questions I was too young or naïve to ask before. Now, experience goes back and strips the cloak off innocence. Before, I was like the young Jamesian heroine peeping through the keyhole for a glimpse of what went on behind closed doors. Now, I have the perfect excuse to pull the door open and barge in. Before, I was the child who noticed a friend's volatile father, another's glamorous mother, a classmate prone to bouts of moodiness. Now, the adult, I realize that the volatile father had a drinking problem, the glamorous mother was having an affair, and the moody classmate attempted to take her own life. Finally, I can provide the explications to my own story, the footnotes to my own text.

Why this, why now? one of my old classmates asked when I called to arrange an interview. Isn't this ancient history? Haven't you moved on? Answering, I mentioned a reporter's curiosity, a classmate's nosiness, a social historian's challenge, a midlife woman's reassessment. But I also write as a mother wondering what's best for her sons. My school-age sons constantly bring my own school memories floating to the surface, luring me to stare down into them, like finding my own reflection in someone else's pond. I watch my sons learning to read, struggling to write papers, crinkling their brows over homework, and my own student days come flashing back to me. Is anything more exciting than the moment when letters marching across a page start to add up to words, then images, when literature starts to reveal its truths—or more frustrating than the mind balking before grasping a new concept? I see my sons making friends, in or out with this group or that, and my own social life comes wafting back over the decades. Is anything more comforting than being understood by a best friend or more agonizing than being excluded? I want to know if I'm making the right choices for my boys by understanding how my own education left its mark on my classmates and me.

CHAPTER 2

Uncertain Graduates

*I*t is June of 1968. My classmates, about to be graduates, are hurtling into the rest of their lives, while seemingly overnight, the world they've known has been shaken and upended. Lining up outside the school's large assembly hall for graduation, the girls flutter with nerves and hormones. Unease, sadness, and fear hang in the sultry midday air, for only the day before, Robert Kennedy was shot, the third assassination, in quick succession, of their adolescence, violence that would mark and change their world. His death is different from the death of John F. Kennedy, an icon; different from that of Martin Luther King, a prophet. Robert Kennedy is defined by being a brother, and while he is too old and remote to be their brother, they see him as somehow accessible, related. A few years before he was shot, my classmate Emma and I hopped off the Eighty-sixth Street crosstown bus on the way to school to shake Robert Kennedy's hand when he was campaigning for the U.S. Senate. Like most famous figures, he seemed shorter than we had imagined, but touchable, courtly. After that, Emma wrote him about her work tutoring children in East Harlem. He wrote her back. His loss feels very real.

Poised today between history and the future, between families and freedom, between childhood and adulthood, the class of '68 finds the world ahead to be infinitely more complicated than what they've imagined from inside the school's cocoon. On their yearbook cover a symbolic senior is pictured, uniform-clad, curled up, fetuslike inside a balloon. Now that the balloon is about to burst and she's about to float free, can she handle the atmosphere, the choppy air outside?

Uniforms

Getting into formation for the graduation processional, the girls all wear the same dress. They are used to wearing a uniform; some have worn one every school day for thirteen years—inky blue bloomers, white or blue oxford-cloth button-down shirts, V-necked, navy-blue gabardine tunics, covered by knee-length, button-down navy skirts, red or white belts, navy knee-high socks. So many layers of material cinched the girls' waists every day that even the sveltest looked chunky and the slightly chubby looked like the Michelin man. Beneath their layers, the secret core of a self was so well hidden that it would take a long, circuitous journey to find out who, underneath it all, that self really was. Today my classmates are about to take the first step on the journey to find that buried underself, to separate each individual voice from the collective sea of their peers.

For graduation, fittingly, the girls are wearing their last uniform, a knee-length high-necked tunic, made by a seamstress in the Village out of rough white cotton and trimmed Cossack-style with a green-and-white braided ribbon. It is faintly countercultural, thus uncharacteristic for Brearley, a nod to the folksy world of peasant blouses, hand-hewn sandals, and "Blowin' in the Wind" just unfolding beyond the school. Flaunting these hippie dresses, my classmates are desperate to be cool, to throw off their cookie-cutter schoolgirl garb.

Despite the matching dresses the girls no longer look alike, but span the gamut from little girls to femmes fatales. They have all hit puberty at wildly different speeds. Some still have the plain, fresh, freckle-faces of children; their dresses hang straight and formless over shy bodies used to curling up with a good read, not with a lover. Others have real figures that chafe against their dresses, womanly and sexual. One girl will get married the day after graduation, head for art school, and bypass college entirely. The rest are bug-eyed at her daring, the sophistication they imagine her to have, the know-how about sex.

Most are virgins, and few would talk about sex if they had had it. Nice girls still don't, in 1968, though it will be only a blink of an eye before girls will start to "say yes to boys who say no," no to fighting in Vietnam, that is. But in high school in the mid-sixties, talking about sexuality—doubts about it or pleasure in it—is still taboo, one of many, many unmentionables: a parent's drinking or depression, an eating disorder, or anguish over identity confusions are never spoken of. No one yet has the freedom or the vocabulary to name these unnameables. Some will spend decades finding these words, honing the emotions to catch up with their academic prowess. So each girl agonizes in private; each believes she's the only one not invited to the dance, the only one to plug her ears against parents' fighting, the only one to cover up when a parent slurs her words after too much to drink. Each aches in silence over becoming a woman, thinks she's the only one hurting over acne, being overweight, gorging herself on chocolates and cookies, then throwing up behind a locked bathroom door.

Much that is central to my classmates' lives goes on behind closed doors, never spoken about, never acknowledged.

But on graduation day, the girls become one sisterhood. Right now they're still sheltered by closeness and tradition. One tradition requires that the school flag be carried by two of the class's handful of "lifers"; the others toss off the prison analogy with droll affection for the girls who've been at the school from kindergarten through senior year, a full thirteen years. Sarah and Jill bear this honor and carry the school flag, a proud blaze of red and white with the beaver mascot. Behind them the class of '68, twenty-five strong, marches in to the swelling strains of "Pomp and Circumstance," past the nursery-yellow walls of the auditorium, past the portraits of the school's founding fathers, staring down oblivious to the changing tides of history, past the rows of parents and teachers, sisters and brothers, who know the varying degrees of angst that have brought the class to this moment, this place, this crossroads between what the girls dream they can be and what they already are. The group settle themselves on folding chairs on the stage, surveying their well-wishers, brooding about their pasts, fantasizing about their futures.

Senior Year

The girls are grateful to put their year of highest stress behind them, for the academic intensity level, always high, has been amped up several nerve-racking notches during senior year, as they've pushed for the finish line. A history teacher red-inked "95" at the bottom of one of my tests, cattle-prodding me toward perfection. "But in all cases I think you could and should think more about the relationships between the historical figures. Get a 99 next time!" Girls have retreated to the school nurse's office with stomachaches and headaches in unbroken succession, bearing their inadequacies in private. Support groups or rap sessions about stress do not yet exist at Brearley; by the 1980s they will be invented in response to the past's hard-learned lessons.

Once I literally take to my bed, like a nineteenth-century neurasthenic, when an SAT score does not match my rigorous inner standards. A few girls amazingly thrive on stress. "I think stress is a necessary part of a high-powered education," one will say years later after not one but two careers, one as an opera singer, another as a businesswoman. "I don't think I could have survived if I didn't feel comfortable with stress." But others crumple beneath the pressures, and some will never work so feverishly again.

My classmates have been been testy as well as tested. They've had spats with siblings, drawn imaginary lines down the middle of shared rooms, and chastised younger sisters for breathing *their* air. They've yearned to blossom like older sisters and taste the liberty of older brothers. They've chafed against boundaries and fought for freedom with parents, been given concessions, taken more than they were given, been grounded, sneaked around corners and done what they wanted to anyway. Then, sweating with the liberties they've won for themselves, they've woken shaking in the middle of the night, and ached for their parents' comfort and to become little girls again. They can hardly bear to live with parents anymore but are still afraid to live without them.

They've been obsessed with finding and defining identity. Who am I? they've asked themselves in the still center of the night before dreams claim them. Am I my mother, my sister, my best friend? Who am I? they've asked each other, seeking mirrors and counter-points against which they can understand themselves. Who am I? they've asked a society that is turning inside out, whose compass has gone haywire.

They've asked questions and looked for answers everywhere—for they still believe in answers—found mentors in teachers, searched out guiding lights in the books passed conspiratorially among themselves. Reading hungrily, they've looked for self-definition between the contradictions—from Sylvia Plath to Allen Ginsberg, from Robert Rimmer to Hermann Hesse to Jack Kerouac, from Ayn Rand to Antoine de Saint-Exupéry ("It is only with the heart one can see rightly," reads my yearbook quote from *The Little Prince.* "The essential is invisible to the eyes"). These characters' quests be-come the wells I stare down into to initiate my own.

Asked in the tenth grade for an essay describing the most attrac-tive man in English literature, I answer without hesitation—Dean Moriarty in *On the Road.* Iconoclast and wild free spirit, he'd be more than I could ever handle in the flesh. But in my imagination, we are a perfect pair; he's the longed-for animus to my too-well-behaved anima. On an eye-opening, mind-expanding trip to San

Francisco the spring before I graduate, I discover North Beach and Berkeley's Sproul Plaza and come home clutching a book of poems by Lawrence Ferlinghetti, ready to proselytize a new dawn. Beneath my polite exterior, beneath the teal-blue suit and yellow silk blouse I wear to my college interviews, a hippie lies in wait, ready to spring.

All year my classmates have dissected and discussed the classics, down to the cleverest double entendre, the most complex pathetic fallacy. "We've worshiped at the shrine of text," explained one inspiring and demanding English teacher, recalling her department's academic mandate years later. In the subtext girls have hunted for the emotional lessons they craved but weren't getting elsewhere. In Hamlet's breakdown, in Macbeth's manipulation, in Cordelia's unstinting honesty with an impossibly demanding father, sensitive students, emotionally hungry, have seen their own lives reflected, their families described. In Virginia Woolf's *Mrs. Dalloway*, they've tried to fathom the gulf that separates and the emotional ties that bind the serene and proper party-giving heroine, Clarissa Dalloway, and the shell-shocked, suicidal Septimus Smith. They've seen them opposite yet somehow twinned. Mrs. Dalloway is the mistress of social conventions but her smooth surface belies the cracks beneath; Septimus is all cracks, no conventions. His death somehow allows her party to go on.

In these polarities the girls have seen their own. They've seen the smooth faces they're taught to show the public, the gracious hostesses they've been raised to become ("Don't shuffle your feet or you'll never be femmes fatales," chides Mrs. Broderick, senior homeroom teacher and also a favorite English teacher, whose wit and compassion make her a mentor and role model to me and many others). But girls have also heard the fighting behind closed doors at home, seen the chaos of parents' woes breaking through unruffled surfaces. They've seen their classmate Alice go footloose off to boarding school, studying, dating, listening to her dreams, a typical teenage life. But they are also aware that her twin sister, Lily, is troubled, fragile, confined to a mental institution. One twin still has choices—college, a work life, falling in love. For the other, choices have become painfully circumscribed.

College Choices

Choices preoccupy the class, and the college-admission process has been the fiery crucible in which they've tested dreams and realities senior year. It's been a stormy rite of passage, a transition that years later family therapist Jay Haley will call one of life's most difficult. Now the tight-knit band of '68 is finally leaving the sheltered cove of childhood for the uncharted, unprotected seas of late adolescence, young adulthood. Each girl has sat squirming beside her parents in the headmistress's office as her capabilities are assessed, her plans for the future probed. "Do you want a large or small campus? Urban or country? All-girls or co-ed?" Miss Mitchell has asked each one. Then, Oz-like, she has offered up a short list of possibilities— only four applications are allowed—and with these each girl has had to gauge the distance between her hopes and the school's expectations for her, between her own desires and her parents' aspirations.

During the college-admission process, every girl has bounced off the deep end at one moment or another. They've all agonized over whether, if their real selves are revealed, they'll be accepted. They've worried that their friends have become rivals for the few spots available. And all this uneasiness has been played out against the struggle to separate from home, against their parents' struggle to let them go. Helping daughters get into college has been the last gasp of parenting for some, prompting panic that the job of child-rearing has been incompletely done. Getting into a top college has been a chance for daughters to assuage the guilt over leaving home, a final gift or reparation to ease the pain of parting.

Getting into Radcliffe has been my Holy Grail. How I've pined for that bluestocking blend of academic intensity and literary history (Henry James! Gertrude Stein! Robert Lowell!) and the seductive ratio of four men to every woman. I strive for my goal single-mindedly, putting too much of the rest of my life on hold. Saturday nights find me hunched over my desk, polishing essays, cramming for tests. "Isn't there a party to go to?" my father asks, peering in worriedly. But in my mind's eye it's the next year in Cambridge and I'm sipping sherry, surrounded by budding Harvard poets and leather-jacketed philosophers. I have deferred so much gratification that I could pile it in vats, like the thirty-one flavors.

When I am finally accepted at Radcliffe that April 15, the relief is sweet but anticlimactic as well. Could any place ever live up to all those expectations? Perhaps I've let myself get too out-of-kilter with anticipation. And in the effort to prove I can succeed, I may have overlooked a more important lesson: learning how to fail gracefully.

Cordelia—Passionate Leader

So poised on the stage between childhood and liberation, my classmates are eager to take one last, deep breath, longed for and, they think, well deserved. They want to bask in their accomplishments, preen in the glory they feel is their due. But this mellow respite won't be entirely allowed, because the world is cracking apart, changing faster than can even be imagined, and the girls must use every shred of energy to catch up. Indeed, world events are so outstripping a teenager's understanding that it will be decades, even lifetimes, before their impact becomes decipherable. For now, change is an invisible virus in the air, inexplicable but catching.

Just the night before graduation, after the news of Robert Kennedy's death broke commencement's usual protective bubble, Cordelia, the school's student government president and the class's fearless and forthright leader, tossed out the speech she was going to deliver and wrote a new one from scratch. The old speech was soft at its center and nostalgic, singing the song of friendships made and not to be forgotten. The new speech is hard-hitting, political, exhortatory.

Now Cory stands in front of her classmates at the lectern, a big blond presence, more womanly than most, with accepting blue eyes and a big heart. She is the country girl more than the city slicker, for she transferred to the school in ninth grade from the soft, rolling hills of western Massachusetts, and seems easy about moving back and forth between the two worlds. She can also be gawky, even a little goofy, and that saves her from self-seriousness, also from envy. "We've been aware of the world around us and will continue to be," she reminds the graduates, startling them with her urgency. She cites the small steps they've already taken to be responsive to the world, from organizing interschool dances—the first in twenty years—to tutoring reading in East Harlem to inviting liberal speakers to schoolwide assemblies to open the girls' eyes to the wider, needier world.

Cory speaks from the heart, caught between her own ideals and her love for an older brother who has chosen to fight in Vietnam. So for her, the war is far more tangible and more personal than for anyone else in the class. And she also speaks for a saving remnant of classmates who've marched for equality and protested the war. Reflected in her eyes, in her descriptions, classmates feel themselves growing bigger, more empowered. I am awed, but also humbled, by her idealism, her conviction, so fully realized while mine is yet embryonic. For me Cordelia represents the group's best possibilities, its best promise for making an impact on the world.

Poised at this threshold of change, most in the class are still more sensitive than political; certainly I am more emotional than activist. For most of childhood, our politics were rubber stamps of our parents'; straw polls at school for presidential elections just mimicked parents' choices. Girls stood on street corners in the Silk Stocking district, handing out flyers when John Lindsay ran for mayor in 1966 because their parents liked the handsome, well-spoken, comfortably upper-class candidate who looked like them and reflected their interests.

Now the girls are trying to wrench themselves away from their parents' ideologies and starting to make up their own minds about the world. Still, most stay more contemplative than activist, more inner-focused than storming the barricades. Until now political consciousness has meant lying on ruffle-skirted beds, listening to Buffy Sainte-Marie sing "The Universal Soldier" or tacking up on a bulletin board, somewhere between Donovan and Paul McCartney, a picture of a starving Biafran child. And many in the group remain glaringly apolitical, oblivious to the tidal waves of the times. ("While other classmates went to marches, I was checking out the sales at Bergdorf's," one unapologetic classmate will remember years later.) So the politicized waning of the sixties and the rabble-rousing dawning of the seventies will be a shocking wake-up call and, for a few, seem like the wrong number entirely.

As Cordelia speaks, confident beyond her years, no one realizes what a tough year has brought her to this seemingly steady place. She has gotten deft at dodging minefields, skilled at transcending her own distress. At home her parents have parted not too amicably, and her mother, a social activist herself, is being courted by a wealthy older man who shares her beliefs and her habit of hard drinking. Cordelia often comes home to find her mother and her suitor still in bathrobes at midday. Cory will rarely speak of her home life to anybody. She feels less and less comfortable at home but is close to her mother nonetheless, and is inspired by her mother's passionate political convictions.

While her mother's head was turned, Cordelia played out her own wild streak—drinking, carousing, falling for older men. One night she went out on a motorcycle with a guy she hardly knew. After a few drinks she ended up naked on a couch, wondering how she got there. Later she'll refer to it as the night she almost got raped. Still later she'll say, "If my mother had been paying attention, I might not have grown up so fast." Even later she'll hover protectively over her own fair-haired, porcelain-skinned older daughter, making sure that history doesn't repeat itself.

Around college-application time Cory's mother tried to make up for lapses elsewhere with zealous overinvolvement. Overriding the headmistress's cautions, she filled her daughter's head with big dreams and insisted she apply to the most competitive colleges. But despite Cory's good mind and other considerable talents (acting, for one—she was a memorably earthy Polly Garter in *Under Milk Wood*), her grades were not up to it. When the letters came back, she'd been turned down everywhere except for a small school in California she no longer cared about. For a while, she was devastated. Maybe she wasn't a heavyweight. Maybe she wouldn't be able to change the world after all. Would her spotty record hamper her grand designs? She feared the chaos at home had undermined her self-assurance in moving forward in the world.

Somewhere deep inside she knows she's bigger than all those C's, bigger than her splintered family. So eventually she hatched a new plan. She'll take a year at an international school in Switzerland and regroup. It will give her a chance to save face, a chance for a new perspective. Still, as she ends her speech in a crescendo of confidence with a triumphant call to the class of '68 to save the world, inside she feels shaky. Ever the actress, she tries to cover up the uncertain little girl inside with bluster and panache. But still she wonders if she'll ever be able to land on her feet, if her capabilities will ever catch up to her ideals.

Miss Mitchell, the headmistress, speaks next, and though she might wish to, she cannot avoid referring to the darkening climate of change and crisis and protest. But with her resonant, upper-class Scottish brogue and her conservative, conciliatory nature, she urges the graduates toward "responsible dissent" and away from "extracting demands" from institutions defined as the enemy. The specter of the angry confrontation in April between Columbia University students and President Grayson Kirk just a few miles uptown hangs heavily over the podium but is pointedly, nervously, not mentioned. Listening to her, my classmates and I absorb the double message. Protest injustice, we hear her saying, but by all means do it in a ladylike manner; do not alienate or infuriate your opponents. Put up your fists, but by all means keep your white gloves on.

Tess—Ambition in Bloom

After her remarks, Miss Mitchell turns to the business of handing out prizes. This is known ground, and here she's more comfortable than she is when scanning the barricades. Three classmates win Certificates of Merit and eight are awarded Letters of Commendation from the National Merit Scholarship Competition. These are the good test-takers who've soared through their SATs, the girls with the highest academic reach and those "school brains" who can easily digest a wealth of information and spew it out multiple-choice style. Cory is not in this group—her strengths lie elsewhere—but I receive a letter and so does Theresa, the class president. Tess bounces down the stage steps to accept her letter, buoyant and full of purpose. Short and charismatic, with long chestnut-brown hair and warm almond-brown eyes, Tess is one of a high-voltage Catholic family of ten. They live on a huge estate, now past its glory days, perched overlooking the Hudson, almost two hours from Manhattan.

Tess is used to being looked at, used to feeling special as she and her lawyer father and sisters commute into town. It's two hours on the train every morning and two hours back again at night, as they make the transition each day from country life to urban pressures. These smoke-filled, joke-filled, homework-heavy four hours every day tell me and the rest of the class just how much Tess wants this education, how much her family wants it for her. Tess is one of my closest friends, and we often hang out together after school on Fridays. But when she eyeballs her watch in the middle of a conversation and knows she has only twenty minutes to sprint for Grand Central and catch her homebound train, I'm brought up short. Tess has to work four times as hard for the education the rest of the class takes for granted. But she's also hungrier for success than most, and something tells me she's going to fill her plate.

Tess is one of the very few who already know what they want, who have already set their eyes on a goal. Most other classmates have dreams but not ambitions. They know vaguely that they want to get out of town, escape their parents' clutches. They're itching for new experiences while not quite able to identify what these might be. But few have plans beyond college; fewer still have thought about a career. As if answering this unspoken need, Mrs. Broderick arranged a couple of tea parties the spring of our senior year and invited several of her friends to talk about their careers. Financial planner, editor, fashion designer, these women led lives that seemed enticing but foreign. "I looked in the mirror one morning," one of these working women confided, "and said, Self, you'll have to take care of yourself because no one else will." Around the room, jaws dropped. Their father's daughters, their mother's graces, not one imagined she'd ever have to take care of herself. Being *able* to seemed as remote right then as the moon.

But Tess is different. Tess already has big plans. She loves plants, loves mucking about in the dirt on her family's rolling property, making gorgeous things grow, changing the face of the landscape. She's also a born organizer, and with nine siblings she has a ready labor pool. Weekends she has them pulling weeds, setting in plants. She's going to Barnard in the fall, and then she's going to get an advanced degree in horticulture. When she announced her scheme to her father he was as shocked as if she'd said she wanted to become a fireman or a priest. He is a high-powered Wall Street lawyer who hopes his children's success will come in equally traditional careers. "You'll get over it," he says of her dreams. But she keeps on puttering, greening their eighteen-acre estate to fulfill her vision, taking advantage of the huge playground he's given her in spite of himself. And in her spare time she makes artful felt banners, splicing together images from folk songs with lines from E. E. Cummings and arresting splashes of color, Sister Corita–like. "Flowers never bend in the rainfall" is her favorite saying, and when she gives me a banner as a graduation gift, she appliqués these words in magenta felt upon an optimistic pink background. But can she rise above her father's objections? She worries silently that she cannot move forward without the faith of her all-encompassing family.

Judith—a Competitor's First Fall

Judith strides to the stage after Tess, a trim, athletic, slightly boyish girl with short dark hair and olive-dark eyes, determined but self-conscious. She trusts her brains, depends on her skill at sports. But she's anxious that she's not quite pretty enough, that her skin breaks out, that her hair doesn't swing. She's not the slightest bit interested in boys yet and doesn't know she's just a late bloomer. She feels awkward, can't yet see the swan getting ready to burst from the duckling.

Still there's a resolute bounce in her step as she accepts her National Merit letter and Miss Mitchell's handshake. Judith is one of the basketball cabal, one of the class jocks, who spend their lunchtimes shooting hoops in the gym, while others dawdle over lunch, dissecting teachers' foibles, comparing parents' unjust demands. Judith's maroon school blazer is covered with athletic awards; she's won them in every sport. Judith's a great competitor, on and off the court. Life's a game to her, and she's used to driving to the hoop, going for the goal. She's accustomed to winning, and her standards for herself are the highest. Even an 89 or 90 on an English paper upsets her. Only the best will do.

But this has been a touchy spring for Judith. For one of the rare times in her highly successful school career she's had to cope with losing. Her heart was set on Radcliffe and she knew all along the competition would be intense. Her closest friend, Jill, turned out to be the most competitive. "If you win president of student government," calculated Jill, "you'll certainly get in and you'll edge me out." But Judith didn't win the presidency—that honor went to

Cordelia—and she also got turned down by Radcliffe. She went to Miss Mitchell's office to hear her fate and Miss Mitchell sat solemnly, like a judge. "Radcliffe says no," she said. "Vassar says yes." But Judith hardly heard the rest. She was crushed, devastated, ran home weeping to her parents' comforting arms. How will she hold her head up among her friends (especially around Jill, who did get into Radcliffe)? How will she pick herself up and make something of her life anyway? She fears she'll never find that academic edge she craves at Vassar, among all those Brearley-like girls.

But years later she will tell me that being turned down by Radcliffe was one of the most important lessons of her life: it taught her to face and learn from failure, taught her that life has a way of working out for the best in spite of dashed dreams, interrupted plans. Years later Judith will turn out to be one of the class's least predictable successes. A slow starter, overlooked by the flashier girls, when she hits her stride, she'll make the others take notice.

Maisie—Among the Aristocrats

Maisie is called to the stage next, a tiny, tidy, well-mannered, and well-spoken brunette whose perky looks give the lie to darker currents underneath. Shaking Miss Mitchell's congratulatory hand, she collects a National Merit letter, as well as the history prize. For senior research projects each girl wrote a lengthy paper on the subject of revolution. Revolution is still just an academic issue for most of the class, though the wind of change that blows through the curriculum now will soon tear through the rest of their lives. Maisie's topic was a French aristocrat whose salon during the French Revolution embraced radical movers and shakers. Maisie poured herself into this project. She's a nose-to-the-grindstone student, the kind who works on her homework all weekend long, not just in a burst on Sunday nights. She labored long days and nights at the Columbia University library, reading original documents in French. Her finished piece took the form of a play, a rather disappointing play, as it turned out, but a stunning piece of research, for which she is justly rewarded.

There is a hint of French aristocrat to Maisie, too—that regal bearing, that silver tongue in conversation—but it is still latent; she is more schoolgirl than femme fatale. On her yearbook page, she is listed as class housekeeper and plant-waterer, sketched in eighteenth-century regalia, all bustle and furbelows, watering a geranium. Maisie's parents are divorced—she rarely sees her mother—and she lives in an elegant brownstone in the East Sixties with her father, stepmother, and older sister. Their life is gracious and aristocratic—late dinners and a glass of wine at every place, including Maisie's. But their home pivots more around adults than children, and Maisie must turn to her grandmother or the maids for moral support. As a result, she's very good at pleasing adults but can be awkward around kids her own age. And her knowledge of the opposite sex goes no farther than what she's gleaned, white-gloved and party-shoed, at dancing school. So she's sophisticated enough to pick up on the sexual undercurrent in the class, the whispered scuttlebutt about who's gone how far. But as for herself, she's virgin-pure and innocent and knows she hasn't got a clue.

At college, she hopes, the pace will quicken. She's known since September that she'll be going to Pembroke, Brown's sister college. She was the only one in the class to apply to college early decision. She carefully appraised her options, ruling out Bryn Mawr, where her older sister went, because it was too much like Brearley, and ruling out Radcliffe because it was too intense, beyond her reach academically. But her stepsister went to Pembroke, so that made it a known quantity, if still the backwater of the Ivy League, years before Amy Carter and the Kennedy children helped to make it a plum choice. It has a good reputation and is only three hours from New York so she can come home any weekend. She's beginning to chafe at her family's tight reins but can't imagine herself pulling away entirely. She knows she wants to grow up but isn't sure she wants to rebel. So how will she fare when rebellion sweeps her campus freshman year? More aristocrat than revolutionary, whose side will she be on?

Jo—on the Fringes

Jo squirms a little in her seat as the prizes are awarded, knowing she will not get one. Academics have been a struggle for her, and she's wondered many times whether she would have been happier and more successful elsewhere. Her talents are those of the right brain— music, art—talents the school gives a nod to but doesn't reward. It will be years before Harvard educator Howard Gardner publishes his work and emphasizes the value of "multiple intelligences"—arts and sports and personal skills beyond just the three R's. But for now, those like Jo who are not quick with words or numbers often end up seeing themselves as dumb.

Jo's a free spirit, a daredevil, pushing the envelope at home and at school. Compact and intense, with floppy dark hair and searing eyes, big silver hoop earrings, and a signature purple blanket serape, Jo is a truer child of the sixties than most of her classmates. She adapts chameleonlike to the coloration of her times. She plays guitar in a band with several other white-lipsticked, black-stockinged girls: "It Ain't Me, Babe" and "Baby, Let Me Follow You Down." After school they hang out in a funky neighborhood coffee shop, smoking and drinking black coffee. Jo hates the taste of the bitter black java, but she knows it's cool, and at sixteen, seventeen, eighteen, she'll do just about anything if she thinks it's cool.

On the weekends she escapes academic pressures and flees to her family's weekend house in Vermont, where her other life begins. Her parents rent out an annex of the house to a bunch of guys from a small college nearby, and Jo hangs out with them around the clock, groupie-like in her devotion. In conversation she refers to them as "the boys in the shed." "Oh, wow" is often the only thing she says to them for hours on end, raptly listening to their guitar riffs, their stoned or boozy teases. To her they're minigods, older men in their twenties, some back from Vietnam, rough around the edges. To them she's a mascot, sometimes a plaything. Occasionally they'll toy with her sexually, use her to satisfy cravings, shore up shaky egos. She's unflinchingly loyal and still has too little sense of her own worth to talk back.

Jo's a party girl, and she wants the world to believe she's always up for a good time. Outside she's Annette Funicello, all bounce; but on the inside she's Janis Ian, brooding, lost, displaced. She's the only girl in the class who was adopted, not that it's ever talked about—this is long before the age of open adoption—but at times she feels it separates her from others. What's more, after her parents adopted her, they went on to have a whole passel of their own kids, a brood of blond sprites at whose head she stands out like the one dark kitten in the litter. Her style is blunter, more forthright; the rest of the family is more evasive and veiled. Besides, the younger kids seem to please their parents effortlessly, while Jo feels she has to try harder to stay in their good graces—and she doesn't always succeed.

Sometimes she gives up entirely. Once during a bad poor-me spell she ran away to the Village and hid out with friends. She lay low for several days, hanging out at the Café Wha, at the Night Owl, playing out her fantasies, strumming her guitar on street corners, making her family miss her, driving them a little nuts. When she came back, her wings were clipped, but she wasn't entirely chastened. Now she's fairly panting to cut loose. She waited to hear from the college she fantasized about, an artsy, progressive school in Vermont that she chose because it was not so obsessively fixated on scholastics. But although she was accepted, she wasn't given enough scholarship money to make it feasible in her parents' eyes. She's heartbroken. What's worse, her parents insist she go to the small local college of the family's tenants, the boys in the shed. The idea is painful—it's too close to home. Has all the running away only led her back to this? She wonders how she'll be able to carve out her own niche under her family's watchful gaze. She worries that she'll always feel like a misfit, a failure, that her talents will never be recognized.

As the prize ceremony comes to an end, the familiar strains of "Jerusalem" swell to fill the hall. *And did those feet in ancient time walk upon England's mountains green?* Blake's stirring poem, his diatribe against industrialization set to Hubert Parry's soulful cadences, pour from the class in one voice. Although the school has its own anthem, this hymn has become more familiar than any other song. The girls have sung it at every formal gathering, every symbolic transition of their Brearley lives. *And was Jerusalem builded here, among these dark Satanic Mills?* As they sing, memories and images of the selves they've left behind flood them with feeling. They are tiny kindergartners about to take on the awesome reading and writing responsibilities of first graders. They are fourth graders in short-skirted tunics about to put jacks and hopscotch behind, as they leap up to the middle school. They are eighth graders, turning moody and broody, as they make uncertain strides into high school. Each time a piece is left behind, a piece is gained.

Bring me my spear! O Clouds, unfold! Bring me my Chariot of fire! As they sing, the faces of old classmates also swim into view, still part of the larger group portrait. There is Emma, who joined the class in seventh grade and left junior year when her minister father was transferred to another job in another state, for what felt to Emma like the hundredth root-wrenching time. He yanked her, with no ifs, ands, or buts, from her Brearley class of twenty-five and set her down in a sprawling, suburban Maryland high school class of six hundred. Once or twice she ran away and tried to make her way back to New York, but her attempts proved futile.

Emma—Rebel Without a Cause

Emma is the classic clergyman's daughter, acting out against her parents' stringent, perfectionist demands in the fishbowl of church life. If she doesn't show up for Sunday services, people know, people talk. Emma loves to give them plenty to talk about. She already has a suicide attempt behind her, and a parade of therapists whom she could never trust long enough to let them help her.

Emma has an appealing pixie face, a pug nose and keen blue eyes. She's almost too cute to be bad. She keeps her bangs long and her skirts short. Her parents are very controlling, and these issues become hot buttons between them. What a battlefront hair becomes between classmates and their parents! Too long, too unkempt, covering too much of the face. Get your hair out of your mouth, parents chide daughters, as girls absently nibble on their hair or twirl long strands around their fingers. No wonder *Hair* was the number one Broadway musical in 1968. Even on the fringes of the Age of Aquarius, Brearley girls responded to its drumbeat.

In Middle School Emma and I met at the bus stop every morning and amused ourselves by talking about crushes on distant boys, which rarely came to fruition. But where we both talked a bigger game than we played, Emma, as an adolescent, started to make good on her threats. She embraced the counterculture with ready arms, while I hung back, still too dutiful a daughter to jump in. Senior year in the Maryland suburbs Emma missed eighty days of school, getting stoned with friends, smoking hash, and taking off for the zoo. Good stuff, she'll later have the distance to admit with a wry smile, that looks great on college applications.

But Emma didn't make any college applications senior year. Unlike Jo, whose talents were more arty than academic, Emma could be a scholarly star but took a conscious stand against it, against the tyranny of the A-minuses that her parents never failed to remind her could have been A's. On her family's hierarchy of values, the most important is not occupation or annual income but academic achievement, and especially *where* someone went to school. So Emma, high on the sixties zeitgeist—tune in, turn on, drop out—made sure to hit her parents where it would hurt them most. While the rest of the class slaved over college applications and sweat out getting in, Emma dreamed of becoming a working-class heroine, college no part of the picture. While in other families, in other settings, a daughter might brag about being the first in her family to go to college, in her overachieving family, Emma boasts about being the first in her family *not* to go.

Emma's family—liberal, political, believing-in-God types of the William Sloane Coffin school—have taught her to work within the system to make change. Her parents have taken her to civil rights marches and antiwar protests, whereas mine have marched me around museums or to see *Peter Pan* or *Camelot*. But cynicism is beginning to creep in, as she sees nonviolence apparently ineffectual and student protests quelled by violence. Robert Kennedy's assassination is the final blow. Even people you believe in are not going to survive, she thinks. Her cynicism hardens into a distrust of all authority. She will not be bulldozed by the powers that be. But she also unwittingly boxes herself in, trapping herself with the dopers and dreamers in her Maryland class who haven't her brains or capabilities. Will she be able to carve out a useful path for herself, staying true to her values and not slipping into apathy? Or will she have to sink deeper into an angry hole before she figures a way out?

Sophia—Wild Child, Prep School Girl

Sophia is another wild child who started in first grade with the class but later left for boarding school. She's an early beauty with pale skin, great bones, an unruly mass of brown hair, and an aura that attracts boys as well as other girls. Until she left in ninth grade, Sophia was a controversial presence in the class with a cluster of admirers as well as detractors. She was boy-crazy wild, stealing liquor from her parents' cupboard and sneaking up to the roof of their East Side apartment house, boozy at midnight with friends she lured to follow along. Her parents divorced when she was five and her mother, another great beauty, remarried a few years later. The household is charged, electric with an energy missing in the staider homes of the longer-marrieds. But the family is also conventional, and Sophia, too, though going through a long unbridled phase, retains her family's values deep down.

Her mother married at nineteen and had Sophia while she was still at college. In her class graduation picture she held baby Sophia in her arms. Though this first marriage did not last, her mother's belief in marriage never faltered, through three of them. Sophia appraises her mother's rocky marital landscape and vows she will never marry. Through her teens and her twenties she holds on to this dogma like the fiercest ideologue. Getting married and having kids is the single most boring thing she can imagine, the epitome of middle-class banality. Not till she's thirty-five will her perspective turn around.

Boarding school is the expected rite of passage in Sophia's family, for it provides that polish of social finesse, that elitist glow, as well as protection from rumbles on the home front. Sophia and, more precisely, Sophia's mother had their heart set on Madeira, the Everest of the social set before headmistress Jean Harris's crime of passion tarnished the Madeira image. But Sophia's grades were not up to Madeira and she had to settle for a small school without much cachet. Socially confident, Sophia was less sure about her brains, but at the not-so-competitive boarding school she got straight A's and finally was accepted at the citadel; her graduation from Madeira was the same June as Brearley's graduation.

Buoyed by her prep school success, she, too, applied to Radcliffe but was turned down. Graduation finds her accommodating herself to the idea of attending a big East Coast university, a place, she'll later say, where she can let her wildness run its course without creating a reputation that will come back to haunt her later. In Cambridge everyone would know her business; she'd never outgrow her past. Lost in the protective anonymity of a huge university, she can be as outrageous as she wants and no one who will ever matter later will know about it. How wild does she have to be until her wildness plays itself out?

Pamela—Dubious Heiress

The year Pamela left the class for boarding school in Massachusetts was the year her world turned upside down. Her parents divorced after years of fighting behind closed doors. The family cook died, the mother stand-in who nurtured and coddled all five children when Pam's parents were too busy to look in on homework, a skinned knee, or a broken heart. Even her beloved cat died, the only family member she remembers missing when she went away to school. In a flash, everything that anchored her was suddenly gone. At home in their stately uptown brownstone all remains understated elegance. A Calder mobile sways serenely over the stairwell, and miles of books silently survey her father's study. The smooth surfaces give no hint of the tumult beneath.

Pamela has had to listen at her parents' keyhole to find out the truth about their crumbling marriage, because they acted so civilized during the day. Though full of surface bravado, she's a little afraid of both of them at times. Her father is a powerful and ambitious newspaper editor, quick and confident with opinions, a Wasp of aristocratic bearing. Her mother is a brilliant, proud, nonpracticing Jew whose family wealth goes back for generations. So possessions are plentiful, but even at a young age Pam knew something was missing, some faith, some sense of tradition, some continuity. Like many of her generation, Pam has every material comfort but still feels deprived. Without having the words to name it, she yearns for a spiritual life, a deeper connection to something bigger than herself, bigger than her complicated family and its nagging problems. The only place she finds peace is skiing down the slopes winter weekends in Vermont. That icy, liberating blast of wind links her to nature's vastness and lifts her out of herself. Driving across the border to her family's Vermont house every weekend, she finds herself mumbling the Lord's Prayer very quickly and under her breath, so no one in the car will notice. Praying hardly jibes with her tough-girl image. But the prayer is heartfelt, and she can feel her spirit soar.

By the time Pam was ready for boarding school, the vibes had gotten so weird at home, it was almost a relief to go away. Maybe she'd be in better hands, she thought, with teachers who are savvy about teenagers. But nobody was quite skilled enough to see beneath the tough-girl exterior she affects to cover up the lonely, vulnerable child inside. "I was like a gang member," she'll later say, "who tried not to show how scared I was." Only once, when a biology teacher held her after class for poor work, did she break down and cry. Otherwise she strode through campus, head held high, jaw firmly set, long blond hair streaming behind her. She was desperate but too afraid and too hung up on what people would think to let her real self out. She needed help badly, she will say years later, but she could no more have asked for it, no more have gotten therapy, than cut off a leg.

So when it was time to apply to college she didn't follow her heart and take a year off. She only fantasized about exploring the world and finding out who she is, what she's passionate about, what she's good at. When she broached her fantasies with her mother, she could feel her mother's fear. Smart people just didn't drop out, people with brains, people with money. People like us. Pam knew she couldn't put her mother through that shame and couldn't put her own ego on the line that way. So she took the safe route, the spirit-crunching route and applied to Vassar, where her mother and both her older sisters had gone. And when she was accepted, she pushed her real desires to the bottom of her brain, like someone stuffing garbage to the bottom of the can to make room for more. She vowed she would make the best of it. But will she really be able to tune out the messages of her deepest self or will that frightened, feisty, vulnerable, vocal person come out in spite of herself? Where was I when I needed me? is the phrase she uses about herself years later, about her lifetime quest for her truest self.

Poised at the threshold of the rest of their lives, every graduate of '68 is asking herself this question in one form or another. All the graduates are probing their own hearts, as they accept their diplomas, as they hug and kiss each other, as they cry in each other's arms. Now they vow they'll be friends forever with these girls, who are like sisters beyond family, whose little-girl braids they've dipped in paint and painted hearts and flowers with, whose victories and vices they know as well as their own. In the passion of the moment they are sure they will be connected forever—and they will be, but in ways they cannot yet know. Many will, in fact, hardly ever see each other again, but the invisible thread of common history will link them on their common journey, as they struggle to define their separate selves, to find their own voices.

"By truth and toil united, we strive with loyal heart." They raise their voices in the school song one final time, teary-eyed and hesitant at first. *"To gain life's deepest blessing, and learn life's nobler part,"* they sing, gathering confidence and momentum. *"Truth cometh not unsought for, the spirit's purest light, must burn undimmed and clearly, To guide our minds aright."* Still novices at truth-seeking, they will all become more experienced.

Just five years later, Mrs. Broderick will send my sister's class out into the world with three rules to live by:

Get a file cabinet to keep track of your precious papers, she will advise.

If you marry, make sure that you maintain your own bank account, kept in your own name.

And, one final caution: In personal relationships, always make sure that the other person feels at ease.

But that is five years later, after the world has settled down a bit. In 1968 the old rules no longer seem to apply, and new ones have yet to be imagined.

Unlearning the Rules of Nice and Not Nice

*H*ere are the old rules; the class of '68 was brought up on them. Good manners are the patrician backbone of nice. Nice is the social graces, dressing for dinner, and putting the other person's needs before your own. It's smiling to cover your fears, camouflage your pain, a lesson learned as early as third grade when the teacher instructed one too-emotional girl to look up at the ceiling every time she felt like crying. Nice is thank-you notes and firm handshakes and calling your friends' parents Mr. and Mrs. Nice is knowing the difference between the meat fork and the salad fork, between a wine goblet and a champagne flute, between when it's a must to cut the chicken on your plate and when it's okay to pick the bone up and gnaw it demurely with your teeth. Nice is "What would people think?" and "One doesn't do that, does one?" (like eating dessert before dinner or wearing shorts to the theater).

Not nice is "Who the hell is 'one,' anyway?" Not nice is doing what you please and consequences be damned. Not nice is putting yourself first, making your presence felt. Not nice is first names only or Ms., not Miss or Mrs. It's Sisterhood is Powerful, Dare to Struggle, Dare to Win, Hell No, We Won't Go.

Nice is handing out flyers for John Lindsay for mayor, because he lives in your best friend's apartment building and your parents and her parents want him to win. Nice is Parents know best. Not nice is Never trust anyone over thirty. It's cutting classes for a demonstration and skipping exams for a campuswide strike. Nice is respecting institutions, not occupying them.

Nice is saving yourself for marriage. It's a discreet good-night kiss and knowing when to say no. It's putting the brakes on to stop his animal advances. Nice is listening wide-eyed to your date and drawing him out with a practiced string of questions, becoming a mirror that amplifies his size and diminishes your own. Nice is keeping your own opinion mum unless asked, speaking only when spoken to, being seen but not heard.

Not nice is going all the way, playing fast and loose, making out in public. Seriously not nice is enjoying all of it as much as he does. Not nice is calling him before he calls you. It's daring to disagree and flaunting your opinions. Not nice is making an appointment at Planned Parenthood all by yourself and being fitted for a diaphragm, and not nicer still is carrying around your own supply of condoms. Way beyond not nice is getting pregnant before you're married and light-years beyond that is having an abortion. A pregnant Brearley girl is about as common as a California condor. But pregnancies and abortions do very occasionally happen, and they are kept just as hush-hush as everything else not nice, like drinking or abuse or heartbreaking despair.

Nice is uniforms all week and skirts, stockings, and heels for weekend outings. It's everything matching, no checks with plaids, a subdued palette and makeup, swinging hair. Not nice is black tights, short skirts, and no bra. It's wild and woolly hair, bangs to your nose, baggy jeans, and army boots. Nice is Saks and Bonwit's. Not nice is thrift shops and Army-Navy stores. Bloomies straddles the chasm between the two.

Neither too thin nor too fat is perfectly nice. So is developing the mind and remaining blissfully ignorant about anything from the neck down. What's going on "down there" is particularly not nice. So is being excessively concerned about your body. Not nicest of all—unspeakable, in fact—is gorging on chocolates and pastries and Schrafft's ice cream, then skulking to the bathroom to vomit it all up, as at least one classmate did silently but religiously to preserve her model-like figure.

Nice is tea parties and birthday cakes, Shirley Temples and a sip of sherry. It's being picked up at the door by your date, whose parents are nice people your parents know. It's going to the movies and out for a soda afterward and then waiting for him to call again. Not nice is getting stoned or getting ripped or, God forbid, dropping acid. It's going to bed with someone you don't really love, sleeping around.

Nice is housekeepers and hospital corners. It's picking up for company and sitting with your ankles crossed. Not nice is an unmade bed, dirty dishes in the sink, and the Worker-Student Alliance. Not nice is picketing your college dorm so that the maids' hourly wage will rise or massing in Washington, thousands strong, to show solidarity with the murdered students at Kent State.

Nice is marching straight off to college after graduation—your mother's college is the nicest of all—and getting your diploma in four straight years. Nice is finding a dependable career, one you can pick up or put down when your children are young, something that meshes well with marriage and motherhood, like photography or interior decorating. Nice is finding Mr. Right without too many false starts, a good man to protect you and support you in the style to which you've grown accustomed. Nice is working only part-time to supply life's extras—theater tickets, a weekend away.

Not nice is taking a year off before or during college. Not nicer still is dropping out, staring at your navel, having nothing to show for yourself. Not nice is also being too ambitious—wanting to become a doctor or a lawyer, for instance, who takes a worthwhile job away from a man who really needs it to support his family.

The apotheosis of nice is the Kennedys, especially Jackie, who is the queen of nice (Caroline went to Brearley for several years and later sat on the board of trustees and sent her own daughters to the school). The Kennedys and their catastrophes frame the class of '68. John Kennedy's election in 1960, when my classmates and I were ten, marks the earliest dawning of political consciousness (how passionately I memorized the names of Kennedy's cabinet members for current events class, so that to this day I know them better than the current crop of presidential advisers—Abraham Ribicoff, Robert McNamara, Dean Rusk). President Kennedy's assassination in 1963, when the class was thirteen, collides with the beginning of their adolescence; and Robert Kennedy's assassination in 1968, the day before graduation, closes the curtain on childhood and darkly shadows the transition to college and the world beyond.

So the p's and q's of nice are defined by Kennedy-style—Chanel suits, pillbox hats, "little nothing" black dresses with a single strand of pearls—that understated chic that's Jackie. Nice is Jackie's breathless little-girl voice when she's televised showing the nation around the White House or charming Nikita Khrushchev (but the secret weapon of nice is the steely mettle and mask of propriety she shows after her husband is shot down and she must carry on alone). Nice is Jackie's Vassar-polished erudition; she's able to deliver a speech in flawless French and so outshine her husband, the president, that he jokes that he's the man who accompanied Jacqueline Kennedy to Paris. Awfully nice is being the power behind the throne.

Horrible, unspeakable, are the assassinations, John Kennedy collapsing into Jackie's arms, blood splattering all over her elegant pink suit. Not nice is never being able to forget exactly where you were that fateful November day when childhood innocence was abruptly shattered (Maisie and Lily were rehearsing their parts as Mary and Joseph for the Christmas play; Emma was riding up in an elevator to visit a friend and thought the elevator man who reported the grim news was kidding; I was smitten for the first time with a boy who had finally noticed me, and I skidded from my own private elation to the global despair that instantly followed the news).

Confusing is Walter Cronkite breaking down in tears, as he announces on national TV that the president is dead. Walter Cronkite, a distant father figure to the country, is a not-so-distant father figure to the girls, since his daughter is a classmate, a freckle-faced free spirit whose dog perpetually "eats her homework."

Here on Walter Cronkite's tortured brow is the cusp of nice and not nice, the seismic shift between propriety and chaos, between the smooth, unruffled surface and the troubled underbelly where unexpressed emotions are caught. For the essence of nice is saying something only if you have something nice to say. It's smile, smile, smile, no matter what's happening inside. And the essence of not nice is baring your soul, telling all, letting it all hang out. Nice is *There's nothing going on here*—and don't talk about it! It's keeping secrets and keeping mum. Not nice is speaking up, speaking out, shaking your fist at injustice and hypocrisy. Nice is being a lady above all else and beaming reflected glory on your family. Less nice is the messy business of becoming your own person.

It's only when nice and not nice collide—raggedly, haphazardly, outrageously—that young adulthood for the class of '68 truly begins.

CHAPTER 4

After '68: The Copers

*T*he summer of '68—somewhere between Brearley graduation, all hell erupting at the Democratic National Convention, and entering the college of her choice—Alexa heads for Paris. After much debate, her parents, a wealthy business magnate and a chic Frenchwoman, are allowing her to spend a summer as an au pair for a French couple with two young kids. Until now, Alexa has lived the heavily sheltered life most Brearley girls have, hers in a huge Park Avenue apartment, palatial enough to have separate dining rooms, one for parents and one for nanny and kids. But this summer is to be her coming out, her emerging from the cocoon of sheltered innocence into the bright, blinding light of society.

But history intrudes, as it does for everyone, while Alexa is making other plans. After the tumultuous Parisian spring of student strikes at the Sorbonne and citywide unrest, her prospective employer has lost his job. Although he'd signed a contract earlier to employ Alexa all summer, by the time she arrives, he can't afford to keep her on. Instead he offers to put her up in a small hotel—he knows the perfect one—for a week or so, until she can come up with another plan.

The hotel is in an unfamiliar neighborhood, a little sleazy, but picturesque—everything in Paris seems charming when you're eighteen and wide-eyed innocent. As the concierge helps her carry her bags to the top floor, Alexa wonders fleetingly why so many of the female guests are hanging out the windows. When the concierge confronts her at the end of the week and demands she share her take, she is *boulversée*. But when she calls her parents to discuss her change of plans, they size up the situation immediately. They get her out of that flophouse faster than you can say Charles de Gaulle. Alexa spends the rest of the summer sequestered in the country with a nice, respectable couple her parents know, out of harm's way.

The Fall of '68

So it went for the graduates of '68 as they stumbled from innocence to experience. They hungered to embrace the world with both arms, naïvely trusting, trying to behave like the adults they desperately hoped to become but were certainly not yet. Their schoolgirl resources paled before the tasks ahead. Like Alexa, they often had to be bailed out by parents and taken by the hand back to the gated kingdom of being little girls. Finally, the waves of history crashed so relentlessly over their heads that even parents' protections no longer protected them.

Overnight it was the fall of 1968, and my classmates and I were tossed unceremoniously out of the womb, into college and free fall. Leaving home and pulling away from parents and the long shadow of the school, those thirteen years of habits and memories, would have been emotionally taxing under the most benign of circumstances. But leaving home and arriving at college in the midst of a social revolution was a blow that blindsided most of the girls and sent some reeling for decades.

Suddenly, nice and not nice were spontaneously combusting, and my classmates were caught in the fallout. Everywhere on campus— both inside and outside the classrooms, inside and outside the dorms—the old order was being challenged and overthrown by the new. Propriety was giving way to open sexuality, traditional academics to politics and mayhem. When I arrived at Radcliffe, ardent but utterly ingenuous, parietal hours—when boys and girls were allowed in each other's rooms—ended sharply at midnight. Within months student pressure got these hours extended till two A.M., and then abandoned altogether. By my sophomore year most of the dorms were co-ed, and both sexes shared the bathrooms. Having barely seen a boy off a dance floor until then, I was now brushing my teeth, half-clad, next to them. Freshman year, strict dress codes were maintained for the boys at dinner—jackets and ties in the freshman dining hall; by the next year, dress codes were history. Studying was often eclipsed by protests, and by spring, exams were canceled by a student strike, the one and only time in Harvard's history that the inexorable forward momentum of academic ritual was interrupted. When I called home in a panic and described the campuswide upheaval, the constant political meetings and calls for action, my mother said comfortingly, "Won't the boys take care of those things, dear?"

For any girl-turning-woman, defining her truest self, recognizing her deepest longings, her starkest strengths, her tenderest vulnerabilities, is an awesome task during any freshman year. But during this particular year of global social upheaval, nationwide campus unrest, and burgeoning feminist ferment the task was all the more formidable. Now childhood's overprotectedness turned out to be no life raft. My classmates were tossed about in the choppy waters of late-sixties college life, churning with the Pill, pot, and politics. They were stranded between two shorelines. They could backstroke to the known but stifling clutches of Mom and Dad or swim furiously forward to the tempting but radical seductions of their peers. Caught in the middle, only some figured out how to navigate a safe passage, what reeds to cling to for support, how to maneuver against the waves. Others drifted, waiting for the tide to turn. And a few threatened to go under entirely.

The Copers and the Strugglers

The juncture between Brearley and college, between family and the world beyond home, was the first of several transitions in this group's coming of age. I call it the crisis of separation, and how my classmates negotiated it reflected both where they had come from and where they'd be able to head. Strategies were divided between copers and strugglers. The copers dug deep into their intellectual and emotional resources to manage this period of separation and begin, first tentatively, then with growing confidence, to carve out a separate sense of self, build a new support network, and reach forward toward newly evolving goals. Meanwhile the strugglers floundered. Their resources were not yet accessible; their talents had not yet flowered; they found themselves depending on the whims and dictates of others rather than generating their own agendas, their own sense of purpose. Some of the strugglers would find their way later on; indeed the very process of struggling would help lead them eventually to a stronger sense of self and direction. But for many strugglers this transition between adolescence and young adulthood was filled with emotional land mines and fraught with self-doubts and pain.

From Brearley to College

"The two hardest things about going to college," Maisie would say years later, "were leaving home and being around men." Academically my classmates were Amazons. Socially and emotionally, they were wobbly and naïve as toddlers. "We might get into the best colleges," a high-powered Brearley senior confessed to me even recently, "but once there, I don't know if we'll know what to do." Socially, she said, Brearley was a backwater.

But, ah, could those Brearley grads study. All the library research skills, the close textual analysis, the assiduous note-taking, the elegant essay-writing, the bleary-eyed test-cramming, and the buttery-smooth oral reports had them so well prepared that many of my classmates came home after fall semester of freshman year confiding to each other that the curriculum had been a breeze compared with high school. The Psychoanalytic View of Man, Government and the Social Contract, Twentieth-Century Drama—I sailed right through my freshman courses. Just losing myself in a crowded lecture hall where the professor never knew if I'd finished all the reading was a relief, compared with my tiny Brearley classes, where every student had to be thoroughly prepared every moment. In a class of ten or twelve, if homework wasn't done, it showed like a flowered slip drooping beneath a tweed skirt. In a college survey course I could cultivate anonymity until I was ready to make a move. Better still, my mind was left unfettered for those extracurricular activities with the longed-for opposite sex that would become the heart of my higher education.

Still, leaving the seclusion of Manhattan schoolgirl life was at first a mind-boggling jolt. "Brearley let you be a child," Judith explained about those warm, protected waters of childhood and early adolescence. "You were nurtured in the bosom of the school like in a womb." But this hermetically sealed world was slowly fading into oblivion as inexorably as an old photograph.

Just years before my class arrived at Brearley, in 1955, legend had it, the school nurse would march from room to room, checking its temperature with a thermometer to make sure it was neither too hot nor too cold for the girls. But if this quaint custom had lapsed before my classmates' tenure, their environment was still highly controlled. They wrote in small, black notebooks on diminutive lined paper that was available only in the school store. They had hot lunches every day with gravy-drenched meat, mashed potatoes, and lima beans, finished off with rice pudding or prune whip, perfect nursery food. And they were expected to act like ladies both inside the school and out.

The Manhattan of the 1950s and 1960s that this group grew up in was neither the melting pot of social mythology nor the criminal underbelly described in the tabloid press. Their New York City was a severely circumscribed area that stretched about forty blocks north from, say, Saks and Bonwit's in the Fifties, past the fashionable parade of Madison Avenue boutiques, to the Metropolitan Museum at Eighty-second. My apartment building at Ninety-fourth and Park was about as far north as any classmates dared venture. East to west their horizons were just as limited—from Bloomingdale's on Lexington Avenue to the Museum of Natural History on Central Park West, with a stop at Carnegie Hall on West Fifty-seventh Street, where, when young, they listened to Leonard Bernstein's Concerts for Young People and, later, screamed like banshees for the Beatles' first New York City appearance and lingered by the Russian Tea Room waiting for a glimpse of Rudolf Nureyev.

So within a city that spread dangerously in all directions, my classmates were cradled in a comfort zone that felt as safe as any small town. They knew instinctively there were places they dared not tread. They rarely ventured far over to the West Side—Columbus or Amsterdam Avenues—where the city pulsed with street life, and exotic cuisines (that is, anything beyond egg rolls and chow mein) peppered the air with savory smells. They rarely went to the Village, that bohemian hotbed, and, God knows, never crossed the invisible Maginot Line at Ninety-sixth Street and Park, where the Silk Stocking district suddenly stubbed its toe on Harlem. Those ironclad boundaries were observed as rigidly as the DMZ.

Their world was still as precious and rarefied as that depicted in *The World of Henry Orient,* the 1958 novel alumna Nora Johnson wrote about two gently rebellious, hero-worshiping teenagers from Brearley. The novel was later popularized in a movie with Peter Sellers that came out in 1964 when my classmates and I were fourteen, the same impressionable age as the movie's heroines.

Even in the late sixties, with revolution a hot breath on their necks, many classmates were used to having decisions made for them. They were used to bowing to parents' authority and uncertain about how to claim their own. Parents' values still framed and defined them. Parents' rules for what was nice and what was not nice seemed unassailable. Parents' wealth bought daughters privilege and insularity; it dangled choices but quickly circumscribed them. Daughters' territory—both outer and inner—felt as contained as a cloister.

So leaving home for college and being on their own in strange new places beyond the reach of parents' rules and school-day customs provoked a welter of complicated feelings that threatened to overwhelm many classmates. Both copers and strugglers at times experienced confusion, anxiety, a profound sense of loss, and depression that sometimes played itself out in drug use, eating disorders, acting out, and dropping out. Struggling to separate, to understand and manage this flood of feeling and find a comfortable autonomy, was as crucial a piece of this sheltered group's college curriculum as any required course.

Besides separation, another great shock to the equilibrium freshman year was going to school with men. For many lifers at a girls' school, knowledge of the opposite sex had been limited to a brother, a cousin, the odd boy or two who moved them stiffly across the floor at dancing school or chatted them up uneasily at a holiday dance. "Until I got to college, I thought boys always came in tuxedos, carrying flowers in their hands," joked older schoolmate B. B. Hiller, later the author of *Teenage Mutant Ninja Turtles*.

My father loved to imitate these sweaty-palmed holiday dance encounters. "What's your name? What school do you go to?" he'd say with feigned nervousness, box-stepping me across the dining room floor, rehearsing me for the impossible-to-imagine man who would one day dance me away from him.

Even the few worldly-wise exceptions—the wild, not-nice, early deflowered girls—knew boys more as romantic or sexual partners than fellow travelers with hearts that ticked just like theirs. Very few classmates as schoolgirls had hung around boys enough to see them as just as uncertain, brave, quirky, and complicated as they themselves were. And as for revealing one's deepest natures to men, here no one had practice.

My Freshman Year: Walking the Streets, Then Writing about It

When I finally arrive in Cambridge to start Radcliffe, I am heady with euphoria and queasiness. My parents drive me up from New York and unload my boxes and bags into the tiny cubicle I share with my new roommate, a television writer's daughter from Los Angeles. Our room, like our lives, is a blank slate. Soon our beds will be covered with Indian bedspreads, our walls with Matisse prints, our shelves with slender volumes of Sylvia Plath, and our windows with bamboo shades and spider plants putting forth their improbable babies. This is the first room I've ever decorated without mother's advice—she chose the turquoise eyelet bedspread and flowery wallpaper of my room at home—and I labor lovingly over each choice.

My parents drive back to New York with my roommate's mother, who reports to my roommate, who loses no time reporting to me, that my parents cried all the way home. Our family does not separate easily.

I, too, feel a bit unmoored. But I am quickly swept along by the rising tide of novelty and freedom. After dinner, I linger in the dining hall with girls from places I've never even heard of—Casper, Wyoming; Hudson, Ohio—giddy with conversation. I hang out in coffeehouses, savoring the first taste of adulthood along with the bitter brew. I walk the streets around Harvard Square for hours on end, soaking up the atmosphere I coveted for so long in the golden cocoon of my Manhattan childhood—that intoxicating Cambridge mix of Marimekko dresses and green canvas bookbags, Bergman and Bogart festivals, ice-cream cones with jimmies and chocolatey espressos, posters announcing visits from all my icons in a single week—Erik Erikson, Anne Sexton, Joan Baez. Striding through the gate to Harvard Yard—Enter and Grow in Wisdom—past Widener Library, Memorial Church, Seaver Hall, I feign a confidence I don't always feel inside. Like every other freshman, I desperately want to be worthy of this place while secretly fearing that I'm not.

There are three flavors of Radcliffe girls, *Crimson* writer Faye Levine has written famously several years before my class arrives: The peach are preppy, perky, social, and well-dressed. They fill the fine arts courses and treasure Radcliffe for "its people." Chocolates come from big public high schools and are obsessed with work; they're brilliant and tend toward too-long skirts and unkempt hair. Limes are sophisticated and have a sense of style—black tights, pierced ears, primitive jewelry, and classically waist-length hair. They gravitate toward creative-writing classes and wrote poetry as dreamy-eyed high school girls.

I ardently hope to renounce my intrinsic peachiness and cultivate the lime. Still, every morning I dress for classes like a nice peachy girl in skirts, stockings, and heels. Every afternoon I trudge back through the Commons, dodging spare-change artists, leering construction workers, and street harassers who turn out to be as much a part of the landscape as the stately homes of Brattle Street. Reaching the safety of my dorm, I toss aside my peachy togs for lighter shades of lime—the blue jeans, big handknit sweater, and don't-mess-with-me boots that become the uniform Ali MacGraw affects when she immortalizes her *Love Story* Radcliffe girl soon after. Indeed, when I return to Cambridge after Christmas vacation freshman year, my dorm has been taken over by the *Love Story* film crew, and Ali and Ryan O'Neal are being filmed coming in and going out of our front door, hurling insults at each other, over and over until they get it right.

Encountering men en masse and in particular for the first time overshadows other experiences of my freshman year. Walking the streets of Cambridge those first few weeks and months I am taken aback by their presence. I am used to a landscape of girls and women; men seem at first like a foreign presence, like invaders. They hurry confidently along the streets, never doubting ownership, never questioning their right to be there. Sometimes I can hardly make eye contact on the street, in class; other times I'm emboldened to catch someone's eye and linger. Will anyone emerge from the pack of strangers to be my confidant, my soulmate? By October I've made my first real male friend, Ezra. Ezra is appropriately arty, has a harpsichord in his room, and sits next to me when the lights dim and the slides go on in Fine Arts 13. My heart knows immediately he is not romantic material. He's too precise, too good a notetaker, just like me. I need someone messier for love, someone more dangerous and inappropriate. But we go to the movies together—*Persona, Jules et Jim, King of Hearts,* which plays longer in Harvard Square than any other film before or since. Afterward we dawdle over hot chocolate and gossip as shamelessly as girlfriends. When Ezra laughs at my jokes or shares a confidence, I'm startled, and then the light dawns. He has humor and feelings just like mine. At eighteen, I'm getting this for the very first time.

I have not come to college with any particular aspirations beyond a vague desire to play the field and find out who I am. So I poke in and out of friendships and romances, and while remaining schoolgirl chaste, I start kissing so indiscriminately that by November, I have caught a bad case of mono and must come home to Mom to recuperate for a few weeks. Academically I am also playing the field. This is not the era when thirteen-year-olds declare themselves premed or pre-law. Experimenting is the norm, and to have too much sense of direction, even at goal-driven Harvard, would be uncool.

I poke in and out of activities and classes—literature, politics, psychology, sociology—until I realize that it's in my creative-writing class that I feel most myself—that is, where I feel most comfortable speaking my own truth. "Be no more ashamed of a story that you've written than of a dream that you've had," reads a small hand-lettered sign hanging over our instructor's desk. Here I begin to probe for the first time beneath the surface of everyday life, the places too deep to speak about, the heartland between dreams and responsibility.

Soon after my first writing class begins, our instructor, Carter Wilson, holds up the novel he published at twenty-three and assures us that any of us in the room can do the same. Around the room we are wide-eyed and rabbit-still, absorbing his message, processing his permission. We labor with even more intensity over our manuscripts about broken hearts, fragile psyches, the wine-dark sea. We are tingling with promise and with self-seriousness. "Why are you staring at that crane?" Carter chides one of my classmates, whose attention is fixated out the window. The boy is the son of a famous baseball player and frequently comes to class high. "I'm not staring at the crane," he replies with a confidence only a Harvard freshman can sustain. "I *am* the crane."

Not too many years later at least three of us from this class will publish our own books. And when I take Carter Wilson's upper-level class in the spring of my freshman year, my work catches the eye of an editor from *Newsday* who's there on a Nieman Fellowship for working journalists. He likes a story I've written about a troubled Swedish actress—my Bergman phase—and offers me a summer job at *Newsday,* the Long Island newspaper, then published by Bill Moyers. In daydreams I see myself as the starving artist in her garret, churning out passionate short stories the world will never see. Meanwhile my career creeps up on me from behind and tempts me to mix it up in the grittier world of freelance journalism.

Sometime the next year I try out for the editorial board of Harvard's daily newspaper, *The Crimson*. Comping—*Crimson* slang for competing—means writing a series of pieces under the guidance of a tutor, an upperclassman who's already on the board. My tutor is a brash, brilliant writer, charismatic, if middle-aged in his ambitions. He is an old soul, typical of many of the *Crimson* writers who know they are just a heartbeat away from lifetime careers at *The New Yorker* or *The New York Times* (which, sure enough, is where he ends up a few years later). I am hopelessly in love with him. At first I feel as if each word I write will be measured and evaluated by him and my worth, no, more than that, my entire appeal as a woman, will be weighed on his scales of merit. But little by little I lose myself in what I have to say.

The relationship heaves and sputters and eventually crumbles. For a time my heart is broken, until I find the man I will ultimately fall in love with for keeps and marry many years later. Still, I keep on writing, thus proving to myself for the first of many times that writing is both a shelter from crises and a life raft that carries me through them. Writing about my own experience both deepens it and makes it more manageable, less frightening, less overwhelming.

Despite having lost the affections of my tutor, I make it onto the editorial board and start seeing my pieces printed for the first time. Watching *Crimson*s rustle around the breakfast table while classmates read what I've written is a secret thrill. I'm hooked.

My *Crimson* pieces comb the territory between the personal and the political. Grounded in my own experience, they also listen for the wider ripples. In one of my first pieces, "Walking the Streets," I try to make sense of some of my encounters with the opposite sex freshman year, from the impersonal to the all too personal. Sybil, the stand-in I create, is a "typical Radcliffe street walker with typically long dark hair and a typically purple canvas satchel" to lug her books. On a walk from her dorm to her classes she's hassled by a parade of harassers, from a street person hustling her for spare change to a guitarist offering "LSD for the lady" to a pack of bicycling schoolchildren—innocents, her last great hope—who pedal by her, reach over, and poke her in the chest. "What is absolutely vital to every legitimately sexist street confrontation," I conclude in a voice that is new to me, a righteous voice of assertion and outrage, "is that the woman must never feel as though she is being singled out for her individuality, her good spirits, or her charm. She must always be made to feel like an object under appraisal. Slim and rich, like a good cigarette."

But there is another, more tender, voice behind that piece as well. For at the end of her long walk home, Sybil encounters her old boyfriend, Stanley, whom she hasn't seen in months, and Stanley simply stares at her, "stares right through her as if they have never met." "It is worse than all the 'Hey, blondies' in the world," I finish. Being ignored is even more painful than being recognized for the wrong reasons.

The piece wins honorable mention in the annual *Crimson* writing competition, and slowly, very tentatively, I start to think of myself first as a writer and then as a woman writer, exploring the landscape between hurt and outrage, between my personal stories and a wider, collective narrative. I follow "Walking the Streets" with a piece for *Newsday* about advertising that exploits women, and later, for the *Crimson*, a critique of Norman Mailer's *Prisoner of Sex.* By early April, I'm back at Brearley's alumnae luncheon giving a talk, "Male Chauvinism at Harvard," which is later published in the school's alumnae bulletin. Still torn between being a nice girl and not so nice, between peach and lime, I'm starting to learn to use my pen where I may not yet be able to raise my voice.

But when campus politics erupt in the lilac-blossomed spring of my freshman year, I dash for cover. When hundreds of students march on President Pusey's house to protest Harvard's policies as a landlord in the community and the galling presence of ROTC on campus, a presence inextricably linked with the escalation of the Vietnam War, as unpopular at Harvard as on most other campuses around the country, I support my fellow students' demands but remain safely on the sidelines. When hundreds continue marching and take over the central administration building, University Hall, evicting deans and rifling files in the name of morality and honesty, and encamp in the building overnight to stand up for their beliefs, I feel a rush of ambivalent pride, but am too inhibited to be among them.

When, in the earliest dawn hours, President Pusey gives the word and scores of policemen swarm into University Hall in a tsunami of blue helmets and blue uniforms, smashing their clubs down on students' heads until they bleed, when students are sobbing and screaming and jumping frantically out of windows to escape the melee, I am safe and sound, oblivious, in my Radcliffe dorm. When a lone night crier races breathlessly from the scene of the University Hall bust to the middle of the Radcliffe quad and shouts, "The pigs are coming, the pigs are coming," so that her words echo in the silent dawn and merge seamlessly with our dreams, I toss fitfully in my bed, but do not rush out. I find refuge in being an observer, in reporting even where I cannot plunge in, and gradually this skill will become a strength. Writing allows me to share the truths I am not yet bold enough to speak out loud and to bridge the chasm between the old, safe world and the new world breaking open around me, threatening and seductive.

Judith—Drifting Until She Finds Her Way

Entering Brearley as a new girl in the seventh grade had been so hard for Judith her stomach still churned to think about it. That austere, unwelcoming, factorylike building that rose ten stories skyward on the farthest reach of East Eighty-third Street on the East River, glassy and unperturbed in the fall, choppily raging during winter storms, and frothy with whitecaps in the spring. The clusters of old, known-each-other-since-kindergarten girls who sat together in the cafeteria, chatting confidently, oblivious to the handful of new girls eating by themselves or in nervous pairs. The school's cavernous stairwell, walls painted bile-green, which linked the whole building and seemed to go on forever. That stairwell would haunt her dreams for decades, for teachers rarely traveled there, so all hell could break out—hair-pulling, gratuitous kicking, decidedly unladylike mayhem.

It was years before Judith felt at home at the school; a few key friendships and inspiring teachers helped the turnaround. Her Latin

teacher, especially, became a major force in her life. She was a powerful intellect who was also a loving mother and strong maternal
presence, the first who showed Judith it was possible to both work
and raise children, and the pivotal person outside her own family
who believed in Judith and taught her to believe in herself. Only
when Judith was known and accepted did the school finally begin
to feel homey to her. She could curl up in the womblike comfort of
the library with a good book or pore over the *O.E.D.*, deciphering
the fourth meaning of an obscure word in *Hamlet*. She warmed up
quickly to the intensity of the place, thrived on studying, always
pushed herself to do her best. Still, her brother remembers her
hunched over her desk at home, plowing through homework, crying when the workload threatened to crush her. She doesn't remember it that way. She remembers the pleasure the school taught
her to find in reading and studying all by herself. She remembers
country visits to her family's Connecticut weekend house, where
the whole family sat reading in the living room for hours on end,
like an extended group study hall. That single-mindedness, that
fierce intellectual independence, did not desert her even when she
drifted off course.

But for someone who doesn't adapt to change easily, leaving
Brearley she's faced with making not one but two of them, two
transitions to college. Getting to Vassar is the first shock. Her parents drop her off a few days early so they can catch a plane to Paris.
Judith rattles around the almost empty campus for those first few
days and the old ghosts of insecurity come back to haunt her. Even
when the other girls start to arrive and settle in, the place seems
harsh. It feels like seventh grade all over again—being on the outside, trying to make friends, wanting to be accepted, fearing she
won't be. And unlike the thicker-skinned girls, who manage to seem
undaunted—her old classmate Pam, who left Brearley for boarding
school and has now turned up at Vassar, is one of them—Judith
can't hide her fears.

It doesn't help when she hears from home that her mom, back

from Paris, has gone into an empty-nest slump. Like most of the mothers of '68, Judith's mom is a traditional mom who hasn't worked outside the home. Like the rest of her social set she has occupied herself with lunching or doing good works of one sort or another while her kids were at school. Most of these moms have not been sufficiently engaged to settle comfortably into the satisfactions of their own lives beyond child raising. And meanwhile many have throbbed quietly with ambitions that did not have an outlet or social support. Such was the backlash from the feminine mystique that mothers often expected a perfection from their daughters that would, they hoped, assuage their own frustrations, shore up their own self-esteem. They were ripe for living out their dreams through the next generation, and primed for disappointment when daughters left home and took their own dreams with them.

But unlike most of the rest of the class's push-and-pull teenagers, Judith has remained extremely close to her mom. Later her mom will warn Judith to find something meaningful beyond husband, home, and kids, so she won't be so chillingly lonely after her own kids leave her. But that's much later. Now Judith asks herself only how she can separate from her mom if her mom can't be happy without her.

For the rest of freshman year, Judith sinks into her own lonely depression. For the first time ever in her illustrious academic career, she loses interest in her classes. The only thing she cares about is listening to music. Music speaks to her. It feeds her soul, nourishes her more than striving for A's. She slides into what she'll later call a drifting phase, when she stays in her room, smokes dope, and loses herself in Beethoven sonatas. All those years of burning the midnight oil to do well at Brearley have finally caught up with her. She stops worrying about achieving. She just doesn't care anymore.

She does start to care about meeting men, about dating. She starts checking herself in the mirror more often, wondering if her old reliable schoolgirl look—the no-fuss short hair and offhand boyishness—could be transformed into something chic, something to attract the opposite sex, not mimic it. She starts to resent that at Vassar, the only way to meet men is to get on a bus and be shipped off to another campus to socialize. It's a meat market out there. It starts to gall her, to feel unnatural, too much like her all-schoolgirl past.

Like several of the class's most glittering academic stars, Judith has expended such intellectual energy in high school that she threatens to burn out. Indeed, a few classmates seem to peak as teenagers and never shine so brightly again. But if Judith's star flickers for a time, it never entirely goes out. She just needs a time-out to decompress. But her intellectual staying power endures, her internal compass wavers but never totally loses course. Despite her lethargy, she rallies to concoct a plan. The boyfriend of a friend of hers goes to Princeton, and Judith likes what she hears about it—the small classes, the beautiful, manicured campus, the academic excellence, to which she's still at her core committed. Even though she can't always motivate herself to get to classes, she'll run through a load of tough math problems on her own. Now Princeton, like Yale and a few other previously all-male bastions, is succumbing to the feminist pressures of the times and admitting women. Judith applies and is admitted to Princeton's first co-ed class.

This time the transition is more manageable. The wrench of leaving home is already behind her. The uncertainty over who she is on her own is not yet resolved but no longer so acute. Though she continues to smoke dope and listen to music, she begins to get interested in her classes again. What a relief to go to school with guys—she can even study with them—and they don't seem to see her as the stringy-haired, pimpled early adolescent she once feared she was. Her phone starts ringing with guys making plans and dates.

As the late sixties become the early seventies—the invasion of Cambodia, the student demonstrators shot at Kent State—Judith becomes more and more politicized. She's energized, not overwhelmed, by the political wave breaking over even the formerly white-shoed, bow-tied, Gatsby-like gentility of the Princeton campus. She grabs the opportunity to participate in history, marches on Washington, sleeps in churches. By the time her two years at Princeton are ending, she has reclaimed her sense of purpose and is determined to continue her once almost abandoned academic career.

Cordelia—Taking a Year Off, Coming Back Stronger

Cordelia leaves Brearley with a divided psyche, not quite sure if she's smart or stupid, powerful or ineffective, a leader or a sideliner. On one side of the ledger, she knows the school has empowered her. She has a wide circle of devoted friends, was elected student government president, and proved a forceful, influential one. She's also buoyed by the faith of several important teachers, including Mrs. Broderick, the class's beloved English and homeroom teacher, and Maggie Tucker, her drama teacher, a whimsical, poetic, political, and iconoclastic soul, who has taken Cory under her wing as a kindred spirit.

On the downside, family pressures weigh heavily on her shoulders after her parents' breakup and her mother's erratic behavior, and taking care of her mother has forced her to grow up faster than most. And then there are all those C's, both blessing and curse—a blow to her ego, yet an opportunity to practice coping with not always being the best. "I was used to being worse than everyone else," she'll say with equanimity and more than a dash of pride years later. As she gets ready to harness her red-hot energy to tackle what lies ahead, she won't have to waste a lot of time fearing she'll fail. She's already mucked around in that territory and she knows she can handle it.

Cory's experience suggests a larger truth—that academic skills were not by any means the only route to success among this group, and that good grades were not a reliable predictor of their futures. Some of the class's best and brightest peaked as schoolgirls and drifted uncertainly later on. And some, like Cory, with her straight-C record at school, later learned to draw on other strengths and made names for themselves after all. For certain resilient girls, fighting back against the stigma of a poor academic record turned out to be a better motivator than a path paved with straight A's was for others; the back-talking girls developed early on a gritty belief in themselves that energized them and gave them confidence through life.

So while the rest of the class scatters to campuses up and down the East Coast, Cory retreats, as planned, to an international college in Lugano, Switzerland. This year abroad works magic to pull her head together and boost her confidence. For the first time ever, Cory gets straight A's. More than that, when her English class struggles over a Shakespeare text or a Wordsworth poem, she trusts her own analyses. Amazingly, she can tell she's even smarter than her English teacher! She also has plenty of beaux and acquires a becoming European polish while keeping her country-girl heart.

This time, when she applies to Sarah Lawrence, she's not at all surprised that she gets in. But once she settles into life on the small, rarefied, all-female campus, she starts to feel hemmed in. During the year she's been away, the culture has been radicalized and she wants to be part of it. Sitting in classrooms, being lectured by tweedy academics about crisis and change, about worker-student alliances, about transformation, she itches to be part of the process. She needs, as she'll later say, to get back to basics. She swiftly mounts her own campaign, and suddenly she has convinced her professors to let her do a field project in Appalachia. She is already used to shifting artfully between two worlds. She has managed the change from Williamstown's laid-back country life to New York's fast track and then from the fast pace of the city to the cultured life in Switzerland. Her muscles for starting over—without cutting all ties to the past—are in better shape than most people's.

The beauty of the Appalachian landscape and its grim poverty stir Cory's heart. She eases her way into the community, makes friends, wins people's trust. She builds an organization in east Tennessee that still exists, called Save Our Cumberland Mountains. While she's there she meets an idealistic lawyer, Sam, who is filing a suit against the Tennessee Valley Authority. Sam is ten years her senior—the same age difference as that between her mother and the wealthy suitor her mother will soon marry. Sam is in the middle of a divorce and has two school-age sons he'll be raising mostly on his own. He's an uncertain prospect, but they fall passionately in love. Still, when Cory tears herself away from Tennessee to return to Sarah Lawrence she's not sure she'll be seeing any more of him.

Back on campus, she writes up her research, but she has shifted her sights. After all her efforts to get into college, now she can't wait to get out. "The professors had read about making change," she'll later say, "but I was living it." On the outskirts of New York, among all those overachieving bluestockings, she dreams about the soft green mountains of Tennessee, about the uneducated but soulful people she's befriended, about her true love, who's still fighting for the cause. After two years at Sarah Lawrence, restless for the Real World, she cuts loose.

Tess—Folk-Dancing to Find Her Balance

Like Judith, Tess entered Brearley in seventh grade, but overnight her sympathetic personality made it seem she'd always been there. The other girls warmed up quickly to her bubbly self-confidence, her ease with herself and with others, which was almost a family birthright. Tess was the second child in a lively family of ten—seven warmhearted girls, each more charming and charismatic than the next, and three boys who did their best to keep up with their sisters.

Like Cory, Tess had the gift of flexibility and ease in settings beyond the school. She seemed to move effortlessly between school life, where she was a top-notch student, a competent athlete, and a social butterfly, and held several class offices, and her home life in a small Hudson Valley town two hours away. The family's rambling estate included a formal garden and grounds that seemed to roll on forever. It was there Tess first fell in love with gardening and discovered her green thumb. The house boasted so many bedrooms and so much common space—a huge pool table didn't half fill one cavernous room—that before Tess's family took it over it provided a serviceable extra dorm for Vassar College.

To outsiders the family's lifestyle looked glamorous and luxurious. What other classmate had her own ballroom? There Tess and her sisters gave unforgettable parties filled with earnest boys from the nearby military prep schools. The family dining room was also cafeteria-like in scale with a dining table that rivaled Citizen Kane's. At breakfast there'd be three oversize cereal boxes, several gallons of milk, and multiple loaves of bread, sticks of butter, jars of jam. In twenty minutes every morsel of food would be demolished. The table would be bare except for a mountain of debris, like a beach after a hurricane.

Christmas was the year's peak experience in this devout Catholic family; Tess's mother prepared for it for months. Typically, the family Christmas card portrayed the children posed in their own Nativity scene. Tess's older sister, sporting a white cotton beard, would be Joseph, and Tess would play Mary, holding the newest family baby in her arms; the others clustered around them wearing crowns, staffs, or angel wings. A gigantic spruce brushed the ceiling of her father's wood-paneled study; the rest of the year it was strictly off-limits to children. Since the Christmas spirit meant that everyone in the family gave presents to everyone else—a hand-lettered calendar, a clay project, or one of Tess's exquisite banners—the packages spilled over one another, like a gigantic passel of puppies, blanketing the study floor and overflowing into the hall.

But what looked extravagant to other classmates, with their comparatively meager two- or three-siblinged families and their gracious but small-scale city apartments, took some scrimping to pull off. The temperature at Tess's house was kept at a chilly 55 to offset staggering heating bills, and she got used to always feeling a little cold. And shopping was strictly at secondhand stores, where Tess and her sisters developed a knack for "finding the finds." When lunchroom chatter turned to a sale at Bloomingdale's or a drop-dead dress at Saks, Tess kept mum.

Still, Tess would not willingly trade the pleasures of being part of a big family for a few extra creature comforts. Adjusting to eleven other people—their likes and dislikes, their moods and quirks—was like learning to live in a small community. Tess learned to accommodate, negotiate, fight fair, and organize. She felt at ease with women and comfortable around guys—besides her three brothers, there were all those young men she and her head-turning sisters brought home. She got used to feeling special, high-profile. What other locals used a vintage Checker cab for their family car? And more than that, Tess absolutely never felt alone.

When Tess gets to Barnard freshman year, it's not quite the same jolt that others feel. After all, she's spent her entire childhood living in a dorm, and she makes the adjustment easily. Unlike most of her peers who want to dabble in this and dabble in that, Tess already has her heart set on the goal of horticulture. Greening her family's huge estate first put the idea into her head, and now her passion has become a mission. But since her family is set against it, she knows she'll have to struggle harder than most to prove that her goal is worthwhile. "If you're going to go into horticulture," she hears her father chiding her, "you're going to have to be the best damn horticulturist there is." Barnard doesn't make it easy for her either. The only relevant course that's offered is an adult ed course on microbiology.

Despite Tess's personal sense of purpose, she sometimes finds it hard to swim against the raging currents of the times. Revolution hit the Columbia campus the spring before Tess arrived; the SDS-led occupation of buildings to protest the university's war-related activities and community expansion was one of the student movement's first takeovers. The political fallout still infiltrates every corner of student life. There's very little structure and endless meetings; her closest friend, Jed, is the head of the SDS and goes to many more meetings than classes. Final exams are canceled. "Normality is very difficult to set up," she'll later say. Some of the less put-together crumble under the pressure. One girl in Tess's dorm locks herself in her room and takes a "mental sabbatical" for a year, coming out only to eat.

Tess neither throws herself into the fray like Jed nor opts out entirely like her barricaded dormmate. Beyond her classes and her studies and the gleam in her eye for gardening, Tess has the emotional savvy and the survival skills to grab on to something that gives her pleasure, structure, and focus. She has always liked to folk dance, has flirted with it all through high school, and now she finds a folk-dancing group on campus and devotes herself to it whole-heartedly. The intricate steps and patterns, the blood-warming ethnic music, the openness to other cultures, the acceptance of all shapes, colors, and sizes, the profusion of eager men, even, she admits, the lovable weirdos in socks, sandals, and too-short pants who often turn up at dances—folk dancing both grounds her and lets her spirit soar.

Soon she's getting very good at it, too, and quickly emerges as one of the group's talented leaders, invited to folk festivals all over the area. "If you have an innate leadership, it has to be expressed somewhere" is the way she'll put it later. "Mine found its path in folk dancing." When she dresses in her costume to perform, grabs the hand of her partner in the circle, swirls her skirt around her to the joyous beat of the music, with her feet keeping careful time and marking the complicated patterns, she feels both deeply connected and free, both contained and released. She has found a way to bridge the old world and the new, to push the envelope yet stay within its boundaries, to be at once respectably nice and yet wild and not so nice, too. Like Cory's activism, my writing, and Judith's intellectual intensity, Tess's folk dancing and passion for plants are natural talents and creative outlets that give her tools to cope with troubled times.

CHAPTER 5

The Strugglers

*A*fter 1968, the pressures of a society in transition collided with my classmates' internal pressures and emotional turmoil. Where the copers discovered talents and passions to ground them during these upheavals, the strugglers took longer to plumb their resources. For them the years after graduation were a time of emotional pitfalls, structureless stumbling.

Pamela—Feisty Tomboy, Fragile Child

Pamela inherited a tradition at Brearley that went back a record-breaking five generations in a Jewish family of vast "Our Crowd" wealth and prominence. This legacy was an invisible honor and something of a dubious one; it meant that Pam had more to live up to than most of the other invent-themselves girls who were the first in their families to attend the school and made—or tarnished—their reputations on their own. The challenge of Pam's illustrious lineage rattled a girl who, even at a young age, preferred to live a bit dangerously and not always follow the rules.

From her arrival in first grade, Pamela was one of the tallest, most mature-looking girls in the class and had a charisma and sophistication beyond her years. Strong and athletic, she started out an old-fashioned tomboy with stick-straight, blond hair, cut short and clasped with a no-nonsense barrette. Blue Keds were her footwear of choice, and red-framed glasses her favorite eyewear. Pam loved all sports and had a serious love affair with skiing, which also gave her an early access to the opposite sex. As a girl she was all knees and legs, but she gradually grew into her promise and became a beauty.

Pam was a leader of the boyish, sporty, physical girls who were the most confident in their bodies. They were also the first to be interested in boys, as if all that physicality needed an outlet somewhere. Athletics was one channel for their energy—killer games of blitzkrieg, sweaty five-on-five basketball, field hockey out in Carl Schurz Park, down from the mayor's mansion, several blocks from the school. Boy-lust was another. Pamela led on both fronts.

Pamela had little patience with girls who could not keep up with her. She could be loyal to a small cadre of admirers but was also a master of the put-down and could easily reduce the faint of heart to tears. Years later other girls would still remember a time Pam jostled them down the stairs between classes or devastated them with a lordly remark. Most classmates were too uncertain of themselves back then to see that her sarcasm camouflaged her tender spots and her bravado covered up her fears. Only much later would she herself come to understand how her tough exterior shielded the very scared person inside. "Sweet and vulnerable didn't cut it in my world," she would grow up to understand and admit.

School became a haven for Pam, the one place where she really "felt at home," when, ironically, "all hell was breaking out" at her real home. Beneath her family's socially prominent surface, arguments buzzed. Her parents' discontent finally disintegrated into divorce the year she left for boarding school. So as a young child, she clung to her nanny's comforts, and as the fourth of five children tried not to attract attention to herself. She had a much older brother, around only at holidays, tall as a tower and as unreachable, two glamorous older sisters years ahead of her at school, and a younger brother who offered the camaraderie and admiration she craved. Among them all, she learned to cultivate a kind of invisibility that she preferred to a limelight that could turn out to be dangerous.

But at school, she basked in the attention she got, not only from peers—that attention shadowed by fear—but also from teachers, who gave her plenty of affection for her "badness and humor." She was quick with words and had the kind of shrewd, verbal intellect that the school recognized and rewarded. "I liked how the teachers seemed to give a damn," she'd say years later. "It was pressure, because they had expectations, but it felt caring." That loving attention was a welcome antidote for what was sometimes missing at home, where expectations were also high but never clear-cut, where ambitions were intense but support was not always dependable.

She was torn between two attitudes—high-profile at school, low-profile at home. Keenly intelligent, Pamela nevertheless had an uneasy truce with "this thing of being bright"—to borrow a phrase from Wellesley College educator Peggy McIntosh, daughter-in-law of Millicent McIntosh, one of the school's most famous headmistresses, who left Brearley to become president of Barnard College. This "being bright"—and its corollary, "being special"—would become both incentive and millstone for many in this group. To Pamela it seemed like an obligation she could reach with effort but did not always feel like stretching herself toward when other possibilities beckoned—skiing down fresh powder, a hot romance. "Meeting Brearley's academic pressure took hard work, the kind I haven't put in since," she would say, looking back at midlife. "I don't know if I burned out or what."

Dropping Out

After leaving Brearley in ninth grade and spending three years at boarding school—relieved to be away from her family's complicated clutches but no clearer on her academic goals—Pam arrives at Vassar deeply ambivalent. Does she want to be in school or out, a student or a party girl, her parents' dutiful, achieving daughter or her own freewheeling person? At Vassar, as at Brearley, she bears once again the weight of her mother's and sisters' Vassar histories. And at Vassar again she finds herself surrounded by girls. But this time she misses the sweetness, the relative innocence, of her school-day friendships. These girls—no one is calling them women quite yet—come from big, heterogeneous high schools all over the country and are used to cordoning themselves off in cliques. Pam's not used to being on the social outskirts but fears she's ending up there. Running into her old Brearley classmate Judith at registration, she sees that Judith's at loose ends, too. But Pam's too cool to reach out, too determined to float above her neediness to advertise that she needs a friend.

One evening she's walking back to her dorm, alone when a strange man approaches her in the half-light. Close upon him, too close to flee, she sees with horror that he's swinging a baseball bat studded with menacing nails. He closes in on her. She screams, but her screams disappear into the unpeopled darkness. Not a soul hears her. She marshalls every ounce of strength she has—every slaloming muscle grows taut—and manages to fight her assailant off. He disappears into the night, leaving her alone, but now a different person. She has succeeded in saving her own life, but at a price. It is as if all that energy used on her own behalf depletes her supply, and more than anything else, she wants her freedom, wants to drift away to a country of no cares.

Suddenly she doesn't feel like trying anymore. She feels tired of the academic grind, tired of writing papers, tired of trying to fulfill some increasingly irrelevant academic promise she can't define or accept as her own. It's the heydey of hippies, and she's hungry to be part of it. She tries a pleasure-enhancing drug and finds it sublime. It takes her straight to that carefree no-effort zone she's been craving. "If all my trips had been as wonderful as that, I'd still be doing drugs," she'll later say, chastened after a few too many bum rides. She sees another life tingling in front of her, glowing enchantingly like the lights on her family's Christmas tree. It's a life of freedom, far away from school, from academic pressures, from cliquish girls, from family expectations, from threatening strangers swinging baseball bats in the darkness. It's a life of skiing fast down sugary slopes, of parties and guys, of an athletic rush that's so pure it becomes almost a spiritual joy, its own kind of ecstasy.

Meanwhile the darkness in her family is intensifying. The dream of a big, tight-knit clan has been shattered by her parents' divorce. Her siblings are scattering; her dad's drinking, once social and overlookable, is becoming more obvious and unavoidable. But in her family, no one is saying a word. The silence is deafening, almost conspiratorial. Is each of her siblings, she'll later wonder, suffering in private, trying desperately to protect the others from the obvious, the disintegrating dream of family harmony? Later she'll wonder if the silence reflects their desire not to rock an already unsteady boat, not to make the fractured dreams worse by airing them. Only later, when the pile-up of secrets has become unbearable, will Pam find that airing them diffuses them, makes them possible to bear.

But that insight comes decades later, when skiing and romance stop working and the demands of the inner self become too strident to silence. "It's been a long haul to be my real self," Pam will grow up to admit. Right now, after a year and one semester at Vassar, all she wants to do is get as far away as possible. Right out of the gate, like a horse given its head, she bolts straight for Aspen, Colorado. For the past ten years Pam has spent winter vacations skiing with her family in Aspen. These vacations have been the year's breath of freedom. Now her next-older sister has also settled in Colorado, and so has her father, who's renounced his upwardly mobile, button-down East Coast life for the New Age in Aspen. He's grown a ponytail and is becoming a minor guru for the encounter-group set.

Aspen feels more like home than any place Pam's ever been. Her restless spirit, straitjacketed by East Coast propriety, soars to the majestic mountains, snow-capped for months and then bursting with summer wildflowers, the intoxicating air, the rugged guys, the healthy women, and always and everywhere the skiing. Skiing is so much more than just a sport for Pam. It's passionate, romantic, almost spiritual, her tether to herself, to the deepest part of herself, where she feels most competent and at peace, both free and connected to something larger.

Aspen is a hippie heaven as the sixties swirl into the seventies with the Day-Glo intensity of a Peter Max painting. Besides her sister, there's not a Brearley girl for a mile. Pam tries gamely to fit in with the hippie culture, Aspen style. She has the sleek, streaky-blond-haired, just-shy-of-flower-child good looks and the insouciant style of the upper class. Most to the point, she's got the sizable trust fund to bankroll the lifestyle she wants, so she doesn't have to worry about working for her living. But somehow her East Coast breeding interferes with the sheer wantonness the counterculture requires. She can never do quite as many drugs, she'll later say, or have as much indiscriminate sex with people she doesn't know as the culture demands, a culture just as rigid in its way as the tight mores of Brearley or of boarding school. Here nice and not nice may have traded places but the definitions are just as unbending.

From the outside, Pam appears to have it all: good looks, a good mind, athletic prowess, a wicked sense of humor, an independent income. Still, she doubts her own resources. For most of her adolescence she's come across to the outside world as tough, feisty, independent. She's made sure that nobody sees the fragile child hidden beneath the hard shell. Being a rebel has defined her both in others' eyes and in her own. Diving headfirst into Aspen's subculture, she suddenly has nothing to rebel against. Here everyone does drugs, loves the land and the great outdoors, has dropped out of school and cut their ties to the past. No one works but everyone miraculously has plenty of dough. Having pushed back against everyone's high expectations of her for so long, she's afraid she'll lose her balance completely now that she has stopped pushing. And she's still weighed down with overstuffed baggage from the past.

The night before she flees the East Coast for Colorado she has a major confrontation with her mother. Accusations are hurled in both directions; painful disappointments in each other poison the air between them. Now, weeks and months later, she's still shaking with the desire to be understood, to be loved and accepted.

Every morning she wakes into the crisp mountain air and the clear, unforgiving light and wonders how to get through the day. Every day, she feels she has to create her life from scratch. Work might have grounded her. Though she doesn't need to work to support herself, working might have steadied her in other ways. But now every morning when she wakes, she wakes into free fall, into a vacuum with no limits, no boundaries. For about half an hour she sees things clearly and then suddenly, every morning, every day, the anxiety sets in. Who is she? Where's she going? Does anyone care if she lives or dies? Skiing is her only reed. She can't yet harness her other talents or find a relationship sturdy enough to shelter her. All day long the anxiety builds, and she has no name for it, no words for its causes, certainly no hint for its cure. She tries to go through the motions of a day—she skis, she does drugs with friends, she parties till dawn. But deep inside she is collapsing.

One afternoon she goes to see the movie *King of Hearts* with a friend and the story speaks to her. The message is finally clear. The crazy people are obviously the sane ones and the sane ones are running the world into the ground. The crazy world, she finally understands, is the Real Thing. "That movie saved my life," she'll later say, after decades of soul-searching and outside help have put her back together, let her believe again in her own possibilities. "I stopped fighting it," she'll later say about that scary time. "I went ahead and went crazy."

Maisie—Poor Little Rich Girl

Maisie transferred into the class in third grade from the Chapin School, another private and elite school, down the street from

Brearley. As one of the few new girls—and from the archrival, no less—she remained on the social fringes for a while. Years later she would confide that it took her a good two years to get rid of that Chapin stigma. Maisie's father and stepmother had moved her against her wishes—an older sister was already going to Brearley—and it was more convenient for both to attend the same school. But Maisie missed the more genteel, nurturing atmosphere of Chapin, where there was less emphasis on athletics and more on the arts, in which she was more at home. "At Brearley they moved at march time, at Chapin in waltz time," the playwright Tina Howe remembers her mother saying, before dispatching her from the slightly more liberal Brearley to the white-gloved docility of Chapin back in the forties.

At Chapin Maisie had been "good at everything"; at Brearley, she felt less so. She was a good enough student but had to apply herself furiously for results. All around her other girls seemed to be succeeding effortlessly. With the outsider's sharp eye, she scoped out the hierarchy in the class, with "academic achievement as the Holy Grail," and determined quickly that she was not on the top. She psyched out which classmates were ahead of her on the ladder and which were behind.

Maisie was a tidy, pixielike girl with doughboy-white skin and piercing brown eyes trained to tune in to adults in her very adult-centered household. She looked young for her age but had to grow up faster than most. At times she seemed like a miniature adult trapped in a child's body.

Maisie had a stringent sense of right and wrong, and strong opinions that sounded, at times, wiser than her years. In a fourth-grade essay on explorers, she philosophized on the difference between dedication and selfishness; at an age when most nine-year-olds had no concept of an inner life, Maisie was already discriminating between external and internal rewards.

Maisie began her life in California, but her parents were divorced before she turned five, and, unusually for the times, her father got custody of Maisie and her sister. Her mother was supposed to share custody of the girls, but emotional problems interfered. Maisie could never quite shake off the image of the day the family split up. Her mother and father each held one of her arms and literally pulled in opposite directions. After the divorce, Maisie's mother remained on the West Coast, and Maisie moved to New York with her father and sister. Maisie saw her mother only a handful of times her entire childhood—once the year she was five, again at twelve and at fifteen, then a final time when she was a senior in college. "She chose not to be in the picture," Maisie would say years later, trying to put a frame around the uncertainty, the emptiness.

In New York, Maisie, her father, and her older sister settled into a fancy brownstone in the East Sixties, territory that Peter Sellers's *The World of Henry Orient* would make famous a few years later. The brownstone was such a plum that when the family finally decided to sell it in the early seventies, Carly Simon and James Taylor plucked it up and turned the library into a recording studio. Some years after the move to New York, Maisie's father, a doctor, married a high-powered lawyer whose own daughter was almost grown.

"I never had the sense that our stepmother wanted us," Maisie said coolly years later, though over the years they made a bond. But in the early years of her father's second marriage, the best nurturing Maisie got was from her grandmother and, haphazardly, from the maids. None of this painful scenario was, of course, visible or revealed to Maisie's classmates. From the outside they saw a perky girl with a fanciful imagination, unusually keyed in to adults, who lived with her father and stepmother and was more attached to her grandmother than most. No mother was ever mentioned and no one probed. "No one keeps a secret better than a child," Victor Hugo once observed, and Maisie kept her secrets with the best of them. No one knew what Maisie knew.

When girls went to her house to play, they saw only how formal and stylish her household was, with an atmosphere as proper as that of a private club—parquet floors, English antiques, and floor-to-ceiling mirrors. Neither Maisie nor any of her friends would ever dream of sitting in the living room. Dinner was fashionably late— eight-thirty or nine—and the whole family dressed for it. Only in middle school and high school, when she had exams twice a year, would a concession be made for Maisie to eat earlier, and then she sat in the kitchen and ate with the maids. At the adult dinner table, the conversation was erudite—her father talked about medicine, and her stepmother about the law. From an early age, Maisie's place was set with a wineglass, and like a good European child, she sipped companionably along with the rest.

The day Maisie graduated from Brearley her father and step- mother took her to lunch at The Four Seasons. Sated with caviar and shrimp and the best wines, they looked at her expectantly. Now what? She stared back blankly. She had no idea of her own heart, of what would give her that internal reward she had already identi- fied, at nine, in an explorer's life. But she knew what would be the right thing to say, the expected thing, the nice thing. Her real mother—the mother she almost never saw but was nonetheless deeply tied to—had been a doctor and her mother's mother had been a doctor, too. "I'm going to major in biology and be pre- med," she sputtered, clutching her demitasse tightly to quiet her thumping doubts.

Culture Shock

But when she gets to Pembroke the following fall, nothing is as she imagined it. Nothing is solid or dependable. Everything is in flux, not the least her plans for the future. Everything is tougher than she had envisioned. She grits her teeth to get through the first few pre- med courses, and then she hits a wall. She's told to dissect a cat, and she simply cannot do it, cannot dissociate herself from her child- hood images of cuddly animals, cherished pets. She's pulling all- nighters to get through her science courses and is just squeaking by with a B. So she tosses aside her dreams and opts for something that feels comfier, easier. She switches her major to nineteenth-century British and American culture, and just as future Clinton aide Ira Magaziner is busily reforming the curriculum, she opts for taking a lot of her classes Pass/Fail.

The truth is, like most freshmen struggling to get their balance, Maisie spends the best of her emotional energy not on her classes but on life swirling outside the classroom. Leaving home, going to classes with men, trying to assimilate into the counterculture, which is as far from her upbringing as Dylan is from an opera diva—each transition unnerves her and unsteadies her a bit more. At first she's desperate to fit in—get stoned, go to parties, stay out late—but she returns to her dorm after these encounters feeling sullied and like a fraud. Her cheeks start to ache from all the false smiles, she's exhausted from the effort to please others and turn away from the person she really is. Fraternity parties where guys get wasted and grab at girls, any girls, make her ill. The private, sheltered, nicely mannered person she's been raised to be shivers deep inside beneath the disguise.

"I was a wreck my freshman year," she'll later have the distance to admit. "Homesick. Blown away." Even though there were rules in place—no men in the dorms after ten, "three feet on the floor in your rooms at all times"—the lack of structure frightened her, made her panic that she'd skid into free fall with no one to catch her. She wished she'd chosen a smaller school, a girls' school like Bryn Mawr or Barnard, where she could have lived at home.

Home for Christmas break her freshman year, she's given a small, tasteful coming-out party in her parents' brownstone. Old teachers and friends from Brearley mingle with her parents' guests and a smattering of her new friends from college. Everyone sips champagne, munches on finger sandwiches, and makes polite chitchat. Compared with the beer-swilling, skirt-grabbing frat parties she's become used to, this party feels almost turn-of-the-century, straight out of Edith Wharton or Henry James. She can practically hear the clash of cultures. After her debut, she tackles another rite of passage:

she's interviewed to become a member of the fashionable Colony Club, where her stepmother and older sisters enjoy ladies' lunches in restricted elegance. She pays twenty dollars a month for this privilege but rarely uses the club. "It's a good place to go to the bathroom if you're on Park Avenue," she'll later say. Eventually she has the gumption to let her membership lapse.

Christmas vacation and her debutante party turn out to be the only oasis of civility in an unruly and terrifying freshman year. Once she returns to school, her most frozen moments of fear come deep in the middle of the night, when the dorm is totally still and the other girls, she imagines, are safely asleep in the comfort of their own dreams. That's when Maisie lies rigid on her bed, fists clenched, staring blankly at the ceiling, waiting for it to happen. Sometimes nothing at all happens and she stares the night away simply waiting. But other times—four, five, six times those first few months of freshman year, when she's most innocent, most gullible, a lamb among sharks—the men come. They stand outside the dorm in the dark, hushed night and scream and taunt. She knows they are coming just for her, just to get her, smelling her innocent blood. "Panties!" they scream, rattling the windows with their raucous voices, banging their chests like packs of gorillas in the jungle, she'll later say. "Panties!" they hoot again, banging against the front door with all their might, as if they're about to enter and haul the girls off over their shoulders, cart them off in the night, like the Sabine women.

Other girls wake and giggle and gaily toss their panties out the windows. Orbs of flowered cotton fly through the night, shaken as innocently as pompoms at a football game. But Maisie lies motionless on her bed, clutching either side with her fists, as if ship-tossed in a hurricane. She goes white with fear, fear that one day the men will not stop at panties (the presence of a guard doesn't calm her one bit), fear that they'll break in, fear that they'll head straight for her.

Finally insomnia has her in its clutches. She can't get to sleep at night and all day long, she struggles to stay awake, struggles to concentrate. At last she drags herself to the school psychiatrist—a huge psychic effort in itself since her family worships medicine but scorns psychiatry. The psychiatrist reviews her records and makes his pronouncement. "There's nothing wrong," he insists. "You're on the Dean's List. You're getting straight A's." He gives her a prescription for sleeping pills and sends her on her way.

How can she trust her own instincts when no one will believe what she's feeling? The other girls laugh off her fears; the psychiatrist denies them; and her parents are too far away and too out of touch to know that she's coming apart inside. She feels more and more isolated. She has no friends, isn't able to go home often enough, and is shocked at how unexpectedly tough her classes are. At the end of freshman year she loses her virginity the way many girls of this generation lose it in those frantic college years, loses it like something to be gotten rid of, something to leave behind so that real life can begin. She loses her virginity to a friend of a friend who "sort of date-rapes her" at the end of the year. It's horrible, hopelessly unromantic, but at least, she can say to herself, "A hurdle was cleared." Her parents, completely in the dark, still remember the boy as wonderful.

Seeking Shelter in an Early Marriage

The next fall, the fall of her sophomore year, Maisie thinks she's found a savior and discovered a way out. She falls in love with a boy named Terry, who becomes completely dedicated to her. He shelters her, takes care of her every need. He teaches her to ride a bike and to drive, two life skills her overprotected upbringing has overlooked. His family becomes a real family to her, more open and less complex than the family that she already has. By that summer she and Terry are married. She's nineteen, he's a year or so older. From one of the class of '68's most innocent, she becomes one of the first to marry. Married, Maisie and Terry are allowed to move

off campus. Under his sheltering arm, she feels the fears start to re-
cede. Gradually the hoots and hollers of men invading the quiet
night start to fade, release their clutches on her dreams. She sleeps
through the night again; the insomnia disappears.

Maisie and Terry stay together for seven years and during that
time she takes her first baby steps to adulthood. Senior year her
mother dies, falls down a flight of stairs in circumstances that are
never entirely clear, and Maisie has to let go of any dreams she's held
on to for a loving reconciliation down the road. She feels bereft, but
it is hard to mourn a mother she was never allowed to know. After
graduation Maisie decides to go to library school—a safe, cozy, useful career. And she's always loved to read, ever since she'd curl up
on the scratchy window-seat cushions in Brearley's Lower School library, alternately reading and staring out at the pewter-gray East
River rolling past Eighty-third Street, until her eyes glazed and she
drifted into dreams. She especially loved to lose herself in books
when her own life pressed in on her.

She starts to think about what job she'd like to take, where she'd
like to live, what friends to invite over for dinner. But Terry is not
used to this independence. He's used to calling the shots, making
the decisions for both of them. Finally, she gets restless under his
wing, starts to grow up and beyond him. Eventually he finds a second wife who Maisie will see is "just as needy and dependent" as she
was when she and Terry first married. But when he and Maisie
part—even though she has instigated the split—every fear, doubt,
and deeply unmothered place in her that her marriage has helped
her contain breaks loose to haunt her. She has counted on Terry to
provide the support and structure she is still powerless to provide
for herself. When that structure fails, she hits bottom. It is the lowest she'll ever go, and she won't realize until years later that she had
to sink that far in order to start the long climb back.

But when her marriage crumbles she feels she has no resources.
She looks back at the past and feels only pain. She scans the future
and sees a dark void, no love, no possibilities. She remembers the

sleeping pills she's held on to against the pernicious insomnia of freshman year. She grabs a handful of pills, gulps them down with water, and waits for oblivion. But before she has waited too long, before it's completely too late, a small voice inside gets the better of her, pushing her out of the haze, out of her lethargy and despair. She calls the nearest emergency room and cries, "I've taken a bottle of sleeping pills. What shall I do?"

"Come in immediately," says a strong voice on the other end of the line, and then, more pointedly, more ominously, "If you don't come in, you'll die."

Emma—Clergyman's Daughter

When Emma joined the class in seventh grade she felt way out of her depth. A clergyman's daughter, used to moving around the country like an army brat with her father's assignments, she won a scholarship to Brearly—$1,250, a princely sum in those days. The family lived on the Upper West Side, which was soon to become bohemian and hip but was the wrong side of the tracks back then. All the other girls seemed to have more money, more style, and, she feared at first, more brains. When she heard the class had read the *Odyssey* the year before—in sixth grade, when her public school class was poking its way through Greek myths adapted for children—she despaired of ever catching up. One day she'd get a 98 on an English paper, the next day a 38 on a quiz. She hadn't a clue why. Her self-esteem would rise and plummet with her grades. One day she'd believe she was smart enough to do anything in the world. The next day, she was convinced she was an utter failure.

It didn't help that her parents held up an impossible standard and that her older brothers always seemed able to handle it more easily than she could. If Emma brought home an A-minus, her parents responded only, "Why wasn't it an A?" Even in the midst of a full-scale tantrum, she'd hear them correcting her grammar. ("It's not 'Me and my friends don't give a shit,'" they'd instruct with exaggerated politeness, "It's 'My friends and I.' ") Nothing she did really pleased them, so after a while, she stopped trying. It really wasn't until she finally got to college, after a long derailment, that Emma began to build her confidence from the inside and let her intellect flower. "That's a little late, isn't it?" she'd ask a friend years down the road.

At Brearley she fell in with the small gaggle of fast girls— the boy-crazy, short-skirted, makeup-wearing, party-going girls— who were already dynamiting their parents' values and going their own way. Several of these families were too preoccupied with their own dysfunctions to pay much attention to their daughters. Emma's family was not as preoccupied as some but became more and more powerless to stem the tide of Emma's rebellion and discontent. For a while Emma kept up one face at home and another with her pals. She'd leave her parents' apartment every morning looking freshly scrubbed, bangs grazing her wide and deceptively innocent blue eyes. Once she was safely beyond their sight, she'd put on makeup, eyes ringed in black, lips suitably pearly pink to greet her heavily made-up crowd.

But finally the effort to separate the two faces started to wear her down. The social pressure, the intellectual insecurity, the isolation she felt in her family, all built up to a fever pitch and imploded. While the other girls bitched conspiratorially about their parents and made theatrical threats, Emma took the threats a step further. That was her signature, she'd later say: she was always one to take things to extremes, willing to try what others just imagined. In the spring of ninth grade, when other girls were getting ready for their Easter trips to Aspen or the Bahamas, Emma tried to end her own life. She downed a whole bottle of aspirin and ended up in the closest emergency room. It was a cry of desperation, a bitterly angry slap in her parents' face.

No one in school heard a word about it. Like Pamela, like Maisie, like most of the class, Emma was an expert at keeping her pain to herself. There was no teacher she took into her confidence, no adult she dropped a hint to. She never let drop a free-floating "My family's driving me crazy" or "I'm feeling suicidal" that today all teachers are trained to pick up on immediately and respond to as the cry for help that it is. Back then the school psychologist was responsible for testing IQ, not mining for feelings, and the school nurse only checked weights and heights and, during epidemics, checked for chicken pox. Though I met Emma at the bus stop every morning and walked companionably to school with her, I, too, was in the dark. When Emma didn't turn up the morning after her suicide attempt and hospitalization, I simply assumed it was a bout of stomach flu, a common cold. Looking back, I'm aghast at my own blindness and at Emma's capacity to conceal. When she returned to the bus stop only a day later, she mentioned nothing amiss.

Emma's parents, well-intentioned but oblivious until then, sent her first to one, then to a second, male psychiatrist. The first was "a fool" who talked only about his own daughters, said Emma. The second was a formal Freudian with an overlay of almost military zeal. Emma clammed up with both of them and spent hours of her time and her parents' money stonewalling. Part of her trouble, she'd later say, was with male authority, especially the iron hand of her own father, the minister, the emissary of the mightiest authority of them all. Through the distorting lens of transference, these doctors assumed the evil face of everything she resisted in male authority. She refused to connect with either of them.

The youngest and brashest and most confrontational in her family, Emma was also the only one among them to go into therapy. Years later, after hours spent dissecting her family's crazies and her own, she'd come to see herself as the family's "identified patient," the one who acted out the pressures that everyone else did their best to keep hidden. Like Pamela and like Maisie, Emma was the family's release valve as well as their lightning rod. She gave everyone else someone to worry about and allowed them to keep their minds off their own troubles.

"I was the one who saw the elephant in the living room and insisted on talking about it," she'd say much later, when hours of therapy and soul-searching had given her a language to name the discrepancies between her family's image of itself and what really went on behind the scenes. "There's a conspiracy of silence in so many families," she'd later say with her hard-won wisdom. "Families think, If we don't talk about what's going on and don't name it, it doesn't exist."

But Emma said it and named it, with her in-your-face behavior and her scathing honesty. She took it upon herself to become the whistle-blower about her family's hypocrisy. "We're not the perfect family," she shouted. "We're not everything we purport to be." What she unmasked was nothing so tangible as alcoholism or abuse, although part of what made living in her family so tense was behaviors typical of alcoholics or abusers, behaviors like denial and masking feelings and responding in inappropriate ways. "My parents tried too hard to be good" was how she'd put it much, much later. "When the negative side came out, it would be inappropriate anger, name-calling, and rage." She made her family scurry, but they didn't want to believe her and certainly were not ready to change. Each side held fiercely to its own reality. In sermons, her father preached about closing the generation gap, about careful listening that could lead to healing on both sides. But under his own roof, the family was torn asunder; and bitterness kept the enemies entrenched.

By tenth grade, when her father was transferred, her family plucked Emma out of Brearley and plunked her down in a sprawling public high school in suburban Maryland. Emma carried her misery along with her, even tried to run away back to New York a couple of times just to assert her fragile will. For a time she found solace in an understanding female counselor in her new school. Here was a therapist she could finally connect with. Here was someone who saw the vulnerable child beneath the cocky exterior and knew how much Emma begged for validation as well as freedom. The counselor won her confidence, and for perhaps the first time ever, Emma bared her soul, shared her most private poems with her. Loving the poems, the counselor helped Emma believe she was loved, helped her start building a shred of confidence in herself.

But the power of peers, the lure of the counterculture, and her ongoing battles with her family were too strong to be counterbalanced by one school counselor. At her new school, just as at her old, Emma fell in with a fast crowd. But this time the stakes were a lot higher than some clandestine makeup and a few sips from mom and dad's liquor cabinet. Her new gang were dopers and renegades and laid-back anti-intellectuals. They hung out together, getting stoned, dropping acid, skipping school, listening to Sergeant Pepper and Ravi Shankar. Few of them headed on to college, so Emma opted out, too, even though her brains and her background and everything about her upbringing would have pointed her unquestionably in that direction.

Over the Edge

While all her old Brearley classmates have left home and moved on to college, Emma continues to live at home, despite her complaints, which, if anything, have grown more intense. She works as a waitress, continues to hang out with her old dead-ended friends who do rock and roll and drugs and will take until their forties to get themselves into recovery. It doesn't take her too many months of filling lunch orders, clearing tables and smiling through clenched teeth for tips to see that becoming a working-class heroine is not as easy and cool as she imagined it would be. Things are rocky at home, rocky at work, rocky with her boyfriend, who seems to be losing interest; he can't handle being a perpetual port in a storm.

Emma begins to feel a frighteningly familiar inner pressure start to build. When her boyfriend finally breaks things off, that rejection pushes her over the edge. No longer loved or understood, she feels too fragile to cope. She ends up in the hospital for two long weeks, feeling as crazy as she's ever felt before. Still, she looks around the ward at the other patients, mumbling to themselves, weaving baskets, staring into space, and somewhere, deep inside, she hears a still, small voice of self-preservation speak to her. "You're not *that* crazy," it says.

It's a lot harder to get out of the hospital than it was to get in, but Emma finally manages it. When she returns home, her parents, deeply scared and chastened, once again urge her toward therapy. But instead of bridging the gap in the family, therapy serves only to push her farther away. She shudders as her father describes his unmet expectations for her. "Our children have gifts from God," he intones as the servant of God. Hearing those inflated dreams, Emma will later say, is "enlightening," to say the least.

These therapy sessions end up saving her, if for the wrong reasons. And that flicker of self-esteem first nurtured by the sympathetic high school counselor refuses to go out again. Instead it catches fire, its embers fanned by a fierce drive for survival, a lust to find out who she really is, a hunger to prove she can stand on her own two feet. "Having that nervous breakdown," she'll later say, "I reached my own bottom."

Giving up drugs is one of the first steps of her long trek back, for drugs, she finally sees, "were not helping me feel not crazy. Acid was scrambling my brain. Chemicals, adolescence, my family—what a stew!" Later she realizes how she escaped by a hair being "one of those people busted for drugs and put in jail." And as her head gradually starts to clear, after all the bum trips and the long, stoned-soul picnics, she has a lucid, focusing moment when the static usually surrounding her decisions quiets down and she sees her own direction clearly. "I realized I was going to have to build myself from within, and to do that I was going to have to move out from my family."

Getting out of Town

"I knew I was going to survive," she says, looking back at that transformative time, "but I was going to have to get the hell out of Dodge to do it." She grabs the $350 she's managed to save up from waiting tables, fills a backpack with her things, and thumbs a ride to Denver. From there she hitches another ride to northern California—"It seemed to be where everyone was going at the time"—all the way out to Santa Rosa, not too far from where she was born. On her own for the first time ever, far from the fishbowl of life as a clergyman's daughter and her family's intense personal scrutiny, she begins to put a life together. "I had to reinvent myself," she'll admit later, "and every day was an awakening"— working as a waitress but this time paying her own rent, taking care of her own bills, choosing her own friends, not to antagonize her parents but because they have something in common with her and will help her become who she must now be.

One day she's in the middle of reading *Crime and Punishment*. Raskolnikov's doubts are somehow familiar to her. She comes up for air to realize she has no one to talk with about the novel. The other waitresses read nothing heavier than *TV Guide* or the latest issue of *Glamour*. At last it dawns on her that she's ready to go to college, ready to have company to share ideas with, professors to open up and enlarge her view of the world. Four years after she's graduated from high school, at a time when most of her old Brearley friends have either graduated from college or dropped out and written it off entirely, Emma enrolls in a local two-year community college. With her waitressing wages she's able to pay her own way, and this financial independence is crucial to her sense of herself and to salvaging any hope she has of rebuilding the relationship to her family. "I began to find my own Emma," she'll later say, "instead of the person she was supposed to be."

The Copers Versus the Strugglers

As they made the first break from family—from the comforts and containment of home and the orderly structure and strictures of school—why did so many classmates flounder and fall and so few manage to find a steady course? This crisis of separation proved to be an emotional standstill for some and a leap of growth for others.

Girls struggled, above all, when they had to face their first separation from home. Overprotected, yet sometimes undertended, they struggled toward independence weighed down by complicated unfinished emotional business. Family histories were checkered; money, opportunity, and privilege were mixed up with stresses like alcoholism and divorce and layered over by secrecy and denial. And from this first vantage point, one step removed from home, daughters wrestled with making sense of their pasts. For both the yes-girls and the no-girls, the compliant and parent-dominated like Maisie as well as the rebellious and parent-baiting like Pam and Emma, separation stirred up fears, anxieties, and guilt. Did they have the internal and external resources to make their own decisions, hatch their own plans, choose their own course—or courses? Could their parents survive without them? Maisie ached all freshman year, wishing she'd gone to Barnard and stayed closer to home. Nor did she really feel grounded, until she tucked herself under the protective arms of her first husband, Terry, who became a kind of parent surrogate throughout her twenties. Emma thumbed her nose at everything her parents stood for but continued to live under their roof four years longer than most of her peers. Intermittently, she'd try to break away and set herself up with friends. When the arrangements collapsed, she'd fly nervously back to the nest.

Even with one foot out the door, the more high-strung classmates remained alert to their parents' subtle messages. They longed for parents' confidence, yet were oversensitive to their doubts. Separation became particularly fraught when daughters got tangled in the skeins of parents' double messages—a mother who clung tightly with one hand while pushing away with the other; a father who expected the highest reaches of success but was too preoccupied with his own ambitions to give his daughter the support she needed to achieve hers.

Being out of sync with parental expectations was another piece of early history that stirred up a cauldron of self-doubts and undermined the separation process for some of the more vulnerable girls. Whether a girl was brilliant or just smart enough seemed to matter less to her future plans than whether her own expectations, her parents', and the school's had all been on the same page. Many parents were more ambitious for their daughters than either the school or the girls themselves—those Harvard dreams for girls who might be happier on a smaller-scale campus without the big-name reputation. These daughters were left with the nagging feeling they'd let their parents down, and no choices they made ever felt quite good enough. So Emma, whose parents had pie-in-the-sky dreams for her, crushed them by refusing to head for college right after graduation, then spent her twenties and thirties making a number of false starts and interrupted forays. Maisie, whose talents were no more or less dazzling than Emma's, at first struggled over leaving home but ultimately felt enough in tune with her parents' expectations to have the confidence to tackle college and professional choices later on.

In the most extreme cases, separation from home unleashed a "catastrophic set of feelings—depression, panic, rage, guilt, helplessness, and emptiness," according to psychiatrist James F. Masterson, the director for many years of the adolescent treatment program at New York Hospital's Payne Whitney Clinic, where a number of Brearley girls went to mend after emotional breakdowns. In an interview, Masterson explained his belief that adolescent separation can provoke an "abandonment depression" that replays a highly charged drama from early childhood. The teenage separation from home recaps the first separation of toddlers from mothers. If the earlier separation has not been comfortably resolved, the later one stirs up painful old feelings that compound the childhood difficulties. Just as the two-year-old needs a steady, loving parent to let her move forward yet comfort her when she wants to touch base again, so, too, does the adolescent. If a parent clings too tightly, pushes away too insistently, or alternates inconsistently between contradictory attitudes, the daughter doesn't feel safe to make a move forward and explore her separate self, her real self.

In the cold grip of this abandonment depression, a young woman will feel deeply alienated from her real feelings and cut off from the emotional supplies she needs to sustain her, suggested Masterson. "At the darkest level of this depression," he explained in *The Search for the Real Self,* "a person can despair of ever recovering her real self, and thoughts of suicide are not uncommon. When one is brought low enough repeatedly, or for an extended period of time, it becomes increasingly harder to imagine oneself happy again or able to push through life with the strength and confidence with which the reasonably healthy go about their daily living. At this point a person can teeter on the brink of despair, give up, and consider taking her own life." Pamela, Maisie, Emma—each teetered precariously on this brink and struggled to find the resources to fight her way back to reasonably healthy daily living. But not every troubled adolescent turns away from the brink. Added Masterson forebodingly, "If the separations they experience in their external lives are painful enough to reinforce their feelings and fear of abandonment, some will commit suicide."

Identity Crisis

But even those classmates whose response to adolescent leave-taking was not catastrophic enough to cause thoughts of suicide found themselves confronting this passage's most soul-searching question: *Who am I?* Who am I beyond the definitions imposed on me by parents, by school, by friends? Who am I in my own eyes, underneath my own skin, down to my deepest, most private self? This question had started to dog all the girls in the class of '68 during their last years at school, as they rounded the homestretch for freedom. But then they were still pursuing answers beneath their parents' sheltering wing. Now nothing stood between them and the beckoning existential choices of their futures. Nothing buffered them from the endless possibilities of how they'd evolve, nothing but their own doubts and questions, their own limits and capabilities.

Leaving home for the enticing but undefined world beyond, every classmate obsessed about who she was, who she had been and would become. But the better-coping girls pursued these identity issues while still managing to move ahead with their lives, while the strugglers kept running around in circles, tangled in their own uncertainties.

Who am I? Am I smart or stupid? worried Emma, as her grades bounced from lows to highs and sometimes down to lows again; as she shook off the academic expectations her parents rigidly held for her and toyed with the anti-intellect; as she churned out poems from the most hidden recesses of her heart, poems she didn't have the courage to show anyone for years; as she struggled to find her own center and not let others tell her who she was.

Who am I? Do I belong to the well-mannered world of my parents or the rowdier circle of my peers? wondered Maisie, as she maneuvered between coming-out parties and panty raids, between becoming a doctor or a librarian, between being on her shaky own or boxed into an early, husband-dominated marriage.

Managing the transition from home to college in a time of so little social structure was another challenge that rattled every graduate of '68 but proved especially overwhelming for some. To move from a rule-bound world of curtsies and social graces to a hang-loose culture where the old rules no longer applied required some fancy footwork, some awesome adaptability. The girls who fared best were the ones who were able to generate their own new structures. The girls who floundered at this transition found the lack of external structure that greeted them after graduation a kind of eerie fun-house mirror of their own unmoored internal world.

"The lack of structure that confronts most freshmen tends to make a lot of them feel pretty lousy," confided a Radcliffe student to fellow undergraduate writer Anne de Saint Phalle in a 1969 *Harvard Crimson* article called "Harvard and Your Head." The girl was one of a subset of Harvard and Radcliffe students—typically twelve to fifty a year—who must leave college for a time-out in a mental hospital. She'd been hospitalized at McLean, Boston's most prestigious private mental hospital, its corollary to New York City's Payne Whitney. "In my case," she explained, "I overcompensated by doing a great many things. I built my own structure but it was a house of cards."

From compulsive overactivity to wild nihilism, these bright college students were desperate to shore up a shaky inner self with a structure that too often became a house of cards. So it was with my Brearley classmates slouching toward the chaotic close of the sixties. The ones who could cope with college found a strong scaffolding to lean on, something that gave shape and meaning to experience. Like my first forays into writing, Tess's into horticulture and dancing, Judith's into independent study and the sustaining life of the mind, the copers were able to find self-definition in an avocation or talent, for a talent or artistic gift, in Masterson's phrase, can provide "added catnip to self-actualization." Most dependably of all, the copers had the emotional intelligence to tap into an unshakable core of self-worth, like Cory, who knew when to take a time-out at an international college and came back with a renewed sense of focus and confidence.

But the classmates who were most shaken during this rocky transitional time either couldn't build an internal structure at all or desperately constructed one, only to find that it didn't hold. Pam busted out of the too-tight-fitting, too-well-known, and too-well-bred propriety of Vassar for the loose and loopy hippie Shangri-la of

Aspen, only to find herself crashing without any boundaries or direction at all. Emma sought alternative shelter with the seductive bad boys and bad girls in her local suburban drug culture, only to find it was no shelter at all. After too many bum trips, busted romances, and a scary motorcycle accident that had her sidelined for months, she finally admitted how cold that shelter's comfort was.

Some of those most shaken up by college found that the old coping mechanisms of childhood—relying on a strong, controlling parent or getting good grades to fuel self-esteem or spacing out when the going got tough—no longer worked in a peer-defined culture in a time of social turmoil. Cultural upheaval threw a lot of these women back on themselves, on their own inner resources or the kindnesses of friends. But many feared, peering deep within, that there was no one yet home to rely on. And those who were used to pleasing parents and were shaky about their own self-worth had a hard time connecting with contemporaries and despaired of ever fitting in. "I never felt comfortable meeting people," said one brilliant classmate whose anorexia drove her to drop out of college and refuel at Payne Whitney. "In college, I did superbly but I couldn't relate; I couldn't manage people."

Maisie, too, had difficulty bonding with her peers. Although Pembroke was still more rule-bound in the late sixties than many other campuses, to Maisie it felt as lawless as the Wild West. Used to adult company and adult conversation, she was bored by the unformed freshmen and frightened by the upperclassmen. She spent much of freshman year isolated, without friends, counting the days until she could go home for the weekend and regain the sense of composure and self-definition she found in her parents' eyes. When, as a sophomore, she fell hard for Terry, she believed she'd found a companion who could bring some order back to her life. That Terry's structure turned out to be untenable was both the most terrifying experience and the most liberating opportunity of her life. When Maisie finally grew confident enough to leave him, she was also able to turn the rest of her life around; once a struggler, she became a success and a survivor.

The Pressures of Perfectionism

The girls who struggled the most also battled the demon of perfectionism. High expectations went with this territory. "Big shoes to fill," inscribed a friend's mother in a copy of *Ulysses* given for a birthday gift. Lofty goals were as unquestioned a part of our background as housekeepers and the summer house in the Hamptons. Brearley girls were raised to believe that though their reach might exceed their grasp—in Robert Browning's memorable phrase—they should never cease trying to attain the heaven of perfection.

Still, some could reach for the stars but forgive themselves when they faltered. But others labored under such a severe inner or parental tyranny that any stumble was equivalent to utter failure. "On the one hand there was a grand vision of what we could become," observed one schoolmate. "On the other hand there was also terrible angst about whether we could fulfill those expectations." Too often perfectionism translated into a kind of self-defeat. "Doing something I wasn't the best in wasn't worth it" was how the hard-driving and hard-on-herself anorexic classmate put it. For if, as in Emma's family, every A-minus was scorned for not being an A, eventually any high goal would become too unattainable to attempt. Some, like Emma, simply gave up trying, at least for a while. Others, like Cory, accepted themselves, despite a string of C's, and made the most of the ample talents and skills they did have.

Beyond the self-defeating demands of perfectionism, the pain of separating from home, the confusion of adolescent identity, the awkward breakdown of old coping styles, and the inability to create a supportive internal structure, those who struggled the most cracked under the pressure of keeping up a façade, keeping the lid on the pressure cooker of secrets. The girls who buckled could no longer tolerate the jarring discrepancy between their inner self and the face they showed the world, between their rowdy, confusing, volatile emotional life and the polite exterior they were raised to present to the outside world. Some simply got very tired of being so nice.

Midway into freshman year I felt sufficiently miserable to take the next rite of passage after leaving home—a visit to a therapist at the Harvard Health Services. My grades were fine but my heart was heavy. The pressure of trying to please my parents, accommodate my roommate, keep my boyfriends amused, be open with my friends, and somehow remain true to my own heart was too much to handle alone. Sitting in the office of this kindly and unrufflable man who had quietly listened to hundreds of self-doubting undergraduates, I released my secrets for the first time. I told him about the pleasant face I felt compelled to maintain and the anguish I sometimes felt that I dared not express. I told him of the pressures that had been building inside and were threatening to explode now that these discrepancies were colliding. He listened very attentively, as if he were hearing not only me but also echoes of hundreds of students who had sat in this chair before me. When I finally finished my spiel, I looked up at him expectantly. Without missing a beat, he offered his interpretation. "Keeping two sets of books," he said.

Like a sly businessman sidestepping the tax authorities, I'd kept two records, one to show the world, the other tracking the real story. On the outside, everything looked rosy. Inside, fears and doubts bored like termites, waiting to bring the structure down.

So it was for so many classmates of '68 and women of their generation in that time of inflated expectations and gnawing self-doubts, that adolescent passage between burgeoning self-awareness and the legacy of secrecy. The ones who struggled could not contain the white-hot emotions that reached the boiling point and started to spill over the edges. Like Pamela, they could no longer turn the other cheek and pretend everything was perfect, when families started to unravel, when dreams started to fray. Like Maisie,

they were forced, at times by circumstances beyond their control—
a turbulent social time, a mother's untimely death, an early relationship that crumbled—to look more deeply inward, to shore up
some painful lacks. Like Emma, they could no longer show one face
to their family and another to friends. These were the girls who saw
the elephant in the living room and would not say it was a mouse.
They did not know it then, but coming apart at this tender age
would allow them to heal later on. For "the world breaks everyone," Hemingway wrote in *A Farewell to Arms*, "and afterward
some are strong at the broken places."

The Youthful Suicides

What about the girls who did not recover? What about the ones so assaulted by inner demons, so shaken by the shocks of the sixties, and so unprotected by families that were themselves troubled that they could not imagine negotiating the passage between childhood and adulthood? What became of the girls so desperate they could not find their way back from the brink?

Along with the copers and the strugglers, Brearley had these fragile wounded, too. There were girls who could not manage the transition from the school's protected walls to the uncharted vistas beyond it, girls so racked by despair that they could not envision a kinder future in which they would be unburdened of pain, free to grow into their promise. Their tragedies also became an inescapable piece of the history of these times. Telling the story of the class of '68, I must confront this sadness, for it is as much a part of the class's legacy as their round, schoolgirl printing, their tidy uniforms that accentuated their idiosyncrasies, their tenth-grade reading of *Jude the Obscure*. Did they ever imagine when they read in *Jude* about the boys who "seem to see all [life's] terrors before they are old enough to have staying power to resist them" that they were reading about girls among them as well? Now I reread such passages for double messages and sift through the past for clues, hoping that the tragedies that were not prevented can at least begin to be understood and learned from.

Gemini

Alice and Lily are the only twins in the class and among the very few sets of twins in the school, and as such they are objects of constant scrutiny. They are not identical, yet they are deeply, inextricably linked, and part of the attraction of becoming their friends is to tease out how they are the same and yet different, opposite and yet overlapping. Part of their influence comes from their power as a couple—the way each twin shadows the other and the other's friendships—and the lure of pulling them apart. Invite one to a birthday party and the other will show up at the door, waiting to be invited, daring you to exclude her. Like Sophia and Pamela, two of the class's most charismatic characters, Alice and Lily have their admirers and detractors. They, too, exert a magnetic pull on the class and seem by their very twoness to divide the other girls into the ones who like Alice better and the ones who gravitate toward Lily.

Lily and Alice are pepper and salt, winter and summer, ice and fire. Lily has skin the color of paper-white narcissus, almost translucent, and coal-black hair cut sharply to frame her face. Her eyes are also dark, and they can be both brooding and incisive. Lily masters early the withering look and does not waste energy on false smiles. Even at a tender age, she has an artist's gift and an artist's eye, which seems to look deeper and farther than others'. That her somber demeanor might already be signaling a deep unhappiness is lost on her classmates. But they know there is something riveting about Lily. The eye is drawn to her first. But at second glance, girls sense they'd have more fun playing with Alice.

Alice looks more like a typical all-American girl. She seems more accessible, with less hidden beneath the surface. Her face is wide and open, and her brunette hair, held back with a headband, flips up in the style Mary Tyler Moore will soon immortalize. Alice tends to be a little more kempt while Lily is unkempt; Alice's shirttails are tucked in, her shoelaces tied; Lily often seems to be coming undone. Alice was born just a few moments earlier, and all their shared life she'll have that older-sister edge, almost maternal at times, even to her twin. She'll nudge her sister to get places on time. She'll be a bridge into a circle of girls who might otherwise exclude her sister.

Once, when they're about twelve, the twins are photographed for a fashion spread in *Vogue* magazine. Their mother is a fashion writer there, one of the class's few working mothers. Their father is in advertising, but occasional layoffs send him home, moodily hovering in the background. For the *Vogue* layout, Alice mugs cheerfully for the camera, arms akimbo, in her Peter Pan–collared tattersall-checked shirtwaist. Lily displays her dark jumper, staring off into the distance, as if she is not there entirely by her own choice.

With the black-and-white thinking fairly typical of young schoolgirls, classmates divide Alice and Lily into opposite camps and line up staunchly behind one or the other. To some, Lily is more serious, gloomier; Alice heartier, more upbeat. An afternoon spent with Lily, her detractors fear, could degenerate into trying to outscare each other with spooky ghost stories or leafing through an art book of Hieronymus Bosch. A date with Alice would offer a rousing game of tag or Red Rover or an all-out board-game battle, sides clearly drawn. Even at six, there's less subtext with Alice.

But others thrill to the exotic in Lily, her insights and humor, "funny in a dark way," Pamela later remembered; they find Alice more knowable, more like everybody else. "Lily's wilder spirit attracted me more than Alice's quieter one," recalled Maisie, a neighbor and frequent playmate of the twins. "Lily had the imagination I felt I lacked," offered Celeste, whose family ran like clockwork and who always colored within the lines.

Later on their classmates will see the subtler shadings in the twins' personalities: that Lily can be broody but uproariously funny, too; that Alice can be all smiles one moment and collapse into cloudiness the next; that she also has an artistic gift, however eclipsed by Lily's.

They'll see that Lily is more obviously eccentric but that Alice, too, can be daring. One day at the park, a boy dares Alice to turn a somersault on the very top bar of the jungle gym. Lily and a cluster of friends stand on the gritty cement pavement beneath and stare up at her. It seems impossibly far, impossibly out of reach, almost crazy to attempt. But Alice can't say no. She brazens up to the stratosphere and spins her somersault on the top bar, uniform flying, navy blue underwear obvious to all passersby. It turns out, her friends duly note, that both twins like to push the envelope, but Alice seems better able than Lily to push past her own fear and carry on.

The Artist as a Young Girl

In a classroom of bright, often gifted, girls, Lily's gifts stand out from an early age and set her apart. Perhaps that exceptionally shrewd intellect, that piercing artistic gaze, is not always easy to bear. Perhaps the distance it puts between her and the other girls—and especially between her twin and herself—is not quite worth the attention that rains down on her for her talents, the attention she alternately seeks and shuns. Did the other girls ever mark her discomfort at the time, or could they see it only in retrospect, when they were looking for signs that portended trouble, trouble they might have helped avert?

By the end of third grade when the homeroom teacher gathers together the best writing of the year, it is Lily's work that dominates the yearbook. While the other girls are spinning age-appropriate froth about ghosts and goblins and horses, Lily's story, "Helicopter Arrest," is literary leaps beyond the others, the longest, most inventive and sophisticated story by far. Its elaborate plot, paced like a good English mystery, concerns a girl, Cathy, who is captured by spies and later engineers the spies' arrest. The language is highly literary, clearly the product of an imagination that ingests books from C. S. Lewis to E. Nesbit, full of old-fashioned turns of phrase like "I've been worried sick" and "I've a good mind to shorten it." As the story ends and Cathy's bravery and ingenuity are revealed, Cathy's brother pins the word "HERO" on her shirt. Even in third grade, Lily's dreams are already grander than anything most eight-year-olds could imagine.

Lily stamps the year-end storybook in another way as well. Its cover is her design—a fanciful potpourri of small illustrations to the stories—a friendly ghost, a galloping horse, two mice carrying suitcases. Each sketch is delicate and perfect as a Fabergé egg; all are executed in her distinctive style, full of confidence beyond her years, clever detail, and sly humor. Girls often stare at her while she draws, as if hoping for a piece of her magic. She would start drawing the foot of a horse, say, and not lift up her head until the whole picture was done, as if the image was already full-blown in her imagination and she just had to get it down. Lily is a perfectionist and will not rest till she gets the drawing right. Her talent gives her a mesmerizing hold over some girls, yet pushes others away.

Jo prides herself on her own artistic flair, but is nonetheless transfixed by the way Lily draws grass—a stylized version, like something folding and unfolding, one blade that is really long and the next one a bit shorter, curling a little more, and the next one curling even tighter into itself, all brilliantly decorative and blazing with life across the page. Jo admires the finesse of Lily's grass so much that decades later, long after the original moment of imitation is a blur, she still draws grass that way herself.

Jill, too, thinks Lily's art is "astonishing and wonderful." Horse-crazy and opinionated, Jill is also a talented young artist. She will be the one to illustrate the class's senior yearbook after Lily is sidelined and her talent has begun to self-destruct. But even early on, Lily's brilliant gift disturbs Jill, makes her confront a part of herself she'd rather not acknowledge. "I was horribly jealous of her, because I was artistic too, but I didn't have the kind of talent that she had," Jill will admit years later. Lily's gift burns its way into the other girls' psyches and they submit to it, as if to something larger than themselves. "Even though I was jealous, I really loved her work," added

Jill. "And I think that was probably very healthy for me, because I was used to being the best at many things. And Lily taught me that you can't be the best at everything, and life was going to be full of lessons like that."

Jill, like many classmates, is drawn to Lily's gifts yet fearful of them. "I tried to talk to her sometimes, because we had drawing in common, but she was so sour and sarcastic," Jill recalled much later. "So she must have been horribly unhappy. But I treated that as brushing me off and not being interested in knowing me. Because I had my own sensitivities, as did we all."

The Hapless Child

On my twelfth birthday, when other guests bring games and hula hoops, Lily's gift stands apart. And long after the games have been trashed, and the hula hoops swirled their last, I still have Lily's gift, and it still haunts and perplexes. Was it another clue, I wonder now, an unconscious piece of autobiography, a message in a bottle I could have deciphered if I'd only known the code?

The gift is a book by the eccentric cartoonist Edward Gorey called *The Hapless Child*. Its story is told in a series of cartoonlike drawings, each exquisitely detailed and macabre, whose impact is unrelievedly grim. Even at twelve, I sense as I flip through the disquieting pages that something about Gorey's vision expresses Lily's own, that his sinister and deeply pessimistic attitude is the adult flowering of her still-childlike imagination. *The Hapless Child* is a kind of fairy tale in reverse. Its heroine, a little girl named Charlotte Sophia, starts out in the land of happily ever after. She has kind and well-to-do parents, perfect crinolines, and a beautiful doll. Then, before the reader's eyes, she endures every kind of humiliation until she ends up with nothing. Each panel recounts another deprivation, until by the end, she lies sprawling in the street, struck down by a car and unrecognizable even to her father.

Could this be, in part, the way Lily sees herself—a creature born into promise and opportunity but then buffeted by twists of fate she is powerless to control?

Separation

Adolescence seems to deepen the differences between the twins and strain the similarities. Lily becomes more and more inward, more cynical, with an edge that puts people off and masks her need for contact, for friends. She develops the most amazing slouch, "a model's slouch crossed with a Beatnik," one classmate will remember years later. Lily's slouch seems to speak of her turning inward, of her dissatisfaction with herself, with her own body. Alice grows more social, starts to go to parties and flirt with boys, is eager to try her own wings. In ninth grade the sisters both apply to leave Brearley for boarding school. Alice is particularly eager to broaden her social circle and get away from home, where her father's and older brother's moodiness are becoming harder to cope with. And though she can hardly admit it even in her own heart, she is growing weary of shepherding Lily from here to there.

Lily, for her part, is not at all sure boarding school is the ideal place for her, and she is also less confident than Alice that she can manage on her own. At the heart of the twins' symbiosis has always been a complicated ambivalence about the full extent of their linkage. Even as children they detested being referred to as "the twins" and always insisted on dressing differently. Adolescence intensifies their doubts and their resentments about maintaining their boundaries and their connections.

Although both girls are accepted at boarding school, Alice easily makes the decision to go, and Lily, less easily, decides to stay. Returning to Brearley for tenth grade, this time on her own, Lily seems to the other girls to start to unravel. For fifteen years the twins have been together every day, shared the same teachers and many of the same friends, rolled their eyes over the same bad jokes, and whispered to each other at night behind closed doors. Now Alice has a whole new world of her own, new teachers and new friends to roll her eyes with, and Lily is left behind, left out and left alone. Depression, always a specter lurking over her shoulder, now sinks over her like a shroud. My classmates and I see only the outward signs—that she becomes thinner and thinner, that she is obsessed with her appearance, that her fingernails grow unnaturally long.

She spends more and more time in bed, sinking into oblivion. Even on school days, she cannot wrench herself up in the morning before noon. Without Alice to nudge her along, she cannot get to school on time. Sometimes she saunters in at one o'clock, after most academic classes are over, affecting a superiority to cover her shame. "Where have you been?" Celeste later remembered needling Lily after one of her irritating early-afternoon entrances. Teenagers are not notoriously forgiving, and Lily's latenesses have started to irk the other girls, who have managed to drag themselves to school on time, even when they're not exactly in the mood. To the others, showing up is a matter of will, and they see it lacking in Lily. What do they know of the unrelenting clutches of depression, the icy dictates of despair? "I can't keep track of time," Lily says, shrugging. It is the last conversation Celeste will ever have with her.

Hospitalized

Beyond the latenesses, Lily starts disappearing from school for mysterious and disturbingly long stretches of time. Rumors fly but no one really has a clue. The school remains glacially quiet; whatever is happening is completely hush-hush. Has Lily run away from home? classmates wonder. Has she gone off to be with Alice? Is she failing academically because of all the latenesses and absences, and is the school not allowing her to come back?

Finally after what seems like ages to the girls but is probably not more than a month or two, a teacher sits the class down and explains that Lily will not be coming back to school. Does she say that Lily has been hospitalized? The atmosphere of secrecy was so silencing, the taboo so total, that I simply can't remember. I do remember that she keeps the discussion as matter of fact as possible, as if passing along the news that a classmate is leaving because her father's business has been transferred to another state. There is no lengthy or probing discussion, no attempt to address the group's concerns or calm their fears. There is certainly no attempt to help the other girls contact Lily or write to her, either to express their feelings or assuage hers. As Celeste will say later, recalling the iron curtain of silence that clanged down when Lily left for the hospital, "It was as if she was erased."

Do other girls wonder, when their own moods skitter crazily or when their feelings are hurt too easily or when they cannot live up to their own daunting expectations for themselves, if they, too, might cross the hazy, undefined line between coping and floundering, between being well enough for school and being fit only for the mental hospital?

Do they chatter among themselves to make sense of the unthinkable? Do they pull teachers aside and beg for explanations? Do they go home and talk over Lily's sad fate with their parents? Not likely. Most just remain tight-lipped with fear and apprehension, stunned into innocent secrecy, as when, in ninth grade, Emma swallowed an entire bottle of aspirin, had her stomach pumped, and stayed out for a day "with a head cold."

The other girls turned their heads away from Lily and from Emma just as they turned them away when another classmate, Melissa, came to school late in eighth grade with razor cuts on her wrist, and with laryngitis, so she literally couldn't speak about what had happened. How loudly her body spoke in a language no one else could yet hear. The others just stared dumbfounded at her bandaged wrists, while Celeste, her best friend, walked loyally beside her, fronting the story that Melissa had accidentally cut her wrists attempting to break out of a locked bathroom.

Some of the class's most anguished souls become artists of evasion, masters at masking the depths of their pain. Years later, classmate Kathy Cronkite, whose father, Walter, was a revered national father figure, would write a book about depression. At forty-four, she would finally admit the childhood roots of her own depressive illness and the lengths she went to cover it up. "I missed classes because I would break down crying on the back stairs and be unable to stop," she recalled in *On the Edge of Darkness,* her very personal study of depression. "I cut myself with razor blades, not in an attempt to die but in an effort to release some of the emotional pain by focusing it in physical pain. I withdrew from my friends. I took drugs in an effort to feel okay at least some of the time. I felt like a failure." Nevertheless, a friend wrote gaily in her yearbook, "It's always such a joy to see your smiling face in the halls." Kathy had this friend, like everyone else, completely fooled. "My pain was mine alone," she would admit three decades later, "my mask of normalcy almost seamless."

Not knowing any better, the other girls accept the mask as the real thing, the fabricated self as the truth. And they buy the alibis for peace of mind, for self-preservation—Kathy's mask of normalcy, Melissa's laryngitis—just as they buy the alibi of a girl in the class ahead, who was said to have accidentally fallen out of a school window and whose life was saved by chance when a snowdrift interrupted her intended fate.

Sarah does remember crying on her parents' shoulders the night after hearing that Lily had been hospitalized. Sarah's parents reassured her that the hospital was the best place for Lily right then, the place that could provide the kind of help and security she needed. But most classmates had neither the language nor the inclination to understand the intensity of Lily's emotional distress. "Nobody talked about it," Jill recalled much later. "That's the way our family handled things back then. That was part of the world of the privileged. Anything that was not pleasant was not discussed." "I knew Lily was uncomfortable, desperate, and wired," Cory added, "but it wasn't my affair."

Mental illness and suicide, like divorce or alcoholism, are never mentioned in this closed circle of classmates, and the gilded cage that protects the girls from life's harsher realities remains untarnished to the naked eye. "I didn't know it had a name," Cronkite would later confess about the black dog of depression that had haunted her since childhood. "I didn't know it could be stopped." Much later, trying to pull away the cloak of secrecy to piece together the story of '68 and this era, I am shocked by all the emotional instability and suicide I find. In this extended group of sixty-four classmates, there turn out to be at least six or seven girls who made youthful suicide attempts, several parents and siblings of classmates who have taken their own lives, and another four or five suicides in the classes several years before and after mine.

One of these casualties would be the girl once saved by the snowdrift, who made a successful attempt at suicide a few years later. Another was a golden girl three years older, the daughter of parents who combined Old World money with Hollywood glamour. After she graduated from Brearley, she danced at the fringes of Andy Warhol's dissipated crowd, married the handsome heir to a natural-gas fortune, had two children, and, after years of tormented restlessness, took her own life a month before her fortieth birthday. When New York magazine ran a cover story about her anguished life and death, the quote beneath her yearbook picture was cited: "Live fast, die young, leave a beautiful corpse." "In her heart she always felt empty," her friend the actress Marisa Berenson was quoted as saying. And her housekeeper's comment gave the piece its sober title, "Too Much Money, Too Much Time."

Indeed both of these girls came from families of great affluence. In neither case did money buffer them from psychic pain; who knows but that their wealth may have exacerbated their despair. A psychiatrist friend with whom I shared these grim stories corroborated my own reaction. Of all the despondent patients she has seen over the years, she confided, one of the most despondent with the most history of suicide on his family tree was also the one with the most sizable fortune. If I can't make it with all the advantages I have, these wealthy young adults may have asked themselves, how can I ever make it? Perhaps someone with less privilege would hold on to the hope that life could improve if fortunes changed—with more money, more education, a better job, happier prospects. But someone starting out with every advantage might despair that that was it—life could never get any better. "Nowhere is it more true that money can't buy happiness," Kathy Cronkite would later write, "than when you're standing on the edge of a cliff and down is the only conceivable direction."

Once Lily is gone, the other classmates try to put her pain and desperation out of mind and throw themselves back into the business of being teenagers. Who do you like? What did you get on the test? But still, Lily's fate lingers at the edge of consciousness, a conundrum they can't explain but sense is linked inextricably to their own lives, their own futures and possibilities.

Meanwhile Lily begins her descent into the city's mental health system, a system that offers the best resources then available to mend a fragile psyche but will ultimately prove fruitless. She spends two years in the adolescent unit at Columbia Presbyterian Hospital, one of the city's most respected programs. She bonds with the caring doctors there and for a time seems to be making progress, inching out of the unrelenting despair that has consumed her like quicksand. But two years pass—the two years in which Alice finishes boarding school and looks ahead to entering college—and Lily is no closer to being ready to live on the outside, no closer to going back to school or handling an independent life. Meanwhile, she is getting too old to be considered an adolescent, too old to meet the program's requirements.

Her family must face the difficult decision of where to place her next. And since financial resources are growing increasingly strained, they cannot afford to send her outside the city to what might have been a more intimate and protected program but also much costlier. Instead Lily is transferred to Creedmoor, a state hospital in

Queens that later Alice will remember as "a loony bin, a gruesome place that from the outside looked like a state prison." Still there is a psychiatrist there who has been highly successful treating patients with a form of insulin therapy, and the family's grave concerns about the setting are mixed with their high hopes for a possible miracle cure.

The anarchy and intensity of the state hospital have a curiously double-edged effect on Lily. On the one hand seeing herself along-side the heavily disturbed cases she's incarcerated with—patients sedated or restrained to prevent them from doing harm—gives her a glimmer of hope that, by contrast, she is not that far gone. She still has her mind and her talents, blanketed though they might be with despair. She still has a family on the outside who cares deeply about her, a twin who is pulling for her, though moving farther and farther away, literally and psychically. By this time Alice has entered her university's division of general education, the place, she'll later say with a self-effacement that becomes her protective shield, that's for "gifted" people who have no sense of direction.

But for Lily, any fragile sense of her own worth is outweighed by the hopelessness that her situation and her surroundings provoke. Looking around at her fellow patients, she is devastated to think that these are now her peers, for most are either withdrawn into their own worlds from the effects of medication or chattering with private obsessions. Once, when Alice visits, Lily points out disdain-fully the patient who is convinced she has a tennis ball in her head. Lily is crushed to think that this loveless place is now her home, and there seems to be no way out. So she is at once motivated toward health and also despairing that she will ever get there. These two contradictory impulses send her, on the one hand, to elaborate ma-neuvers of recuperation that will win her release on her own recog-nizance, and on the other hand, toward a suicide attempt that will win her another form of release, a permanent and irreversible one.

Gradually, the impulse toward health seems to be winning out at last. When she is released from the hospital after almost a two-year stay, she is considered "cured." Together with her family she begins to make plans to set up a life outside, a life on her own, a life where she will finally be able to make her own choices, exercise her own talents, allow her generous gifts to thrive. Although her parents want her to live at home, where they can keep a closer eye on her, Lily lobbies for her own apartment. When that's ruled out as too costly and too unsupervised, she agrees to take a room at the local YWCA, a place I imagine as not unlike the "Amazon," the for-women-only hotel that Sylvia Plath immortalized in *The Bell Jar.* For Lily the Y seems a safe transition between the total protection of hospital life and the unlimited, potentially dangerous freedom of living on her own.

Of Lily's last days I have fragments that I have pieced together, again knowing that she took the most coherent version of the story with her. From the outside, I assume, Lily appears to be going along with preparations for her independent life. She moves into the YWCA on a Sunday; the next day she has signed up to start classes at a nearby private school—one less pressured than Brearley—to finish the requirements for her high school diploma. That Sunday afternoon, she hangs a poster of Michelangelo's *David* in her room, her very favorite piece of art. Later the housemother tells her to take it down, condemning it as "obscene."

Such is the last random detail Alice has of her sister's life, reported angrily by Lily to a friend and repeated sadly, painfully, to Alice after Lily hurls herself out the window early that Monday morning, after that very first night on her own, after she has been hoping against hope that she can make it, when she suddenly loses faith that she can.

Aftermath

When the call comes to tell me the news, I am a freshman at Radcliffe, caught up in pursuing my own dreams. For my first writing class, the class that would inspire my own career as a writer, I have been writing a story about Alice and Lily. The story is called "Gemini," and in it, in sequences alternating between Alice and Lily, Lily and Alice, I am trying to explore what sent one twin down the path to health and the other toward emotional despair. The pages are strewn across my desk when my closest Brearley friend, Sarah, calls.

"Lily is finally at peace," Sarah quotes the grieving and bereft Alice as saying.

Out of all the heartbreaking ups and downs, Lily has reduced all the contradictions to this final, irrevocable solution. "I think there may be some people who kill themselves like this in order to achieve a calm and control they never find in life," writes A. Alvarez in *The Savage God,* his classic study of suicide, published in 1970, a year after Lily's death. There are people, he writes, as if about Lily, who "take their own lives not in order to die, but to escape confusion, to clear their heads." *Lily is finally at peace,* echo Alice's words, trying to contain her sister's pain and her own. No one could be closer to Lily's suffering than Alice or have a deeper need to give it meaning. "It is conceivable to kill oneself so as to count for something in one's life," so Alvarez quotes Cesare Pavese, "Here's the difficulty about suicide: it is an act of ambition that can be committed only when one has passed beyond ambition."

Have Lily's dreams, her drive, the youthful, creative mind that imagined the word "HERO" pinned to a young girl's shirt, all come to this dust, this act beyond all ambition?

She is so young, so untouched by the wider promises of life, that she does not even know how little she knows, can know. But she is desperate enough to risk what she doesn't know against the intolerable pain of what she does know.

Unraveling the Mystery

Any suicide is by definition a mystery that begs to be solved yet eludes solution. The only person who could begin to explain the murky and labyrinthine underground tunnels that led to it has taken herself beyond explanation. So any interpretation can be conjecture only, more a comfort for those left behind than a true epitaph for the departed. And if suicide in any context seems, at first, inexplicable, it seems particularly so in Brearley's cloistered setting, where, as Judith put it, looking back years later, "we were protected from any bad reality. It was a kind of storybook world"—with no poverty, no despair, certainly no self-inflicted death.

By eighteen my classmates and I had, of course, all had a first taste of disappointment, depression, glorious dreams unfulfilled. But now suddenly everyone was measuring these stresses and strains against the yardstick of Lily's fatal act. "I may have felt I had acne or I wasn't pretty enough," mused Judith many years later, "but there were not deep psychological issues. I had a loving mother and a father who was stern and strict but whom I admired immensely. I did my homework, had dinner, went to bed, got up, and started over." But what depths of despair, baffled classmates now asked themselves, could so preclude any hope of improvement that they'd be willing to defy their fates and futures by ending their lives forever? Lily's death was a troubling, complicated omen for every classmate, and when Lily went, a piece of their childhoods went too, a piece of their innocence, a piece of their faith in happily ever after.

So talking to classmates about their intertwined lives during Brearley and afterward, I also asked each of them, What do you remember about the twins and what did Lily's death mean to you, how did you explain it to yourself both then and now? Then to pull back the curtain of secrecy and break the taboo of silence, I consulted with psychologists both about twin psychology and about the complex roots of adolescent suicide. I asked them all the questions that could not be asked at the time—why and why again and could anything more have been done and would things have unfolded differently today?

"It was hereditary" was one classmate's instinctive explanation. She was especially intimate with the family and saw its emotional instability up close. In Lily the doctors labeled the problem schizo-phrenia, but that was a catchall phrase (to Alice, Lily was "extremely depressed"), and in different family members emotional pain man-ifested itself in slightly different, wrenchingly sad ways. Shortly after Lily's suicide, her older brother went to Vietnam and was so trau-matized by his experience there that when he returned, as Alice later described, he "gradually withdrew from the human race."

Certainly an unstable family history leaves an indelible mark on a daughter's chances to grow up healthy, strong, and independent. In his study "The Parental Factor in Adolescent Suicide," Dr. Mi-chael H. Stone pointed out, "It is noteworthy that the patients who did the worst usually came from the sickest families, in which at least one parent had been given a diagnosis within one of the major func-tional-psychotic categories." Examining the six suicidal adolescents with whom he worked at the New York State Psychiatric Institute in the late sixties, a bright and comfortable to affluent population, similar to Brearley's, Stone found that three of the four teens who did commit suicide had at least one parent who was considered schizophrenic. In these families the parents' preoccupations with their own troubles presumably prevented them from being able to support their troubled teens, particularly as their children sought independence from the family.

Although Lily's parents' histories lay beyond the scope of my interviews—both had died before I began this book—what seemed likely, in retrospect, was that emotional and financial resources in the family grew strained to their limits. Whereas Alice was able to stay centered by drawing on her own inner reserves and support outside the family circle, Lily's more fragile psyche needed extra shoring up that the family could not always provide.

"There was a downward spiral with Lily that we couldn't stop" was the way the twins' mother explained Lily's unraveling to a close family friend. With an unalloyed bleakness that I found hauntingly resonant of *The Hapless Child,* Lily's mother described each of

Lily's symptoms as following so relentlessly on the one before—the depression, the anxiety, the obsessiveness, the withdrawal—that the family felt powerless to arrest the cycle. Nor did a wider safety net exist back in the sixties to catch an unstable girl when she stumbled. No network of savvy and psychologically minded friends, no support groups, no school counselor specifically designated to offer guidance to struggling girls, no parent education, such as exists today at the school, on everything from eating disorders to substance abuse, depression, or suicide. Today the school, like the wider society, has made dramatic strides in emotional support and awareness of the warning signs of emotional trouble. But in the late sixties, silence and secrecy prevailed; some hands reached out, but other heads turned away out of unawareness, uncertainty, misplaced politeness.

"When Lily did herself in, everything was hush-hush," said another classmate and close early childhood friend whose two brothers suffered from mental illness heartbreakingly similar to Lily's. One of the two, a gifted artist like Lily, finally "went the same way in his thirties." More than a decade later this classmate can't talk about the suicides of her friend and her brother without tears and anger. "The sheltering of anything 'not nice' in the fifties and sixties was unrealistic," she observed. But she also found comfort that social changes and medical advances give the mentally ill a better prognosis today. "Today their chances would be better because of all the new medications and the greater degree of openness." From her point of view and somber history, it was the secrecy of the times, coupled with a relative lack of awareness about depression and schizophrenia and a paucity of medications and treatment options, that contributed to her brother's premature death and to Lily's. Certainly the society and the subculture were much less sophisticated about reading signs of despair—the turning inward, the hopelessness, the veiled or not-so-veiled suicide threat—and there were far fewer effective treatment responses available once mental illness or depression was diagnosed. An adolescent had to be a lot farther gone to be picked up for treatment, and therefore chances of full recovery were slimmer.

For Lily, as well as for numbers of other fragile Brearley schoolmates, it seemed to be the psychological stress of trying to separate from home and school that provoked the first serious emotional crisis and need for therapeutic intervention. Certainly each teenager in the class of '68 had to dance this dance of separation from parents, and find a comfortable distance between self and family, between autonomy and connection. Even those who struggled the most to establish balance—like Pamela, Maisie, Emma—were able to take advantage of the years beyond adolescence to negotiate the separation.

But for Lily, the psychological demands of separation from parents that every teenager faces head-on in high school were compounded and intensified by the simultaneous need to separate from her twin before she may have felt ready. For fifteen years the twins had been as emotionally linked as a deeply enmeshed couple. They shared life and breath, family and history, friends and enemies. Their intimacy began in the womb and continued powerfully when they were little girls, and then waxed and waned during their middle school years, both closeness and distance fraught with ambivalence.

As with many twins, their psyches seemed to interlock, giving them more weight in the world than either could have on her own. Alice was more confident in the external world; she knew how to maneuver bus schedules, homework assignments, getting books back to the library when they were due. Lily was more attuned to the inner world, more sensitive to subliminal messages, emotional undercurrents. Alice got them places on time, Lily interpreted the dynamics when they arrived. Their interdependence could be a source of strength, but it also provoked resentment and guilt.

So when Alice left for boarding school in tenth grade and Lily was left behind, the separation may have been well-timed for Alice, but for Lily it must have felt confusing and untimely. The part of Lily that saw Alice as her "drill sergeant" was relieved to be rid of her sister; but the part of her that depended on Alice for survival was deeply frightened and shaken. Indeed, she may have felt as if a vital part of herself was gone. The specter of depression, always a cold breath at her back, was intensified by the complicated feelings surrounding her separation from her twin.

Wondering about this emotionally freighted crossroads, I consulted with Eileen Pearlman, Ph.D., a psychotherapist in Los Angeles who specializes in the impact of separation and loss on twins. "Lily may have felt abandoned," she suggested. "Some twin pairs unconsciously divide up areas of expertise that complement each other. Together the twins' personalities are blended into one 'whole.' Alice appears to have been more stable and responsible, whereas Lily appears to have been more fragile, less responsible, more of a free spirit. When Alice left Lily for boarding school, Lily may not have yet developed the other part of herself which Alice provided at the time."

Issues of separation are particularly heightened for multiples, Pearlman explained. "When twins go their separate ways in high school or college, they are separating from each other and from their twin identity. They are forced to ask themselves, 'Who am I alone without my twin?' The one left behind may feel deserted and her self-esteem may be lowered; this may feed her sense of worthlessness."

For Lily, adolescence meant not just the separation from parents that every teenager must negotiate but this additionally equilibrium-shattering separation from her twin and from the particularly enmeshed identity they had shared from the womb. This double-layered separation proved more than she could manage; it precipitated a crisis from which she was never able to recover, even with hospitalization and some of the best therapy available at that time. Despite intermittent signs of recovery and periods when her fragile and divided psyche seemed to be healing, the symbolism of her suicide—its timing and location at the ambivalent brink of inde-pendence, when she was about to live on her own outside the hos-pital for the first time—seemed to suggest how insurmountable a problem separation had become. And beyond that, as Alice would explain many years later, "She lacked an optimism about her own future or her ability to survive it."

The Twinless Twin

"In this life it is not difficult to die / It is more difficult to live," wrote the Russian poet Mayakovsky in the aftermath of the Revo-lution and after the suicide of fellow poet Sergei Esenin in 1925. So it must feel for Alice after Lily's death. How could she carry on in the face of such pain, such loneliness, such spirit-crushing uncer-tainty? Like most twins, she must feel their fates are intertwined—they have come into the world together, and she must have always imagined they would leave it together, too. Now overnight Alice is the one abandoned, the one left untwinned behind. And this sepa-ration cannot be undone.

After her sister's suicide, emotions churned inside Alice, filling up the void left by her sister's death with the bleakest, blackest thoughts. Unspeakable sadness roiled with anger and guilt—anger at herself for leaving Lily before Lily could cope on her own, and corrosive anger at Lily for leaving her, more hopeless and defense-less than she could have imagined she would be. And horrible, gnawing guilt that she could have done more, could have read the signs earlier, could have saved her sister's life. Perhaps she couldn't credit herself for having helped prop Lily up, for carrying her along for years when Lily might have faltered earlier. Instead, she could only blame herself for having been too hard on Lily. "I clobbered her into getting places," she'll tell me much later. "I was her en-abler," she'll say. "You're in these roles even if you don't choose them." But at the time she agonized with self-blame, with mis-placed blame, for how can a teenager be responsible for another's life? And who mothered Alice while Alice mothered Lily? Nevertheless, she ached with survivor guilt. Why was she the one chosen to go on?

The Survivor

But just as Lily seemed to have an irrevocable impulse toward death, so Alice has it toward life. Slowly and imperceptibly over the course of months which become years, Alice opts for survival. She draws deep on her own resilience, the sources of coping she discovers in herself and deepens, which Lily was not able to access. Above all, Alice relies on the kindnesses of her friends. Where Lily's broodiness and eccentricities pushed people away at a time when she needed them the most, Alice has a large network of friends who are drawn to her humor, her sense of the ridiculous, and, now, her need, and she is not afraid to lean on them. It is as if the closeness she had with Lily—intense, unequal, and difficult as it sometimes was—demands another expression, a chance to get it right, rebalanced.

There are childhood friends from Brearley who are comforting in that they knew Lily, too, but do not push Alice to talk about her. There are more recent friends from boarding school whose attraction is just the opposite—they did not know Lily and thus do not relate to Alice as the left-behind half of a couple. Alice will continue to connect and reconnect with these high school friends once a year for decades, redefining and reinventing their friendships through closeness and separations, travels and reunions. When they stay married and she doesn't and they have children and she doesn't, their families will become her "many surrogate families," and their children will become her godchildren and honorary nieces and nephews, giving her a link to the next generation.

But if friends help her gradually lessen the painful hold of the past, her chance to build a future, she comes to believe, lies in cutting loose, starting over, cobbling an identity from the ground up in a place where she is not seen as the diminished half of a larger whole but as an independent woman, capable of standing on her own feet. A few years after she graduates from college, she says good-bye to the East Coast, which has been the only home she has known, and moves to France. Exiling herself there for fifteen years becomes another route to survival. Much, much later, when her self-imposed exile is over, she'll still refer to it as the "flight to health." She'll quote the shrink whose counsel she sought in Paris, the shrink who reassured her that escape is not necessarily a negative, a running away, but can be a positive thing.

The move to France is unarguably a positive thing for Alice. It's a place far removed from her family and her history, where she finds some breathing space to find out who she is. It's a place where she takes comfort in the certainty and foreignness of another country's customs ("There's only one right way for the French," she'll later say. "Only one salad dressing and that's vinaigrette"), a place whose culture provides welcome camouflage ("I can do a very good French person imitation," she'll say, and even after she returns to the States, she'll keep her dual citizenship for life).

In Paris she falls in love with and marries a Frenchman, whom she stays with for more than a decade. He is not the love of her life, it turns out, but years after their divorce, she still calls him a "very sweet man," the right choice at the time, a partner who helps her find stability and security when she needs it the most.

France also provides the incubator where her own artistic talents first flourish. For the artistic genius that had blazed so brilliantly in her twin had overshadowed Alice's considerable artistic talent, and after Lily's death, Alice can gradually reclaim her own gifts. Lily's talents were for Lily double-edged, a source of pride as well as pressure, and Lily destroyed every piece of her artwork before she died. But for Alice, art becomes another route to survival. During Alice's fifteen years in Paris she develops a high-profile career as a graphic artist, working with internationally known clients. She starts her own graphic design company with two close friends and travels around Europe, consulting about package design, so that she becomes something of a figurehead in her field and is profiled in industrial design magazines.

But as the years go on and the excessive eighties become the more reflective nineties, the things about France that so attracted Alice and nurtured her survival start to wear her down. Her high-powered career, which mobilized her talents and became a source of pride and self-sufficiency, starts to become too stressful. Her marriage, which had given her such comfort, starts to grow stale. And everything French that had seemed so charming and seductive when she first expatriated begins to look rigid. Now suddenly the French seem "old, cold, and set in their ways"—she paraphrases Joni Mitchell's line. The French, Alice comes to believe, are "turned toward the past," while "Americans are turned toward the future."

One lovely Parisian night, romantic as in a movie, Alice sits in an outdoor café with a friend, looks around, and realizes, "Nothing is going to happen here; it's a dead society." She had come to Paris to escape her own past; now she could finally see a future opening up back in America. "I suddenly realized I could bail," she would later say about her epiphany. "I wanted to return to my own context." Moving back to Manhattan, once the scene of intolerable misery at the time of Lily's death, now makes her "euphorically happy." She finds an appealing apartment in the Village and secures steady freelance work in the art department of a major book publisher. Still, she keeps her French options open. For a year and a half after her relocation she holds on to her old job in Paris and sublets her apartment there, until she's finally ready to sever her French ties and jump foursquare back into American life. Still, it's this flexibility, this ability to make change, to reinvent herself to keep up with her own growth, that is her saving grace, the hallmark of her resilience.

Bearing Grief

When I finally catch up with Alice it has been almost five years since she's returned to the States. We meet in her small, neat office, where she works on book jackets; museum postcards are tacked on her office wall in orderly, aesthetic arrangements. We've spoken several times in the past couple of years, but each time we've come close to meeting and trying to sort through the past, she has canceled our interview at the last minute. I am eager to talk with her, knowing she holds many of the clues to an understanding of this story. But I honor her timing, respect her privacy. The last time we saw each other was at the twenty-fifth reunion dinner party, shortly after her return from Paris. Then she was quiet and subdued, still seeming to be burdened by the weight of the past. Did seeing all those old classmates bring back her sister's ghost and remind her of the twinned life that was cruelly taken away from her? Even after twenty-five years, her mourning still felt palpable.

But this time, when we finally meet after the many postponements, I sense immediately that she has made it to a more settled place. The outgoing schoolgirl who was replaced by the somber, shell-shocked twenty-something has now, at midlife, become a mature, confident woman. She looks as chic as the most soignée Frenchwoman but thoroughly American—silk blouse, beige linen jacket, brunette hair now silvery blond. Her tone is wry, bemused; her attitude is droll, taking life with a long sigh, as if she's seen a lot that's difficult as well as sweet and has chosen to come through it.

When we talk about Lily, about her painful life and tragically untimely death, Alice speaks from a place of hard-struggled-for acceptance, a place of devotion but now, finally, some slight detachment, too. Years of introspection, of therapy and exile, have finally allowed her to come home to this kind of awareness and equanimity. "If Lily were alive today, she'd be living a functional life on antidepressant pills," she says, putting her sister's life in its context, as if she has finally relinquished blame—both of herself and of others—and come to see Lily as a casualty of the limitations of her times. "But those medications didn't exist then, and she was a victim of extreme depression. She found life unbearable."

This explanation seems to provide some closure on Lily's death.

But her life and her potential still haunt Alice, as they haunt me and all her classmates, her peers. "Isn't it amazing to think what she could have been if she had lived?" Alice asks me.

It's not really a question to be answered, but it mingles with Lily's possibilities, which hover in the air between us. For Lily's death turned out to be not only about Lily but about everyone in the class, about everyone's possibilities and what would become of them. Lily's death, coming as it did between the last gasp of childhood and the first blush of womanhood, said to every one of her classmates that adulthood was not a given but a choice. Could each of them make something of it both for her own sake and for Lily's memory?

CHAPTER 7

Note Takers at the Orgy

*T*he six months after college graduation can be the most difficult in a person's life," behavioral psychologist B. F. Skin-
ner once observed.

Think of that shell-shocked, expressionless face of Dustin
Hoffman's Benjamin Braddock as *The Graduate* begins. "Dad,"
Ben chokes out, while his parents' guests are beginning to arrive for
his graduation party, the ill-fated Mrs. Robinson among them. "I
have to be alone," he stumbles. "I'm just worried."

"About what?" his dad prompts.

"About my future"—the reply.

"About what?" his dad presses.

"I don't know. I just want it to be"—pregnant pause—
"*different*."

The Graduate came out in 1967, five years before my classmates'
college graduation, but the film describes their anomie as well, their
own yearning for something "different" and confusion about how
to find it. Like Ben, they too spend aimless hours, psychically speaking, floating on their back in a pool. That they don't give up and go
under, as Lily had, is an accomplishment of sorts. But for many, buffeted about by the fierce headwinds of a changing world, simply

surviving absorbs so much energy that not much is left over for fashioning the future, finding a place in the world.

Their parents, well-educated, affluent, and well-meaningly pushy, still expect great things from their daughters. They will not let go of ambitious post-Depression dreams, even for daughters weaned on the sixties and dubious about ambition, ambivalent about achievement. The ante is clearly up, but are these graduates up to the ante? Like Benjamin Braddock, they find themselves drifting, waiting for the rest of their lives to begin.

The Graduates

All the questions my classmates had asked themselves, all the doubts that plagued them, standing on the threshold between Brearley and college, resurfaced more insistently as they left college for the world beyond ivy-covered walls. This time the stakes were higher; it was no dress rehearsal. Who am I as an independent person in the wide world? Do I have the resources to take care of myself? Can I find fulfillment in work and love? Can I carve out a path for myself, sound out my life's meaning and purpose?

When my classmates asked these questions at eighteen, their search for answers was still confined to the relatively comfy constraints of college—which course to take, which demonstration to attend, which lover to pursue or abandon. Now, with four years' maturity, they recognized the old decisions as expendable. But they feared that the choices they were making now, they were making for keeps.

Some postponed the inevitable by extending college years into graduate school. They cordoned off a safe space in which trial and error could continue before the demands of real life got truly serious. Thus they created a "moratorium," as Erik Erikson once called it; a buffer zone between the anything-goes of late adolescence and the playing-for-keeps of adulthood. So Maisie, already married and, she thought at the time, settled, went on to library school at Simmons. Loving to read and feeling womblike safety among books, she was seduced by the cozy security that a career as a librarian seemed to offer. Tess, dreaming of horticulture and having transferred from the urban jungle of Barnard to the more plant-friendly open spaces of the University of Arizona for an undergraduate degree in landscape architecture, sharpened her focus as well as her employability by continuing her training at a graduate program in public garden administration. Judith stayed on at Princeton for a Ph.D. in math. She was turning out to be one of the most high-powered academics in the class, as well as a late starter socially who was now beginning to hit her stride.

I burned with a desire to write but had no idea how to structure a life around that dream. So I enrolled in Stanford's graduate creative writing program, whose reputation had recently been polished by Wallace Stegner. Going to Stanford catapulted me across the country and gave me a rationale to put some necessary distance between myself and my doting but overprotective family. I had fallen in love with California on a trip there at seventeen and vowed to call it home one day. But beyond gifts of geography and individuation, my year and a half at Stanford gave me uninterrupted time to write and reflect on the temper of my times (my master's project was a series of stories called "Waging the Peace," about the fallout of the Vietnam War on the lives of Americans at home). The graduate program also introduced me to the pleasures of the writing life and to a cadre of working writers—among them Alice Hoffman, Ray Carver, and Richard Price—who showed me that writing need not only be attic-garret pure—my image until then—but could propel a career and support a life. By the time I received my M.A. at twenty-four, I had the courage—call it youthful chutzpah—to move to Berkeley and call myself a freelance writer.

More than anything, my interlude at graduate school, like the planned moratoriums of other classmates, had bought me time to delay heavy-duty decisions about my future. But now, in my mid-

twenties in the mid-seventies, I had to admit my adolescence
was over. My classmates and I had come of age with the Vietnam
War, Richard Nixon, and Gloria Steinem. Now the war had wound
down to its anticlimax, Nixon had resigned, and Steinem's *Ms.* was
the flagship of a new movement that could revolutionize future
options. Once again the world was shifting gears and my class
was scurrying to keep up with it. Suddenly our decisions felt adult
and irrevocable. But many in my class and my generation would define and invent themselves now, and then several times over again
later on.

The Without-a-Blueprint Generation

If the task of the late teens was to separate from home and school
and begin to chisel out an independent identity, the task of the
twenties was to consolidate and refine that identity by shaping a
purpose and setting out on a path toward love and work. This time
the internal agenda involved deepening a capacity for intimacy and
cultivating an ability for self-support and independent sailing.

But as the upheavals of the late sixties trickled down to the
mid-seventies, the paths to love and work for this group and this
generation were not straightforward. Instead, decisions were perpetually complicated by roads diverging in that fabled yellow wood.
This was the generation without a blueprint, making their lives up
as they went along. The old models were being debunked; the new
models were yet to be born. Everything and nothing was expected.
Should they play it safe by choosing the traditional, accepted, and
"nice" path they were raised to follow or defy conventions and opt
for the confusing, experimental, not entirely nice world that was
cracking open before their eyes? Or would their life's task be to invent a hybrid solution that would integrate and accommodate both
the old values and the new?

Just a half generation before—for older sisters and cousins—the
mandate was clear. Marry soon, marry well, let your husband sup-

port and define you, and make motherhood your lifework. Just a half generation later—for my five-years-younger sister and her classmates—the mandate had been upended. Commitment to a career could define you just as surely as marriage and motherhood, these younger women believed, and the most successful of all would confidently juggle all three.

The transitional generation, mine was caught in the crossfire. Falling in love for the first times, they were pulled between safety and excitement, between the comfort of the known and the thrill of the yet-to-be-discovered. Either they dreamed of a partner safe and secure, the kind of man mother had married, who would support them in high style, or they pined for a new, daring, and as yet undefined mate with whom they'd reinvent marriage as a partnership of equals. They were both attracted to marriage and dubious about it. For some, marriage "was about as hip as a Tupperware party," as my Radcliffe classmate Lynn Darling would later write. So maybe they'd marry late or not at all; maybe they'd have a succession of little marriages, à la Gloria Steinem; maybe they'd experiment with women; maybe they'd live contentedly and unconventionally on their own.

If hearts were pulled in many directions, toward conflicting romantic images, so, too, were plans for working lives and professional prospects. Just as my classmates were thinking twice about marriage, so, too, were they reconsidering worldly ambition and success. Did they want it for themselves or did they want to marry it? Was work about following your passion and the money would follow? Was it for self-fulfillment, serving others, making the world a better place, none or all of the above? Children both of the complacent fifties and of the confrontational sixties, this group was tugged between working inside or outside the System, contributing to the economy or undermining it. They wondered if they'd be defined by their work or if they just needed an odd job or two to get by while finding their real selves elsewhere. They brooded about the elusive nature of success: was it the financial stability and social prominence their parents aspired to or was it something less tangible and quantifiable, more inner than outer reckoned?

And they worried about where motherhood would fit into this equation. Would it be central and defining, as it had been for their mothers, or would it take a back seat to careers, as the new feminist strategists would have it? Certainly in our twenties, the decision to have children seemed as distant as another cosmos. The Pill bought freedom to manipulate and postpone the Baby Question until the ticking of the biological clock got too loud to ignore—my classmates were part of the postponing generation that had the freedom to defer its life decisions until the emotional eleventh hour. For now the choices seemed more intellectual than actual. The newly minted graduates asked themselves if they could eventually balance love, work, and family. Did they want all three, and if so could they have them all?

Standing at the threshold of the rest of their lives, they looked both forward and backward, forward to the new women they dreamed of becoming and backward to the girls who'd been educated and the women they'd been educated to be.

"Did a Brearley Education Prepare Us for Our Lives?"

This is the question Mary Catherine Bateson asked not long ago in an alumnae lecture at Brearley. Bateson, an anthropologist and author of the best-selling *Composing a Life* and *Peripheral Visions,* is the daughter of Margaret Mead and Gregory Bateson and was a member of the Brearley class of '57. Although Bateson's class graduated a decade before mine, she, too, was trying to gauge the discrepancies between the world her classmates were educated to enter and the world in which they ended up coming of age. It's a "very complicated question," she offered, "for when I was a student, my teachers had no way of knowing what kind of life I was going to lead. This was before radical reinterpretations of the sixties of how women would spend their lives. And now we all have to learn new techniques from year to year. In what sense were we prepared for this?"

Similarly, as Brearley graduates and now as college grads, too, my classmates and I had to acknowledge that any education would be limited by the blinders of its historical context. No teacher had X-ray vision to foresee the sexual and social revolution that confronted this post-Vietnam generation. Still, my friends wondered, as they gazed uncertainly into their futures, if they could apply the lessons they'd learned so diligently in the fifties and sixties to the tradition-shattering choices and challenges of the seventies and eighties. Here was the fulcrum of this generation: how to adapt the lessons of the past to a future still revealing itself.

So the class of '68 tallied up both sides of the ledger, their education's pluses and its minuses, how they were equipped and how handicapped.

Unarguably, Brearley taught girls to think independently, to analyze, organize, work single-mindedly on their own. Critical thinking was the school's catechism and its bible was I. A. Richards's *Practical Criticism*. Again and again, students learned to grapple with a text, tease out its meanings, dissect its style, appraise its imagery, and define its strengths and flaws. All this intellectual pumping-up left many believing that they could pit their minds against any challenge and succeed. Judith, for one, was so confident in her ability to study independently that she sailed through not one but two rigorous stints of postgraduate education—first for a Ph.D. in math at Princeton, then, more than a decade later, for an M.D. at Stanford. Often she wouldn't even show up for the lectures but would study on her own and still ace her exams.

But Brearley's near-reverence for verbal skills above all others left those whose strengths lay elsewhere feeling undervalued, often dubious about their talents, sometimes deeply scarred. One classmate whose gifts were artistic remembered through tears, years after the fact, how "the school was attached to one way of learning and it wasn't mine. . . . It did a bad number on my self-esteem." She said she still "can't stand to write even now." Nor did she remember being recognized for her artistic talents at school, although as an adult she has defined herself as an artist and has gone on to exhibit and sell her work. "I dropped out of art class, because we were referred to as 'Easel One' instead of by our name," she recalled, the oversight still wounding.

Besides overvaluing verbal skills and undervaluing other learning styles, the Brearley curriculum, like so many private schools' in the fifties and sixties, reflected its social milieu and was thus lopsided in other ways as well. Girls were taught to sound out the emotional nuances of fiction but not to express their own emotional subtext. "Teachers did make me feel valued and loved, but more for intellectual achievements rather than issues of emotional life," said one high-achieving schoolmate who became an activist lawyer and confessed she needed years of therapy to feel comfortable with intimacy. The girls of '68 became more savvy intellectually than emotionally. As graduates, most felt unschooled in recognizing or naming their own feelings, so that they had to reinforce their academic education with another education entirely—a course of psychotherapy, a spiritual search, the kind of vision quest that attracted Pamela as she dug deeper for midlife meaning.

"If I would fault Brearley, it would be for this," Pamela said later. "Our education was not for the whole person, but just for the brain." But, she added with a sigh of resigned acceptance, "that's how the whole Northeast was at that time." The class of '68 were the daughters of a particular class, a subculture, a slice of history and geography, and the message they got from all sides was to think with their heads and not with their hearts.

"We left knowing how to think," assessed another schoolmate, about another gap in her education, "but not to think and do." To think, but not to do, to "make a life but not a living," in John Dewey's notable phrase—here was another contradiction in the way this education prepared girls, another imbalance they had to confront on the brink of adulthood. One of the benefits of a single-sex education is the intellectual confidence it nurtures. Educated separately as girls and young women, my classmates could find their voices and enhance their self-esteem, class discussion by discussion, essay by essay, project by project. Learning took place away from the competition, intrusion, and social distraction that boys would have provided. In girls-only classrooms my classmates and I were far removed from boys waving their insistent hands in the teacher's face, getting called on first, or shouting their answers, no hand waving necessary. Girls were shielded from that potentially debilitating power imbalance that the 1992 American Association of University Women's study "How Schools Shortchange Girls" would bring to the nation's attention decades later. Many of my classmates spoke passionately of this powerful and empowering influence of their girls-alone education, this early jump start to achievement, this belief, as Judith reflected, that she could "do anything." "The school gave me incredible self-confidence" is how she put it, "I don't feel threatened by anyone intellectually."

But between college graduation and doing "anything" lay a yawning and intimidating chasm. "The biggest problem was getting out of college and not knowing what to do," said Alexa, speaking for most classmates. School and parents may have grandly conceded that their daughters could do anything, but what exactly did "anything" mean? "Okay," said Alexa, "just give me a hint!" Somehow "Plastics!"—the pithy piece of advice given to Benjamin Braddock at his graduation party—was no longer relevant. But what was? Lawyer or secretary, artist or homemaker—preferences shifted quicker than the colors in a lava lamp. The graduates of '68 were overqualified for some options, underqualified for others, befuddled by most. Drifting, they often let choices choose them, rather than actively pursuing the outcomes they wanted, like the girl who went to medical school instead of law school because the lines for premed courses at college orientation were shorter than the lines for pre-law.

Very few of my classmates left Brearley with a clear sense of direction, and though college may have sharpened that focus for some—Judith toward math, Maisie toward library science, for instance—most faced a good deal of stumbling and floundering before they found their way into a working life—or could add in emotional attachments. Nor did this group have a clue about how to combine love and work, family and friends. The skill of juggling roles, which my younger sister had already begun to learn in consciousness-raising groups in high school in the early seventies, was a course that was missing from my class's curriculum. So my classmates' education was circumscribed by history's limits—and their adulthood would be preoccupied with redefining and balancing marriage, work, and motherhood.

For those who thrived on stress, Brearley was a good training ground, but it was spirit-breaking for those whom stress crushed. "I felt so insecure, because everyone else seemed so smart," said one schoolmate, who went on—defiantly—to become a nurse rather than a doctor, opting for the lower-stress choice, because she realized that it better suited her temperament and her emotional need to spend time with her husband and young children.

Being able to turn to a mentor either inside or outside school also took the edge off stress, and for those who made this connection, it turned out to be pivotal, a crucial influence on making fulfilling choices as young adults. Tess found role models in several teachers, "brilliant women," she called them, who opened her up to the pleasures of following your passion. But even these mentors, influential as they were, could not always guide their students to places they did not yet know existed, to opportunities as well as uncertainties still revealing themselves.

The day I found out I'd gotten into Radcliffe, I raced to tell one of my favorite teachers the news. "You'll be married in a year!" she laughed. I was curiously flattered—she saw me as marriageable!—but also deflated—what about my dreams? She was a French teacher, droll, earthy, ironic, and like all of the distinctive native-born Frenchwomen in that department, a marvelously sophisticated woman of the world, one whom many Francophile classmates hoped to pattern themselves after. Still, her response was constrained by her own experience—after all, *she'd* snagged a Harvard man while still in college. But more than that, her reaction reflected her knowledge of how the world had worked until then. Until then, marriage was the brass ring college promised. So it was with many Brearley teachers and mentors—brilliant and beloved, they could not steer their protégées into territory that had not yet been perceived.

As newly launched graduates my classmates were intellectually confident, but emotionally naïve, sensitive but not psychologically sophisticated. They could analyze and categorize but hesitated to take action, make dreams become realities. They alternately thrived on and were crushed by stress. They could depend on their families—or felt burdened by their families' dependencies. They wanted to break free and start fresh but were lured by the safety of the known and traditional. They looked up to teachers and mentors to show them the way ahead but could not trust their guides to know what they hadn't yet lived.

On the threshold of adulthood, the only certainty was change. My classmates and I craved it and feared it.

California Dreaming

I fell in love with California at first sight. I was seventeen—it was the spring vacation before I would graduate from Brearley—and I flew out to the West Coast on my own, invited by two San Francisco friends I'd met on a trip the summer before. They toured me up and down the heart-stopping hills of San Francisco, took me dancing to acid rock at the Fillmore, and then scooted me across the bay to Berkeley. And it was there, in Berkeley, in the sun-dappled, incense-heavy, jasmine-scented, springtime air that I breathed deep, like a shut-in sprung for the first time in months. I finally saw that here, another self, a self far removed from the uniform-clad, nice New York City girl, a truer self, could incubate and emerge. For several seductive days I bounced around Berkeley with my friends. We rambled through the sprawling campus to Sproul Plaza, where protesting students had only recently been leveled by tear gas, down to Telegraph Avenue where hippies, panhandlers, and poets blowing bubbles slouched on street corners, and then we hiked up the eucalyptus-cloaked hills where San Francisco beckoned in the distance. It was there, three thousand miles from my birthplace, that I knew I had incongruously found my home.

So after Radcliffe and after Stanford—the roadstops I had to make because I was, after all, a dutiful daughter, a nice girl, a Brearley girl with academic promises to keep—I hotfoot it to Berkeley. Berkeley means starting over, starting fresh, for California has been, historically, the farthest edge of this country's possibilities. Its landscape of towering redwoods, cascading rivers, and awesome mountains has provided, since Gold Rush days, what its bard Wallace Stegner once called "the geography of hope." For me, at twenty-four, California means freedom; it means breathing my own air, my own way. It means no one looking over my shoulder if I skip a meal, stay out all night, dance naked on a beach.

Berkeley is about as far from Brearley as a girl can go. From Park Avenue to Telegraph Avenue is a psychic head trip even more than a geographical one. But many of my classmates make the trip in the seventies, either temporarily or permanently, wanting all that glorious, buffering distance from the person they had been and were expected to become. Pamela comes to California after dropping out of Vassar and between long forays to Aspen, which will ultimately become her true spiritual home. She falls in with a Tibetan lama in Berkeley and gets into Buddhism for a while, because, as she writes me at the time, "that's what the people I was with were into." Periodically she'll return to California over the years for a spiritual recharge, just as I'll return to New York City for a tune-up with family and old friends once California becomes my home base.

Emma knows to survive she has to "get the hell out of Dodge"—read: Washington, D.C., and her too-righteous churchgoing parents. So she hitches to Santa Rosa, where she'd been born, and enrolls in a community college. She comes to California, because "that was where everyone was going at the time," and once there, she basks in the independence she has wrenched from her family's nit-pickingly "close scrutiny of her personal life." Emma stays in California longer than any other place she'll call home as an adult, although by midlife she has bounced back east again, first to Orlando, then to Boston.

Later still, Maisie comes to San Francisco too, to put a failed marriage and ill-fitting career behind her and start again with a better-fitting second marriage and reinvented career; and Judith comes for medical school at Stanford and to find a marriage and start a family.

Out of the sixty-four girls who make up the extended class of '68, only eleven end up settling in New York City. Only a sixth of this group is content to replicate the lives they'd known as girls or to become adults under the shadow—sheltering or intrusive—of their parents' established lives. The others scatter to every corner of this country and beyond. California beckons me, but others find their way to Vermont, Colorado, Illinois—even England and Chile. This diaspora reflects the restlessness and mobility of our generation. It also speaks to my classmates' and my need to rebound from the cloying closeness of thirteen years at the same school, fishing from the same still waters. As adults, each needed to dig her own new pond.

Berzerkeley

I move to Berkeley a scant month before Patty Hearst is kidnapped from her apartment only a few blocks away from the brown shingle house I share with four friends. Her story transfixes me, and I identify with it by proximity and history, if not intensity. Like me, Patricia Hearst is a nice girl, a private-school girl, raised to do all the right things. Like me, she yearns for transformation. I watch her story unfold on TV by the hour—her abduction at gunpoint from the campus apartment she shares with her bespectacled fiancé, her captors' demands that the Hearsts donate two million dollars in free food to the city's poor, Patty's metamorphosis into Tania, and her declaration that she has chosen "to stay and fight," her participation in a bank robbery, her ultimate recapture, imprisonment, and release—and eventually her marriage to her bodyguard. Her life is a metaphor for my craziest yearnings and deepest fears.

She is a poster girl for the marriage of convention and wild unconvention that will characterize so many of my own classmates and friends. Like many, she will come full circle from tradition to wild caprice and back home to security again.

Berkeley in the seventies is Berzerkeley, a hotbed of experimentation and change. Berkeley is a birthing place and testing ground for every harebrained scheme, as well as for most of the profoundly life-altering ideas that will either transform American society or be hooted off the edge of the continent into oblivion. There could be no better place for "finding oneself." And indeed, everyone in Berkeley has come from someplace else—Chicago, Los Angeles, many New Yorkers like myself—and everyone is busy becoming someone new. No one knows exactly who that will be, but the possibilities seem limitless. Sometimes I wander up and down Telegraph Avenue, bug-eyed as Alice at the wonderland of posters and announcements stapled to telephone poles, and I feel almost a psychic rush from the choices. Consciousness-raising groups, journal-writing classes, t'ai chi and yoga, radical therapy, Grateful Dead concerts, appearances by David Harris, Tom Hayden, Angela Davis.

Looking among all these tantalizing choices for the path that best suits me, I experiment according to the two methods I know best: either I fall in love with them or I write about them. From one lover, a dedicated yogic practitioner, I learn all the asanas, including a few of the Tantric ones; from another, a heavyweight in the free speech movement, I get my graduate education in activism and learn what strange bedfellows radical politics do make; yet a third, a beatnik throwback, introduces me to San Francisco's North Beach and the pleasures of Beat poetry and cappuccinos. But the man I fall in love with for keeps is a Harvard-educated East Coast refugee like myself, who has no gimmicks except that he loves me and wants to build a life together.

But more permanent commitment comes later in the story, as the seventies settle into the eighties and I, too, start to yearn to settle down. In the middle of the seventies, in the middle of my twenties, I am still hoping to find my truest self by madly trying on new identities, and writing about them is the most accessible route I know. Researching an article gives me an excuse to test the rushing waters of alternative lifestyles without really getting my own feet wet.

Freelancer

Fittingly, my very first published piece is one for *Newsday* about the metamorphosis of a straight, suburban, college girl into a hippie chick. "Good-bye, Manhasset," I call it, nodding to my Long Island readership, but it could as likely have been the more accurate "Good-bye, Manhattan," for, though tongue-in-cheek, it is my story, too. For a sequence of before-and-after photos, I pose in a variety of countercultural haunts around Greenwich Village, settings that could as easily have been Berkeley. At first I am prim and tentative in a nice-girl black sheath, ladylike clutch in hand. Then scene by scene, I don rose-colored glasses and a velvet vest embroidered with the face of Jesus, lace leather Spartacus sandals up my leg, sample vegetarian fare, and groove to Dylan, until I am transformed by the end of the story into a hippie for the day, swathed in tie-dye and puffing uncertainly on a hash pipe.

I make my way through the seventies, trying on possibilities in print, experimenting vicariously with successive disguises. I investigate a rainbow of alternative lifestyles without having to commit to any of them—single parenthood, motherhood after forty, radical psychiatry, the women's self-help movement, natural childbirth, men's liberation. All the while I am doing research for my own life, my own choices, the person I am hoping to become. Camouflaged and buffered by my intrepid-reporter disguise, I am braver as a writer than I'll ever be in real life, more radical in print than I'll ever be in practice.

In a cover story for *Ramparts* on "the feminist view of childbirth," for instance, I lambaste medicated births and male doctors' unnecessary interventions into the natural process of childbirth. But my own two sons are both born—joyfully—by cesarean section a decade later. Sometimes when I propose a Berkeley-inspired story idea to my mostly New York–based editors, they'll reject it for being too way out, too "California." Three years later, when the rest of the country has caught up with the West Coast, I'll see a similar topic featured on the covers of those same New York–edited magazines. I, too, am farther ahead of myself in my writing than in my emotional development.

And sometimes when I agonize over a manuscript, when the words stick like peanut butter on the roof of my mouth, when I worry that each sentence could be written one way and then scrapped entirely and turned inside out, then I realize that my struggles are as much about writer's block as about identity block. I'm writing "to find out what I know," as Joan Didion once observed about why she writes, but even more, I'm writing to find out who I am.

Reporter at the Orgy

One wintry Friday evening I find myself in San Francisco at a lavish Pacific Heights mansion doing research for yet another piece on countercultural communities, which will eventually appear, somewhat blue-penciled, in the Sunday supplement of the *San Francisco Examiner* as "Games Liberated People Play." This particular group meets once a month, I have been told, to explore their sexuality, re-vitalize their relationships, and reach out to like-minded souls. This exploring, revitalizing, and reaching out, I soon find out, is done entirely naked. For when I climb up the sinuous spiral staircase to the group that's gathering in the stately common room, its gleam-ing hardwood floor muted by a huge Persian rug and accented by overstuffed couches, I realize I've stumbled into an orgy.

At first people are awkward with each other, sizing each other up without committing, like orientation at summer camp. The pace builds slowly, restlessly. People of all sizes and shapes—many of them quite ample—drift around the living room and then into other nooks and crannies of the grand Victorian, which surely was not constructed for this purpose but has turned out to be ideally suited for it. I respond to peer pressure and take off my own clothes—I want to be a good sport, after all—but also, wanting somehow to remain a nice girl, I continue to clutch my notepad as conspicuously as possible. It becomes my shield, my alibi, my fig leaf.

Gradually the momentum intensifies. Pairs find each other, and couple up around the sumptuous quarters, falling onto couches, at odd angles to each other on the Persian rug. The more private—everything being relative—sequester themselves in one or another of the mansion's endless supply of bedrooms. Moans start to pene-trate the air.

I am left, naked and dubious, holding my pad, scribbling from time to time in a more and more desultory way, asking myself what it all means, wondering why I've come. I'm not exactly the wallflower at the orgy, in Nora Ephron's famous phrase. Men ap-proach me, we share a few ironic remarks—not mixing business with pleasure?—and they move on to more willing players. One man I find attractive—he plays the harmonica, has a sense of humor, a great body, and a headful of dark curls. He asks me for my phone number. I scribble it on a piece of notebook paper, tear it off, and give it to him. Later, off the job and back on my own turf, I see him a few times. Orgy Pete, my roommates dub him. But like a shipboard romance, ours flounders back on shore. Clothed, we seem to run out of things to say.

Note taker at the orgy—it's a role I've stumbled into during college, more social observer than activist, and continue to refine during my postgraduate, who-will-I-become? years. It's a role that's allowed me to blend in with my subculture but not inhale. But now, by the mid-seventies, it's the metaphor that also seems to define my cohort of classmates as they try to make sense of the orgy of choices surrounding them, choices just as noisy and demanding, ecstatic and disturbing, as the bodies coupling across the San Francisco mansion's Persian carpet. Uncertainly, the women of '68 peer at the action from the outside, sticking their necks out, trying to see where they belong. They're gathering data but are not quite ready to transform it into action. They're not yet gutsy enough to mix it up in the center, sweaty and engaged, but hover on the fringes, trying to assess the meaning, trying to discover what blend of the comfy old world and the sexier new one will fit them.

The Untraditional Traditionalist and the Unconventional Career-Tracker

*A*mong the orgy of possibilities that confronted the class of '68 as they began to make choices in love and work, four prominent coping styles stood out, I learned from interviews and shared reflections: the untraditional traditionalist, the unconventional career-tracker, the seeker, and the juggler. These patterns also reflect the adaptations of the women of the wider boomer generation as they threaded through the paradoxes of this transitional time and did their best to reconcile the staider, more circumscribed traditions of the fifties with the increased freedoms and opportunities of the sixties and its liberating legacy. So these styles are particularly fraught with contradictions and challenges that would have been unheard-of a generation earlier and would be more easily resolved a generation later.

Each style comes with assets and vulnerabilities, periods of clear sailing as well as choppy seas, as each young woman struggles to craft a story for herself that she hopes will not only answer the conflicting demands of this historical moment but also maximize her own gifts and minimize her liabilities. The women of '68 were pulled through their twenties and thirties by various opposing currents as they sought out different goals, more or less actively, more or less consciously. The untraditional traditionalist is searching for security above all, but typically only after a carefree or eccentric experimental phase. The unconventional career-tracker is tracking worldly success, dreaming of making a name for herself, albeit not the most conventional one nor in the most conventional field. The seeker is traveling a path toward awareness, personal growth, and spiritual transformation, conventional security and worldly glory be damned. And the juggler is striving for balance, trying to integrate marriage, family, and career.

Balance, it turns out, is the one goal that every member of '68 seems to be looking for in one way or another, the one goal most commonly articulated by my classmates and other women of their generation looking back at and assessing their choices at midlife. Balance between work and family, family and self, self and community. Balance between old expectations and new possibilities and between a varied and challenging public life and a rich and sustaining inner life.

The Untraditional Traditionalist

Of the four styles, the untraditional traditionalists and the unconventional career-trackers contrast the most dramatically, yet are also linked: alternative responses to the same complicated questions about how to set priorities and find a fitting balance between personal and professional lives. Overall, the untraditional traditionalists put personal fulfillment ahead of professional, I found, and the unconventional career-trackers put professional goals first. But it's typical of the class of '68's divided consciousness that the untraditional traditionalists also have a strong renegade streak of resistance to tradition, and that the unconventional career-trackers, however ambitious, are also suspicious of ambition and have a strong dose of unconventionality.

Just a half generation before, a traditionalist's attitude would most likely have been an unalloyed embrace of old-fashioned family values; she would have unambivalently accepted her primary role as wife and mother. Flipping through old yearbooks, I see these women with their tidy Peter Pan collars and circle pins, hairstyles as tight and as similar as their values. Just a half generation later, the senior yearbooks reflect the revolution in culture and style, dress as varied, hair as freely cascading as these younger women's options. Among this younger group of women, who entered the workforce five years after my class did and were empowered by the surging momentum of the women's movement, the career-tracker would be pursuing her professional goals more single-mindedly than my group did at the same junction; she would be grabbing for career success without the unsettling ambivalence many of my classmates expressed.

Caught in the middle, my classmates were the daughters of contradictions, so as adults they've had to confront both sides of the oxymorons they've become—the traditionalist exploring the untraditional, the focused career-tracker also pursuing the divergent, unconventional path.

Sophia—the Wild Child
Who Came Back to the Fold

Sophia had always been a wild child from a rather staid, conservative family. She was a girl who pushed the limits of a family that clung to its conventions and outward appearances and kept quiet about its chinks. Horse-crazy from a tender age, she was something of a wild stallion herself, roaring around the more workaday horses, teasing less confident classmates with a flick of her mane. Sophia was an early beauty with debutante-worthy good looks—patrician bones, flawless skin, a womanly figure at a time when tentatively budding classmates were still faking it with "Littlest Angel" bras.

Sophia and Pamela were among the earliest leaders of the class, figureheads who presided over rival factions. Pamela led the boyish girls, the ball-slugging, high-jumping girls whose athleticism wouldn't truly be socially sanctioned until decades later. Sophia was a beacon for the girlier girls, the first ones to appear at school with makeup and short skirts, the boy-crazy girls who turned the lights out at boy-girl parties and played Spin the Bottle, while most other classmates were just beginning to tire of Pin the Tail on the Donkey. Sophia's sexuality and her interest in the opposite sex also bloomed early. And her charisma, her clout, came from this early burst of heat, and from her wild streak. She would dare to do things others would never consider—talk back to a teacher or casually swear. Once in a third-grade game of Hangman on the back of the school bus, she baffled me with the word "intercourse." I stared dumbly at all those vowels—not a bad choice for Hangman—and hadn't a clue. For me, as for other similarly overprotected members of the class, Sophia stood for the attraction of the forbidden, daring girls to go down the dangerous primrose path, all the more seductive for being taboo.

Socially confident to the point of cockiness, Sophia was less confident academically, despite a shrewd mind. Words didn't come easily to her, and concentration could be a struggle. She was the last girl in the second grade to learn to read, a disappointment that no one else noticed but that stung her like a bruise. Years later she would admit that she never felt smart enough for Brearley. "I shouldn't have been there," she said. "I was trailing along." Only when her daughter attended the school three decades later—an obvious smart cookie and good test-taker, but a late reader, too—only then would Sophia feel intellectually vindicated.

Like Pamela's, Sophia's family was social and prominent. Her mother was an elegant Wasp beauty Sophia would alternately adore and reject and finally model herself after. But the "let's not discuss it" veneer of family life was ripped forever by her parents' divorce, when Sophia was five and her sister three. In an era of "Ozzie and Harriet" myths of nuclear-family harmony, her parents' divorce—one of the very few that early in the class's history—set Sophia slightly apart. Groping her way through it gave her a boost toward maturity as well as an earlier glimpse than others had into the fragility of relationships, the uncertainty of commitment. And when her mother remarried three years later, and the family configuration changed once again, it threw Sophia "for a loop," as she would recount many years later, a loop that took her a mini-lifetime to unfurl.

Here lay the contradictions out of which her later choices would emerge, the tension between stability and chaos, between convention and rebellion, which becomes the hallmark of the untraditional traditionalist. Sophia's more tradition-bound side yearned to create the stability she'd known so fleetingly before her parents divorced and her security was shattered; she dreamed of that mother-married-to-father insularity that old traditions applauded. But another side of her wanted none of what she feared she couldn't have; her nose-thumbing, convention-defying side wanted to jettison tradition and cut loose. And it was that rebellious, tradition-smashing side that dominated her early years, the years at Brearley and the years of college and just beyond when she was trying to define herself outside the sway of her family and was wildly experimenting with lovers and jobs.

"Our class went through a disorienting time," she can say now with the wisdom of hindsight. "All the givens were unreliable." Marriage and having children, ambition for success, earning big money or graciously accepting being taken care of—all the pillars that held up her mother's comfortable, traditional life crumbled in the late sixties and early seventies when Sophia was checking out her choices. At the big eastern university where she'd gone reluctantly after getting turned down at Radcliffe, she hardly took her studies seriously. She whiled away the best of four years "doing drugs and living with a guy with hair to his waist." Most classmates of '68 fell in love with at least one of these renegades or a whole string of them, the more inappropriate, the better; these romances were a critical rite of passage, a badge of honor for these times. In retrospect Sophia was glad she'd had her hippiest fling in a lower-profile town where she "only made a small splash" rather than in Cambridge, where the wider ripples might have caught her in the undertow later on. She put in her most untraditionalist stint away from the prying eyes of the very traditionalists with whom she'd eventually hobnob when she finally returned to the New York City fold.

Journey to Find Herself

After graduation, like many shell-shocked veterans of '68, Sophia feels lost and disoriented. She scorns her mother's path, for her mother married for the first time and had a new baby at nineteen, while still a Barnard college student. "Getting married and having kids" is to Sophia right then "the single most boring thing, the epitome of the middle class." Marriage and motherhood are synonymous with the tradition, the cultural vise, she's fleeing. But she is also not motivated or focused enough to carve out a career track for herself, nor is she blessed with a talent that might immediately translate into a professional path. Like so many classmates during their early twenties, that transitional time both in their own lives and in the culture, she is obsessed instead with questions of identity. Beyond being a daughter to parents of privilege and social polish, a sister to a sister even wilder and more mercurial than she is, a girlfriend to a rebel without a cause, and a rather reluctant student, who was she?

Shunning conventional choices at this early crossroads, she chooses instead that unofficial pilgrimage of the soul that attracts many similarly stranded members of her generation. She sets out on a journey to find the self who has been lost since earliest childhood. And because she is lucky enough to have the privileges and wherewithal of affluence, in a flush economy fueled by military spending, she takes two years for this journey and it leads her around the world.

Her trip proves a graduate school in self-reliance and a moratorium on decision making. Two years on the road, fending for herself among strangers, negotiating constantly changing languages and customs, teaches her that she can get around "with no one knowing who my parents were or that I was in the *Social Register*." A long stay in Australia also, surprisingly, opens her eyes to the seductions of stability, seductions she has always before dismissed. There she gets to know "people who were married and stayed married without having affairs." Their fidelity gives her hope, holds up a different kind of model than the footloose solo life she has imagined until now.

Her journey proves a "big breakthrough" of self-discovery— "just to be known as who I was." It also gives her a chance to reinvent herself, to rediscover her values and ideals, a transformation that will come to characterize many women in this group and this generation. Her independence is intoxicating, but also scary; she doesn't know where it might lead.

But Sophia would never exactly find out where this particular journey of self-discovery might lead. Shortly after she returns from her round-the-world travels, the old, reliable givens of her universe are irrevocably jackhammered. Walking out of a movie theater with a pack of friends one night, her younger sister, Samantha, is hit by a car and killed. Samantha, two years younger, is the sister whom Sophia has alternately loved and hated (usually many times in a day). She is the sister whom Sophia rescued after their parents' divorce but couldn't quite prop up through academic struggles at Brearley and later floundering at boarding school, where her reputation got wilder and wilder. In one irreparable instant, her only sister is gone. Samantha is twenty-one when she is killed, Sophia, twenty-three.

The family keeps its grief about the accident very private, as is its style, and friends keep a respectful distance as they watch Sophia gamely try to get back her bearings, try to shore up her shattered family with her presence, her dignity. Her old schoolmate Alice is especially sympathetic. Lily's death five years earlier still aches like a fresh assault. Sisterless both, Sophia and Alice bond in their powerlessness before fate.

Samantha's death shakes Sophia to her core and forces an about-face in her plans. Any residual lust for adventure, any yearning for nonconformity or wanton rejection of her family's values, suddenly drains out of her, like a long, weary sigh. "After my sister died," she would say years later, "I knew someone had to hold things together, someone had to keep the family together. I knew that my mother could only take so much, for rebelling is inflicting pain." That crisis marked a big transition in her life, a transition from "thinking about herself to thinking about others." "We were late bloomers," she remarks wryly in retrospect, "even though we thought we knew it all at thirteen."

Wake-up Call

In the lives of many classmates, an unforeseen catastrophe proved a wake-up call, a painful shock to the system that would ultimately transform a life course. For Alice, it was Lily's suicide that forced her to confront the depths of darkness and finally catapulted her to France to build a more satisfying life for herself. For Maisie, it was the shattering blow of her divorce and her grief at its aftermath that ultimately catalyzed a shift in career and a better-fitting marriage. For Sophia, it was Samantha's senseless death that made her want to retrench and get more serious about her own prospects.

Suddenly she was embracing the very values she had gone around the world to question and escape. Security was foremost among these, and financial security most of all. Part of her, the most traditional part, was biding her time, waiting for her prince to come along. But there was also her untraditional side, that surprisingly self-reliant person who had traveled around the world and kept safe during two adventurous years. That was the self who knew she would have to lay the groundwork for her own security. She set out to find her first job.

Submitting résumés, she proudly offered up her educational credentials and her hard-won if unconventional international experience. But this was the mid-seventies, and the new expectations of the women's movement had just begun to trickle down to personnel offices. Only one question greeted her: "Can you type?" So she put in two years as a secretary in Baltimore and then networked her way to a job at a glossy fashion magazine, capitalizing on her own intrinsic sense of chic and earning a princely nine thousand dollars a year. But several years of just squeaking by financially made her assess her future again. Her mother had married at eighteen. Sophia was nudging thirty with a decade of dating behind her but no serious marriage prospects in sight.

Determined to feather her own nest if no one else would do it for her, she left the gossipy, collegial, but underpaid magazine scene for the corporate whirl of a major cosmetics company. Again she crisscrossed the world, but this time selling her corporation's image of highly polished outward appearances, skin, eyes, lips, all groomed until they glowed. The company paid her handsomely enough so that she started to feel secure again for the first time since her sister's death unhinged her. But traveling and doing international promotion, she was never in one place long enough to build attachments, never mind settle down. Finally, at thirty-five, she had "another crisis," another moment of reckoning. If I'm away so much that I can only say I'll make a date three months down the road, she asked herself, how will I ever meet someone and marry?

It was another watershed between the untraditional life of the high-powered, high-paid, but unattached career woman she could see herself becoming and the more traditional, married-with-children matron like her mother, the role she had once rejected as "the epitome of middle class" but now found herself desperately yearning for. The pull of tradition turned out to be the stronger pull. Purpose redefined, she quit her corporate job. A year later, at thirty-six, she was married. A year after that her daughter was born and two years later, her son.

It took Sophia almost two decades longer than it took her mother to define her dream. But her dream nevertheless turned out to be almost a carbon copy of her mother's—marriage to a good provider, an apartment on upper Fifth Avenue, a summer place in Southampton, two darling children—"Ralph Lauren children," Sophia calls them—both in private schools. Once she narrowed down her options, she got the life that she wanted, and if there were compromises along the way, she accepts them as the necessary trade-off for security. Her husband is a real estate developer, "not a great corporate giant," she admits, but attractive and easygoing, four years her junior. Once she may have fantasized about life on the grand scale; now she's content with the quieter, more contained pleasures of domestic life. "I wanted security, and if it turned out a little boring, so be it," she admits without resentment. "I used to associate interest with disarray," she adds. "It was not until I reached thirty-five that I realized that disarray led to chaos."

Searching for Security

Although the path of the untraditional traditionalist may lead circuitously through rocky terrain, her ultimate goal, the dream that pushes her forward over countless obstacles, is a settled life, a stable life with husband, home, and kids. Like Sophia, she may vehemently deny it in her twenties, scorning marriage and motherhood as middle-class dull, but she will ultimately embrace the married-with-children life with the fervor of the born-again. In her twenties her trail seems headed in the opposite direction from her own traditional mother's. By her thirties she may end up embracing the very life she has gone on record earlier rejecting.

"I imagined more of a career than I've actually pursued," said another untraditional traditionalist schoolmate. "I always imagined a husband and children, but I always imagined doing it differently." Differently for her ended up meaning having a husband willing to take a year off from work when their first child was born (when strangers saw him in the park with the new baby, she remembered, they assumed he either was a widower or couldn't get work). Differently also meant a career that could be picked up and put down around her children's schedules and needs. She became a lactation consultant who counsels new mothers through the stresses and joys of nursing, a career that in itself neatly combines traditional and modern wisdom.

Sometimes the untraditional traditionalist will end up being even more of a traditionalist, even more of a throwback to fifties values, than her own mother, who may be either taking strides toward a more liberated womanhood herself or wishing that her daughter would play out her dreams of glory for her. At times this mother's ambitions end up exceeding her daughter's. "My mother may have been disappointed that I didn't have a big career, but it suits me," said the traditional daughter of one such traditional mom, both full-time wives and mothers, both fully supported by their mates. Her mother's ambitions for her were more grandiose than her own; she was satisfied with the life that had also satisfied her mother.

Still, despite her eventual craving for security, the untraditional traditionalist will often cartwheel experimentally through her twenties before settling down. But even if she toys with the counter-culture, as Sophia did—with drugs, nonmonogamy, an identity quest—it's usually for a limited period, which may become a treasured piece of personal history but won't be a resource drawn on every day. For an untraditional traditionalist like Sophia, the wild phase turns out to be a detour on the road to stability and the work phase an interlude before being married and supported. Working and contributing to the family income is not the ethos for adulthood that it will be for the jugglers who, by midlife, are integrating marriage, family, *and* career.

Every daughter of the fifties and sixties who came of age in the seventies was at some point inspired by the promise of an independent career, by the dream of self-support and self-fulfillment, yet also tempted to stay home and be provided for. For the untraditional traditionalist the conflict between old and new alternatives—the hallmark of this generation—feels especially charged. She both yearns for self-sufficiency and dreams of snuggling into the lap of someone stronger. She's pulled between the excitement of the untraditional (independence, a career, a professional identity, seeing where ambition will lead) and the comfort and safety that harks back to her original family's traditional style—"marriage as a career choice," as one ambivalent untraditional traditionalist put it. And opting for hearth and home, she might still feel a residual twinge of curiosity or envy for the road not taken.

Another schoolmate, two years older, approached the classic career/family tug by scaling back her goals but keeping her career and putting her family first. She called marrying her artist husband and having two kids "the best things that ever happened to me." She also worked part-time at nursing, a career that suited her needs, even while her parents—her mother is a professor who published her first book in her sixties—kept nudging her to get her M.A. and give up "hands-on nursing." But nursing's flexibility made it a good choice for her. "It's per diem work that I can also turn down," she explained, and added, "I'm not a push-push sort of person. I look at other people with envy who have high-powered careers, but I'm not that sort of person." Interestingly, her sister was one of those "push-push people" she sometimes envied. Her sister, younger by four years, is a Brearley alum who stepped right on the career track after graduation and became a professor; she's also single and doesn't have kids. "My sister has fulfilled my parents' academic stuff," said the nurse, this untraditional traditionalist, "and I fulfill their marital and grandchildren stuff." Then she sighed. "And I feel inadequate around academics and my sister feels inadequate around kids." Both the traditionalist and the career-tracker revel in what they've accomplished yet occasionally long for what they're missing.

The untraditional traditionalist often has a complicated relationship with ambition. She wants it / she doesn't want it. She wants it now / she wants it later. She wants to marry it / she wants it for herself. It often makes sense to her to see her life in stages. She may not be able to juggle everything that's meaningful all at once—

being a wife and a mother and pursuing experiments or ambitions outside the home—but she may be able to integrate all her dreams sequentially, as her life unfolds through the decades. So the untraditional, experimental, joys-of-singlehood phase in her twenties may give way to a more settled, traditional wife-and-mother phase in her thirties. But then in her forties and fifties, when children are grown, she may reorient her life again to allow a time for professional exploration or community service. By midlife, she may once again check out the pleasures beyond family and home that were so important in her youth.

One such stage-savvy untraditional traditionalist was a schoolmate whose early working life after college was dedicated to social change. "In my twenties I thought I'd always be out there fighting social evil," she admitted in her early forties. "But now I care most about my own kids." As a newly married career woman, she imagined that after her first baby was born, she'd take six months off and then go back to being a "hard-driving professional." But once she became a first-time mother at thirty-two, her priorities were totally reordered. She left her job and became a full-time mother just like her own mom, "staying at home and volunteering." For now, with school-age children who still need a lot of attention and ferrying around, she's committed to being at home. "Emotionally, I can't imagine any other choice," she said. But she also hasn't closed the door on retreading her career after her children are older, and she keeps her skills current by running a drug-and-alcohol-abuse program at her daughter's school. Right now she prefers to take the long view of her life's many possible incarnations. "My first job was assisting a professor who started at forty-five," she said. "So that's a model for doing things in stages." This untraditional traditionalist knows she may not be able to have it all, all at once. But she also rightly suspects if she's willing to sequence her goals, she may eventually accomplish them all. But for now, at forty, the traditional still takes precedence over the untraditional, and marriage and family come first.

The Unconventional Career-Tracker

In contrast to the untraditional traditionalist, the unconventional career-tracker puts career first and marriage and family later—if at all. But the untraditional traditionalist and the unconventional career-tracker, as illustrated by my classmates, as well as other daughters of this generation, are complementary rather than contradictory lifestyle choices. I've named them with antithetical terms because both are also defined by their shadow sides. Both are beguiled by the choices not taken, the styles not chosen. The untraditional traditionalist is also tempted to shun tradition and the unconventional career-tracker to flout convention.

The untraditional traditionalist reaches security by traveling trial-and-error back roads. Thus she takes advantage of untraditional means to secure a traditional outcome. And the unconventional career-tracker yearns for professional success but often either looks for it in unconventional fields or achieves it through unconventional routes. Thus she also uses unconventional means to achieve her more conventional ambitions.

The strikingly unconventional career or unusual career path seems to be the signature of my classmates' professional lives, another indication of how, professionally as well as emotionally, they see themselves muddling through adulthood without a blueprint, inventing and reinventing their lives as they go along. Where my sisters' classmates followed relatively straightforward career paths toward law, medicine, psychology, my classmates' work lives are full of oddball surprises, backslides, reinventions, interruptions. Many have created not so much careers as quilts of possibilities, weaving personal needs and quirks in and out of professional prospects in a generational style that owes much to its anything-goes late-sixties roots.

There is a lawyer who left the law for motherhood and art and another who entered law school after a stint working in a factory. There is a bank vice-president who took a five-year hiatus to play championship bridge and another classmate who has entered and exited a parade of occupations worthy of a Kerouac hero—from painting yachts to selling shoes to working at a bank to marketing real estate to retreading architectural salvage. These unconventional career histories reflect the dichotomies of the times—the conflict between ambition and suspicion of ambition, between drive and desire to go with the flow.

Meanwhile, both the untraditional traditionalist and the unconventional career-tracker are absorbed in the same delicate dance—trying to accommodate the traditional and the countercultural, the conventional and the New Age.

Tess—the Girl Who Turned Out to Be Good with Both Kinds of Green

Tess was one of the few in the class of '68 to have a dream. Tess had ambitions that were nurtured by preparation and plans and blossomed into success on a grand scale. By thirty-seven she was the general manager of horticulture for all of Walt Disney's Orlando theme parks, heading a staff of 350; ten years later, that staff had mushroomed to 600. She had a national, even international, reputation in her field, and was one of the key people Disney sent over to France to oversee the landscaping when EuroDisney opened in 1992. She had coauthored a book and made a name for herself for her fanciful work with Disney character topiaries, from a leafy-eared Mickey Mouse to a Lion King with a clipped-hedge mane. Among the classmates I profiled, Tess was the only one who had become notable enough to be written about in the press.

By the time Tess was ten, growing up on her family's estate north of the city, she knew she wanted to work in a public garden. That it might turn out to be Disney's colossal fantasy empire was at first as remote as Never-Never-Land. Still, her childhood dream flowered into tangible plans, each choice leading naturally to the next opportunity, like stepping-stones across a mossy garden. And being gifted with a talent as well as a passion helped shape a career choice early, long before many other classmates had even considered professional plans.

But Tess's early path of preparation was not strewn with roses. Creating a career dedicated to plants and flowers was an offbeat choice in the mid-seventies. The juncture between her childhood dream, her youthful preparation, and her future job prospects came at least a decade before gardening fervor swept through the country and became big business. So her dream was met with deep skepticism by her family, particularly by her pragmatic father, a Wall Street lawyer who sanctioned only three careers—law, medicine, and business. Indeed, her sisters, who dutifully obeyed their father's wishes, included a banker, a stockbroker, and two lawyers.

Certainly Tess's family nurtured her dreams in positive ways, both spoken and unspoken. Her parents extolled education, perseverance, achievement. They also provided enough financial security for daily comfort but not so much that she didn't dream of providing some extras on her own. But looking back, she wonders whether her family's doubts—despite her loyalty and love for them—might not have been a better catalyst to achievement than their unerring support would have been. "If I'd been encouraged to follow horticulture," she mused decades later, her success well proven, "would I have had to fight as hard? People tried to steer me in other directions. I stuck true to form."

Indeed, I noticed that this sticking true to form despite outside skepticism, this unshakable conviction in the face of doubt, either at home or at school, was a defining trait of the unconventional career-tracker and part of what fuels her drive. Among those I interviewed there was a grant-winning research doctor who did so badly in advanced placement chemistry that her science teacher told her never to take another science course, and an internationally respected opera singer who hated having to choose in ninth grade between music, art, or drama; now she revels in the combination of all three arts. "If I really want to do something, I go ahead and do it anyway," said the doctor undeterred by her nay-saying science teacher.

Who knows, as Tess observed, whether these successes would have pushed as hard or as creatively if all the doors had been opened for them.

Disneyworld

In 1976, when most other classmates are still making hit-or-miss attempts to find their paths, Tess is hired by Disney as its tree-farm supervisor. Disneyworld is then as newly fledged as Tess—its doors have opened only two years earlier—and their reputations will grow together. Over the years, as the parks' attractions increase and tens of thousands of visitors pour in every day, Tess's domain enlarges as well. She is put in charge of all Disney's horticultural training, then of the landscaping at the Magic Kingdom, then at Epcot Center, then at Disney-MGM Studio, and finally at all the resort properties and the surrounding roadways. When, most recently, Disney opens its Wild Safari Park, her domain stretches even farther to include the new park's native animal habitats. Her landscaping provides the visual backdrop to the park's attractions but has also become an attraction in itself, the country's largest public garden.

Now, in her late forties, Tess has allowed her large talents to bloom with her responsibilities, and her career blends the conventional with the unconventional, like compost mixed with topsoil. On the agenda at a typical biweekly staff meeting might be a proposal to evaluate the high-tech computer system that controls park-wide irrigation, a discussion of how best to move a tree with a four-foot-wide trunk, an overview of the two hundred grass varieties at the new animal kingdom—and an update on the development of the twirling-hippo topiaries with pink-flower tutus! Dressed in a long, billowy skirt, her blouse accented by a diamond-studded necklace of Mickey Mouse ears, Tess shifts confidently from topic to topic, equally comfortable whether the discussion concerns accounting procedures or the color range of chrysanthemums. So, much to her father's relief, she has become a savvy businesswoman after all, albeit in the business of pleasure. She's responsible for the bottom line in a major department of a hugely lucrative enterprise in one of the country's most profitable corporations. "Horticulture—beauty—has to play a role within the economic framework," she has said. "I believe very strongly in business." So sticking true to form, she has also managed to wed her imagination and vision to her company's productivity, and it's that combination that has made her so successful within Disney and such a role model beyond it. Many of the traits that bring her satisfaction also make her a terrific manager: her academic savvy and shrewd mind coupled with her emotional intelligence—her resilience, her people skills— as well as her ability to weather cycles, and her unflaggingly positive temperament, high-energy and ebullient. Facing fifty, Tess remains a human dynamo. Spending the evening with her after a day touring Disneyworld, I felt as energized by her contagious enthusiasm, her lust for life, as I remember feeling as a young girl.

Still, if Tess's career has blazed like a sunflower, reaching ever loftier heights, her personal life has remained in the shadows. In graduate school she fell in love with a fellow botanist; they married, and for the first few years their relationship was lively and animated by their shared passion for plants. But what began with such promise soon started to unravel and eventually came apart. Even today she doesn't entirely understand what derailed her marriage; she still wonders about her former husband and what's become of him, muses about what might have been.

To dull her grief after their divorce, Tess poured even more of her abundant energy into her work. That's the modus operandi she has continued over almost two decades—working around the clock, planting, supervising, going to meetings, traveling, speaking, writing. Surrounded by devoted friends, and still very close to her burgeoning extended family, she likes to keep romance in her life (she calls her current, three-year-old relationship "very warm and comfortable," but probably not destined to be lifelong). She has never remarried nor become a mother.

Being a loving aunt to a passel of nieces and nephews does nurture her maternal side, and she has also made it a goal for her department to think of ways to involve children in growing and appreciating plants. Recently a group of Disney volunteers landscaped a local schoolyard, providing the plants as well as the sweat equity. But for someone raised in a clan of ten, where creating a family dominated all other dreams, the contradictions between her dazzling professional success and her unsettled personal life occasionally bring her up short. Still, Tess is not a brooder. She's an optimistic, energetic, glass-half-full kind of person. When the doubts come, when regrets surface, she rolls up her sleeves and digs in her garden, feeling grounded making plants grow.

Maisie—the Banker Who Stands on Her Head

Waiting for Maisie in the reception area of the respected bank where she's worked for many years, I do a double take when she comes out. Who is this staid grown-up? I wonder. For at first glance, Maisie, at midlife, looks every bit the part of the conservative banker. She's dressed for success in a navy suit and navy pumps; a yellow silk blouse provides a splash of color, but a dark, tightly patterned vest tones it down. Her hair is still brown and still cut neatly around her face, the way she wore it all through school; a streak of dark lipstick is the only update to her style.

But as we speak, the years fall away, and I see both the spirited and the self-doubting girl I remember, both the confident one who identified with the French aristocrat and her salon for revolutionaries and the tentative one who worried about her brains and feared she had to work twice as hard as others to succeed. As we talk at a Chinese restaurant, Maisie starts to reveal some of the contradictions smoothed over by her staid suit and some of the struggles hidden by her polished surface. For like Tess, Maisie made choices that bridge the conventional and the unconventional. But unlike Tess, whose career blasted off in an unimpeded, upward trajectory, Maisie has followed a zigzag course, full of dead ends, self-scrutiny, inner reckonings, and the need for redefinition and reinvention.

The necessity for reinvention characterizes the lives of many of my classmates, indeed, of many of my generation. "When we speak to our children about our lives," Mary Catherine Bateson wrote in *Composing a Life,* "we tend to reshape our pasts to give them an illusory look of purpose." But few contemporary women have the luxury of defining one set of goals and living happily ever after. Whether because of economic, emotional, or professional realities, most confront interruptions or "discontinuities" (Bateson's word) at different stages of their lives and must shift directions or strategies. A career no longer satisfies or provides sufficient financial support; a job is downsized; a marriage shatters; babies don't arrive when wished for; illness intrudes; children leave the nest—all these events can be crises as well as opportunities that prompt redefinition and reinvention. So it was for Maisie—a crisis in work, love, and identity ultimately proved an opportunity to reinvent her own life.

After Maisie's marriage to her college sweetheart broke up, after her first career as a librarian failed to provide the satisfaction and security she craved, after her mother died suddenly without giving Maisie any chance to connect with her, Maisie sank into dark hopelessness. One bleak night in her late twenties, suicide seemed the only way out. But some glimmer of self-protection, some shard of self-respect, propelled her toward the nearest emergency room before it was too late. And after flailing about in the dark, she finally found a therapist who could help her rebuild her life, slowly, subtly, from the inside out, and ultimately reinvent herself both in love and work.

Maisie's first set of choices, the ones she'd made in her early twenties, had been classically traditional. She'd made an early marriage, at nineteen, to her college flame, who'd become a protective husband of the old, unliberated style. He'd sheltered her from the convulsions of the sixties turned seventies in return for her dependence and uncritical loyalty. And she'd also chosen an old-fashioned, safe and cozy, traditionally female career—librarian. Being a librarian was a career that could be picked up and put down at will if family needs demanded it, like a gripping but expendable novel, and, early on, she still imagined she'd have a family.

A Second Set of Choices

By the end of her twenties, Maisie has outgrown both marriage and career; neither fits her needs any more. Hesitantly at first, then with increasing conviction in the private chamber of therapy, she is starting to listen to her own heart, tune in to her own needs, unearth and rely on her own inner strengths. Now she is no longer just the nice girl trying to please her parents with her choices. Now, in her late twenties, as she faces the next decade and that life-altering thirtieth birthday, she begins making decisions for the first time as an independent woman beyond the sheltering arm of either father or husband.

The second set of choices, which emerge from the ashes of the first, reflect her increasing confidence and self-knowledge, as well as the cultural shifts and changing expectations for women that developed as the rebellious seventies turned into the staider, more prosperous eighties. Her second set of choices is far less traditional but instead links convention and unconventionality in the style that singles out the unconventional career-tracker.

The first phase of Maisie's metamorphosis is from librarian to banker. Over the years she has grown restless with the very lack of risk that had at first attracted her to working in libraries. Eventually she decides she doesn't want to limit herself lifelong to an all-women's profession, much as she loves the coziness and familiarity of being around books. As her confidence in her abilities grows, she feels more daring about entering the ranks of a profession once closed to women, using skills that have been traditionally more identified with men—crunching numbers, making financial decisions, negotiating deals.

Taking the first step away from the warm, familiar safety of words and books into the unknown terrain of numbers and money is scary. She signs up to take "baby math" at a nearby university as a prerequisite to the more advanced math she'll need for graduate business courses. Sitting in class the first day, staring at the equations, her mind fogs with anxiety. "I can't do it," says the old, self-doubting, little-girl self. But then the voice of her future, the voice of independence and self-preservation, takes charge. "Girl," the voice instructs, "you've quit your job. You'd better do this." So mining abilities she never knew she had, she plods through the introductory math course and goes on to ace calculus and take business school in stride.

Now a successful banker, Maisie continues to surprise herself with her skills—not just the math skills but lots of writing, which she dislikes but pushes through anyway, plus "boring, nitpicking work that Brearley taught you to be good at." But most important are her problem-solving ability and her people skills which, she comments with a rueful laugh, "did not come from Brearley at all" but from her experience outside the classroom, listening, observing, and sizing up a situation as the youngest member of a very adult-centered household. As a big-time moneylender, she's able to take a packet of financial statements and figure out what story they tell, which companies to finance, which companies to dismiss. And for these major responsibilities she earns a major-league salary, more money, she says, "than I ever thought I'd make."

Maisie is one of the few I interviewed in the class of '68 who could make this boast—or did make it, in fact. Most classmates, though daughters of wealth and privilege, remain decidedly ambivalent about earning money, trailing the legacy of sixties antimaterialism well into the eighties and nineties. Most have tended to choose careers (teaching, the arts) that are personally satisfying and socially useful but hardly offer major-league salaries. As a result, my classmates may feel more fulfilled than their parents did, they may even sleep better, but their family incomes are far less impressive. Maisie stands apart in earning a grand-scale salary and being proud of it.

Once Maisie reinvents herself professionally and learns she can create her own financial security, her emotional options also seem to open up. Now she is looking not for a strong authoritarian figure to provide both financial and emotional ballast, but rather for a partner to share life's pleasures and pains. She marries her second husband at thirty-two, after three years of living together. He's an accountant with a strong business background, so they share their financial interests, but in other ways he's an unconventional choice. He's from a very observant Jewish family; hers is classically Protestant. He's also six years younger. "I fell in love before I realized how young he was," she admits; neither of them give a hoot about the age gap. She describes her husband as "very easygoing and emotionally one of the healthiest people I've ever met." Their marriage is highly compatible, but without children to provide a constant common ground, they often find themselves leading separate lives. "We make sure we spend one night a week together," says Maisie.

It is her passions beyond both work and marriage that seem to anchor Maisie at midlife and add a deeper dimension to her life. And it is her ability to combine these passions with the demands of her professional life that makes her not a conventional but an unconventional career-tracker, someone who has responded to the eighties and nineties messages of achievement and success without forgetting the sixties siren song of self-realization and transcendence. Her passions are spiritual and psychological, and they help her keep a balance between her outer goals and her inner needs. She is devoted to Ayengar yoga, a passionate commitment she shares with her husband. Three or four times a week she practices this very

athletic form of yoga, and periodically goes on yoga retreats and occasionally to India to visit her guru and Ayengar yoga's spiritual
center. "Doing yoga," she says pointedly, "is like taking Valium."
The admission is all the more meaningful coming from someone
who once swallowed a bottle of pills to obliterate her pain. Now she
is saying she has learned how to take care of herself. Yoga has both
grounded her and helped her transcend some of the painful patches
of her past.

Her other commitment is to a kind of peer psychotherapy called
co-counseling. Maisie has been involved in co-counseling for almost
twenty years, since her own therapy turned her life around and gave
her the courage to try a second act after her first act closed so mis-
erably. Once every week she gets together with her co-counseling
partner, one of two women she sees regularly. They come together
not as therapist and patient or trainer and trainee but as equals,
speaking from the heart without censoring themselves or each
other. First one talks without interruption while the other listens
uncritically for thirty minutes; then the roles are reversed. "You
want people who can give as well as receive," Maisie explains,
adding that venting old pent-up feelings can clear out decades of
negative conditioning and allow the basic "strong, zestful, healthy
self" to emerge.

Co-counseling is also called reevaluation counseling because, as
Maisie explains and practices it, it provides a safe space and steady,
reflective, comradely partner to reevaluate one's life and mobilize to
make changes. After years of practicing co-counseling every week
and watching her own life come closer to her dreams, Maisie is now
trained as a co-counseling teacher, training other practitioners in listening skills and helping them learn to discharge their own anger
and lighten the weight of their past. Co-counseling nurtures both
the little girl Maisie once was, the mostly motherless little girl who
more than anything needed someone to confide in, and the independent, resourceful woman she has become, the woman whose
strengths bloom more in a relationship of equals than in one where

authority comes from the top down.

Both yoga and co-counseling have helped Maisie integrate the demands of a high-powered, potentially high-stress career with the subtler and more fluid requirements of a complex inner life. Co-counseling has helped her lighten the pressures of the past and build confidence in her problem-solving skills; yoga has centered her in the rush of everyday pressures and has deepened her spiritual search. Yet she remains unconventional both as a career-tracker and as a spiritual seeker, not completely in one world or the other.

Recently Maisie sent me a postcard responding to an invitation I'd sent her—she had to miss the party because she was away doing yoga in India. Her card is a cartoon that I also read as a kind of self-portrait. Several groups of traditionally dressed businessmen and -women are sitting around a fern bar, drinking and chatting each other up. Standing at the door is another group waiting to be seated; these people are cartooned like cubist figures, all odd angles and eyes on the side of their heads. "Picasso, party of four," announces the maître d'! The unconventional career-tracker, like Maisie, straddles both worlds, conventional as the neatly suited and necktied businessmen, uncommon and original as Picasso's party of four.

CHAPTER 9

The Seekers'
Emotional Education

*I*f longing for security shapes the untraditional traditionalists' choices in their twenties and thirties and dreaming of success and glory propels the plans of the career-trackers, then searching for awareness and emotional authenticity is what shapes the life paths of the classmates I call the seekers. Margaret Mead once called this quest the "drive to insight," and it can be just as powerful a motivator and just as all-consuming as the hunger for security or the lust for worldly glory.

Beyond Academics: A Second Education

This journey inward was a crucial piece of the sixties mandate as it played itself out in the lives of most members of the class of '68 and its generation. Once fifties secrecy collided with sixties openness and fifties pressures to be nice at all psychic costs combusted with sixties psychic freedoms, this journey of the heart, this search for spiritual satisfaction, became irresistible and inevitable. My classmates, like privileged children of the sixties everywhere, grew dubious about achievement, suspicious of the material comforts of wealth. They began to yearn for an emotional education to deepen and make relevant their academic one. And developmentally, the later twenties and thirties was the critical time when missing psychic pieces wanted back in, when emotional holes demanded to be filled. Eager to plumb and define their inner selves, most sought out therapy or support groups, meditated or went on retreats, experimented with drugs, or tried to reeducate themselves on their own with self-help literature or soul-searching with friends.

But in the lives of several classmates, this inner quest came to dominate all other pursuits. For them the search inward was not a short interlude but rather, for quite some time, the main event; many of them kept the flame of the Age of Aquarius burning right through the seventies and the eighties "Me-Decadism" and beyond, until eventually, in Peter Gomes's memorable phrase, their exhaustive pilgrimage took them "from me to meaning." At times their absorption in their journey eclipsed their concern with where they were heading, the journey meaning more than the arrival. And often the journey which began as a search for a source of wisdom outside the self ended by learning to listen to the wisdom within.

The Journey Inward

The seekers' journey inward was often begun out of necessity rather than choice, prompted not by pleasure but by pain. It could be precipitated by psychic upheaval, a tremblor that set off a quest both for self-knowledge and to repair a shaky, tattered sense of self-esteem. For as the negotiations of separation that mark the twenties give way to the thirties' increased demands for decisions about love and work, the seekers find themselves balking. Despite their outward bravado—a headstrong early marriage, cutting all ties with home—the seekers often have the most fragile sense of their own self-worth, the most limited belief in their own capabilities. They deeply question whether they're up to the tasks ahead.

"Where was I when I needed me?" Pam asked plaintively when the choices of her early twenties started to sour, and she feared being thrown back on shaky inner resources. Surely this is the clarion call of all the seekers. This desire to make sure that somebody is home inside sets off first a crisis of authenticity, and then a journey inward to unearth, then nurture, then finally come to rely on a strengthened inner self.

For Pamela and Emma, seekers both, the quests that would absorb them for the crucially self-defining decades of the twenties and thirties were spiritual and emotional; the two strands were inseparable and intertwined. Both were daughters of demanding families whose expectations felt unreachable. Emma's father was a minister who believed his children had "gifts from God." Pamela's mother came from a wealthy and powerful clan; her father was hard-driving and ambitious. As troubled adolescents, both Pamela and Emma ached to define themselves as separate, valuable, and independent. But their outward feistiness masked two vulnerable, lost girls who still ached for parental approval and family acceptance.

So their rebellions from their families skidded between alternating desires for distance and closeness. Their twenties were marked by restless, impulsive perpetual motion as they struggled to separate from home, yet clung awhile longer; as they fell in love again and again but never quite for keeps; as they toyed with and then tossed aside possibilities for vocations, life paths. Accommodating to dramatically different economic realities would prove the defining difference between them. Emma's family considered itself rich in intellectual promise but was by no means affluent. Emma waitressed her way through college in California. Then, from graduation on, the need to support herself always drove her life moves.

Pam, by contrast, was sustained by her family's wealth. Although she would occasionally demur that she wasn't all *that* rich, she never lacked for creature comforts. She could indulge herself at whim. A dazzling ring, a ski trip to Switzerland, her own home in pricey and exclusive Aspen—Pam's inheritance secured them all. Still, never having to work came with its own price. For the impetus to support herself led Emma to a profession that became a vehicle for her intelligence, an outlet for her creativity, a source of self-esteem, and an emotional anchor. Never needing to work, Pam never found the psyche-defining solace nor sense of self-reliance that work can provide. She wandered through her twenties and thirties, experimenting with crafts and causes and looking for her anchor in relationships.

Beneath their striving for separation, beneath their restlessness in love and work, both of them were aware of an intense spiritual hunger. As a child each experienced a religious life that was out of kilter. Pam's interfaith family downplayed traditions and ignored its Jewish heritage entirely. Pam celebrated Hanukkah only once as a child, and that was lighting a menorah at a friend's house. Years later, hearing Hebrew would make her weep, that ancestral language never recited at home. Emma's family went overboard in the opposite direction. As pillars of the church, her parents observed religious rituals on a grand scale, but in a way that to Emma rang false. So for both girls, the inner emotional quest also became a search for an authentic spirituality and a hunger for unconditional love that would make up for what was lost in childhood and would become meaningful and nourishing in adulthood.

Breaking Away

Explosive periods of rebellion against their families' values and overbearing expectations jump-started both girls' journeys. And for both, breaking away meant putting geographical as well as emotional distance between themselves and their childhood lives. Pamela dropped out of Vassar after a year and a semester and drove hellbent for Aspen, Colorado. Aspen had been the "Mecca of [her] heart and soul" since she was eight and took family ski trips there during spring vacation. But it was not just the skiing, the powdery snow, and the crystal cold that made her spirit soar. It was also the thrill-seeking and the seemingly limitless possibilities for romance

and adventure. The whole pace of life in Aspen gave her the freedom, the rush she craved.

While Pam couldn't wait to bust loose, Emma dallied in her parents' orbit for an extra four years. She lingered in and around their
suburban Maryland house, alternately leaving home to set up her
own apartment and coming back to the fold. But finally, after one
romance too many failed and opportunities fizzled—and a scary
breakdown landed her in the hospital and provided a sobering
wake-up call—she hitched a ride out West and mobilized herself to
start over in Santa Rosa, California. Waiting tables, she put herself
through two years of community college and then two more years
of university. Funding herself, she realized years later, "gave me an
incredible drive to do well." Now the good grades she studied for
were for herself, not just a gift to be brought home to Dad and
judged never quite good enough. Her grades and her unfolding intellectual passions could open up prospects for her future. She discovered new interests in education and English and dreamed for a
while of becoming a preschool teacher.

While entering college with an edge of maturity seemed to help
focus Emma's search, dropping out of college sent Pam into a panic
of experimentation and self-doubt. At twenty, she confronted for
the first time just how alone and directionless she was. She'd cut her
ties to her family and the conventional expectations of her past and
her class. Many of her age-mates—certainly her old friends from
Brearley and boarding school—were still wrapped up in their college lives. Anxiety held her in its unrelenting clutches, and she felt
herself, as she later put it, "going crazy" for the first time. That time
may have been the most unnerving. But sadly, it would not be the
last.

To stave off her panic, Pamela embarked on a frenzy of nontradi-
tional pursuits, swirling from activity to activity. With all her material riches, Pam was hungry for self-awareness. She longed for that
epiphany that would make sense of her purpose in life. Whatever the

counterculture offered, she was game to try. Her plans looked like the patchwork of flyers on a Telegraph Avenue bulletin board. She dropped acid. She took off to California for a spell and met a Tibetan lama in Berkeley and got involved in Buddhism.

After a while the pace caught up with her, and her momentum crashed suddenly, if briefly, to a halt. She fell off her bicycle and had to have stitches in her chin. This mishap sidelined her and forced her to slow down. Like Emma, who emerged from a hospitalization with renewed energy and more clarity of purpose, Pam felt an internal shift as her body began to heal: shortly after the accident, she wrote me at the time, "that scared and schizy feeling I had been carrying around with me for months went away."

Back on her feet, Pam picked up where she'd left off, sampling the countercultural smorgasbord of the sixties, now become the seventies. But now she was going to pursue her own passions rather than doggedly following the crowd. So she stopped dropping acid—her world seemed mind-blowing enough without it—and started practicing Sufism, a mystical form of Islam. Now she'd found a spiritual context for her whirling.

Throughout the wanderings of her twenties, there remained two constants—"skiing and romance." Both could be counted on to give her that rush of adrenaline she craved, the high that made her feel most alive, most herself. Blasting down a mountain, gulping the mountain air, luxuriating in her own speed—skiing connected her to nature, to something grander than herself; it became a spiritual experience as well as a physical one. When skiing, she would later say, "I had God in my body. It was my prayer." One of her older sisters, as spiritually famished as Pam was, devoted herself to an Indian guru. But Pam felt she didn't need a guru. "I found the sense of the spirit in me" is the way she described her inner quest. A friend called skiing Pam's "making her arcs of devotion."

Falling in love time and time again, turning male heads with her mane of sun-streaked hair and her agile, taut body—this was the other time she felt most powerful, most alive. And the slopes were a nonstop hunting ground. When skiing and romance combined, the energy was overpowering.

Pam—the Love Quest

Pam falls for Trevor the winter they are both on the ski patrol. He is a Canadian with "long dancing legs, twinkling red-gold hair, and magic, flashing, green-blue-gray eyes." He is mischievous, with an irreverent spirit that matches hers. "He sees things clearly," she writes me in the glow of early infatuation, "and his purpose in life is to live it." When winter's snows melt into summer's wildflowers, they are married on a remote little northern island that belongs to Trevor's family; his mother and grandmother prepare a fabulous homemade feast. It is a festive, romantic time, although neither of them, Pam will later admit, know what they're doing getting married. Pamela's mother most definitely does not approve. Her dismissal casts the first shadow on their "beautiful, protected, little lovers-on-skis world."

All too soon the romance, which has seemed so blissful, so meant-to-be in its early stages, turns cold as Pam realizes she has made the relationship permanent. Now the intuition that propels her forward, the internal radar that beeped her when it was time to drop out of Vassar, time to move to Colorado, time to leave, then to return, flashes her a neon warning sign: she has made the wrong choice marrying Trevor. His diamond-in-the-rough appeal, which had so attracted her on the slopes, quickly loses its allure in other settings. Up close, he is less diamond, more ruffian. His "fuck you's" lose their rough charm and begin to hurt. "It could have been worse," she'll later say, providing a spin control of sorts. "He wasn't abusive." But after four days of marriage, honeymooning miles removed from anyone or anything familiar, Pam cries to herself in private, "What have I done?" And that still, small voice she had disregarded earlier answers her back, "Just stay with him long enough to save face." "I didn't want to be considered a flake," she'd later admit, reflecting on her cool calculations, "so I decided to stay with him for two years." Meanwhile, she'd do what she could to make the best of it, and making the best of it meant taking him along on her quest.

Marriage does not dim Pam's wanderlust nor make her life's purpose any clearer. But now she has a fellow traveler in tow. The year after they marry, the pace of their lust for experience quickens. With money no object, they become hippie jet-setters, trust-fund nomads. Together they parachute out of a plane, ski in Switzerland for a couple of months, return to Aspen, journey through Glacier National Park and into Canada, then head south to San Francisco. There Pam, an instinctive craftsperson still looking to find her craft, learns to weave, spin, and dye, and together they take Werner Erhard's EST. When winter blows around again, the slopes lure them back to Aspen, where, in a brief flurry of stability, they buy a house. By the summer, Trevor is practicing karate four hours a day, and Pam is taking a mushroom-hunting class and providing tantalizing feasts from the field. To outsiders they look like two contented flower children. Only Pam knows the discontent building within.

Even knowing their marriage is not for keeps, Pam can't dismiss it as a lost cause. It turns out to be yet another experiment whose purpose will not be revealed until much later on. Pam's twenties, it turns out, are devoted to getting things wrong again and again in order to find a better balance later on. This wrong-turn syndrome is something of a seeker specialty: an outrageous romance, an ill-fitting career, psychic excavations that seem excessive in retrospect. Many classmates, but seekers especially, spend their twenties and thirties trying to make awkward choices fit. Only with hindsight could they see that these early wrong turns helped them find a more comfortable path by their forties.

Pam's relationship with Trevor, one of a long line of Mr. Wrongs, will one day help her recognize a Mr. Right when she finally bumps up against him, when she finally feels herself worthy of being treated well. Trevor's self-absorption, she will later see, mirrors the self-involvement of her father, who led one life as a power-brokering New York City newspaper editor and, after that life cracked, moved to Aspen and reinvented himself as a New Age seeker. Unable to get her father's full attention as a child, Pam tries repeatedly to get Trevor's, and dreams their marriage will be a chance to repair the earlier oversights. But her strategy turns out to be hopelessly misguided, as rewriting these leftover scripts from childhood inevitably is. Still, her marriage gives her a chance to work through some unfinished business with her father and, perhaps by doing so, helps her unhook from the past and nudges her that much closer to a relationship where her needs can be met and her value cherished.

Leaving her marriage, Pam is thrown back on her own resources, and the first glimmer of a stronger, more resilient, more compassionate self starts to peek through the tough-girl image she spent her adolescence cobbling together. When, at twenty-three, she pours out her heart in a four-page letter to me describing her quest until then, she reveals the first glimpses of an inner self tentatively struggling to establish itself.

Crisis of Authenticity

Somewhere in their thirties almost every daughter of '68 experienced an inner reckoning, a time when the combustion of external and internal events forced a reexamination and redefinition of self. Whatever strategies they'd used in their twenties to find and sustain love, to define and pursue work, to pin down where and how they lived, these strategies were now up for grabs. Parts of their selves that had been rejected or put on hold now demanded to be heard. Those who spent their twenties getting a foothold in the outside world now wondered what was going on inside. Those who were dancing rakishly from high to high now suddenly had an inexplicable urge to settle down. Whatever path they'd carved out for themselves now seemed to preclude other, more soul-sustaining options. Whatever vision they'd pursued, glittering gloriously through their twenties, now, by their thirties, seemed to lose its allure. Sometimes relationships no longer seemed to sustain them either, as they turned inward, preoccupied with their own birth pangs.

In their twenties, many of this group suffered a crisis of separation, as they left the confines of school and family for the wider stage of college and the world beyond. Now in their thirties, most suffered another psychic upending of self-definition and direction which I call the crisis of authenticity. Now they cycled back to the questions they'd posed in their twenties and revisited them with new awareness, new seriousness. Who am I beyond the expectations of parents and school, family and friends? they'd asked at twenty. Now, at thirty, they probed even deeper. This time they sought out what nurtured them, what gave them hope and confidence, what helped them respond to self-doubts. Less innocent now, but also less cocky, the women of '68 were readier to admit they needed a hand on the journey toward self-knowledge and self-reliance.

For Pamela this crisis of authenticity, occurring in her late thirties, became a pivotal juncture on her journey inward, a time of turbulence but ultimately transformation. Her emotional odyssey took the form of an intense "internal housekeeping," in which she tossed out outmoded parts of herself and salvaged the parts that had been neglected for too long. "I reclaimed my inner person in my thirties," Pam explained, looking back at midlife. "If you're an aware person, that's the time when the rejected parts want back in. It's about balance." For Pam, these rejected parts were all the soft, needy, vulnerable sides of herself that for years she had been afraid to expose. For the first time, she felt desperate enough to explore these buried parts with a therapist.

Back in her early twenties when she'd moved to Aspen and started to unravel in all that structureless, open space, she wouldn't have considered therapy. Back then she'd felt therapy was for emotional weaklings who couldn't handle their own problems. This was the dominant attitude of her parents' generation, and for better or worse—mostly worse—Pam bought into it. So instead of searching out help, she just limped along on her own, spinning out of control and patching herself back together the only way she knew how—by experimenting with drugs, by skiing, by losing herself in love. Only later did she realize how much rage and self-hatred she was carrying when she fled the East Coast for Aspen—and how much psychic effort she expended looking "independent and rebellious" to the outside world while tuning out the scared voice inside.

In her late thirties, she was still single and rudderless when more and more of her peers were pairing up, settling down, and finding a life course. Now she was in enough pain to let go of her pose and admit she needed help. Willingly she welcomed the excavations that she'd now come to believe could help her feel whole. Leaning on her therapist, she remembered the shy girl she'd been in second grade, the year she had "a personality change." That had also been a year of upheaval in self-image, a year when she'd been sick for two months with pneumonia and chicken pox, when she'd gotten glasses and had her first filling. It was the year she realized she wasn't perfect, wasn't invulnerable, was, in fact, human. But even at such a tender age she sensed she was expected to tough out her troubles. So she switched from being a "sweet, shy kid" to being a tough girl.

She knew that in her circle of family, friends, and later lovers, she could never expose that tender little girl. "Even to talk about that stuff," she later realized, "you would have been the Lone Ranger. That's why I became tough instead of vulnerable." And over the years she'd kept up her front; she'd propped it up with athleticism, medicated her pain with skiing and later with romance, as corrosive as any addictions.

But finally her addictions caught up with her. She had OD'd on them for so long her body could no longer take it. "Skiing and romance stopped working," she confessed. "I didn't want to be on the ski patrol and be one of the guys," she realized. "And my big romances unraveled. So what then? Self-esteem was a huge problem, really liking myself. It became a big issue once the old game fell apart."

Internal Housecleaning

What finally stops the old game cold is the one thing she has never planned for nor expected: pregnancy. But it is a dangerous tubal pregnancy, and it lands her in the hospital for five days, sick, feverish, and scared. "It was the result of a great romance," she would later explain, that turned out to be a "big fantasy." While Pam lies in the hospital, fighting for her life, her fast-track, high-stakes lover is obliviously abroad, brokering a deal. Never has she felt so desperately alone. "My body really failed me," she would later admit. For a long time after she gets out of the hospital, she can't "do a damn thing, even vacuum." For someone who has prided herself since girlhood on her stamina, this is her lowest ebb. Years later she will call this episode a mental as well as a physical breakdown, a time when her tough-girl carapace cracked so badly she was forced by psychic necessity to look inward. But it is also the beginning of a transformative turning point in her life. "What doesn't kill us makes us wise," she will one day have the distance to say about this traumatic time.

Although her affair with the wheeler-dealer breaks up not long after her hospitalization, as she recovers, she rebounds into yet another all-consuming romance. Finding new lovers has never been a stumbling block for Pam; this one comes from an old-money world similar to the one she has grown up in. He is wealthy and sweet and a recovering alcoholic with "just occasional slips." With him, she feels she has the "safety to become unglued." Still raw from the trauma of the unexpected pregnancy, she slips even further into depression, railing at herself for the slightest blunder, the smallest imperfection, even if she "misses a tennis shot."

When her beau's "occasional slips" become worrisome, he checks himself into an upscale alcoholic treatment center, and Pam, almost on a lark, tags along with him. She sits in on the group therapy sessions and does psychodrama for the first time. After a week, her boyfriend is "sent home with flying colors." But the skilled staff detects how shaky Pam is and tells her to stay on. She ends up staying for six weeks. Those six weeks help her begin to undo the self-hatred that has been weighing her down since childhood.

"I was living in a beautiful house with garbage in the basement"— that's the metaphor she uses to describe herself, looking back from the next decade. "Sooner or later the stink will get to you." She will spend the rest of her thirties cleaning out the layers of garbage. Gradually she will learn how to set free the scared child crouching in the basement, and by doing so she'll uncork new energy and a wellspring of self-esteem. Mostly she'll learn a brand-new self-acceptance, of both her scared self and her feisty one, her vulnerable self and her reliable one. "If my self-esteem gets bad," she realizes years after that intense emotional housekeeping, "I now know what to look for. I have more kindness about how it got there." Finally, in her late thirties, she would learn how to treat herself more compassionately.

Facing forty, she was no more committed, either in love or in work, than she'd been at thirty. She still had little she could report to the *Brearley Bulletin* alumnae news, when other classmates were weighing in with marriages and children and accomplishments in the outside world. But for emotional growth—the kind that's experienced inside even if it doesn't get written up by the class secretary—the second half of her thirties was a time of progress and promise. She was facing forty grounded and centered, proud of the person she'd hacked through the psychic underbrush to become. And for a seeker like Pam, that life-affirming insight was accomplishment enough.

Emma—Colorful in the Convent

For Emma, too, the thirties turned out to be a time of life-transforming upheaval, both emotional and spiritual, a time of suffering, introspection, and change. She, too, experienced a crisis of authenticity, a time when the big questions of her twenties stared her hard in the face once again and demanded to be confronted, if not resolved—questions of authority, autonomy, and affiliation, of spirituality, service, and self-esteem. As a rebellious minister's daughter whose parents raised her to believe that she and her brothers had godly gifts, Emma had always had a complicated relationship with spiritual life. She spent most of her teens and twenties rejecting her father's church-centered, tradition-bound form of Presbyterianism. Though her legacy was different from Pam's—Pam's interfaith parents were both nonobservers—Emma also felt a spiritual void which she hungered to fill. At thirty-three—an age often freighted with meaning, for it was Jesus' age at his crucifixion, a piece of symbolism not lost on Emma—she took a radical step to fill her void.

"I've always been one to take things to extremes," Emma explained years later by way of introducing this leg of her journey inward. Certainly pushing the envelope is a hallmark of seekers' behavior; Emma danced on the edge from her teens through her twenties, toying with drugs and sex, bouncing in and out of school, occupations, liaisons. But now, in her early thirties, the experimenting, the partying, the rushing from one high to the next, was beginning to lose its luster. Her work life was uncertain; her love life was muddled; her family relationships were strained. Drastic times called for drastic measures.

In order to reinvent herself and prove her pure intentions, Emma makes a complete U-turn. She joins an order of Franciscan nuns.

What attracts her to religious life? Perhaps it is the orderly structure after so much chaos, the security after too much self-doubt. Maybe it is the freedom from decision-making after too many mind-stressing choices, the absence of men and sex after disappointment with both. Perhaps she wants to link herself to her father's implicit desires, for he was always "real ambivalent" about marriage and children and felt that a solitary, celibate life devoted to the service of God "had its pluses." Or perhaps she fantasizes for herself the radical creativity of a Sister Corita, whose bold designs colored the seventies from greeting cards to gas tanks. But the reality that greets her in the convent is grim and colorless.

"Talk about the ultimate authority situation with people telling you what to do!" More than a decade later she could laugh about the rigidly authoritarian structure that closes in on her when she enters the fold. Although her order is Episcopal, the group models itself on the old Catholic tradition of religious sisterhood. Emma lives in a dormitory with anywhere from six to twelve women. They wear habits and headdresses both inside and outside the convent. They rise for morning prayers at six, meditate in the chapel, then have mass and finally breakfast. After breakfast they are dispatched into the community to jobs to earn money for the sisterhood. Emma works in a church counseling center. "The idea was to do good," she would later put it, "but with no particular identity," for the convent was not attached to a school or a hospital. "There was nothing especially holy about the work except that it was service." It is that selfless gift of service that attracts her—after all, it was a keystone of her father's philosophy. But for all her good intentions, these acts of service are not enough to fill her spiritual void.

For Emma, rebel extraordinaire and most decidedly "not a morning person," the regime is trying. She may have craved structure after years of living fast and footloose. But she also craves a subtle, satisfying spiritual life, and the rigid structure of the convent turns out to be more spirit-stifling than -enhancing. "I made a colorful nun, but not a good one," she later admitted ruefully. "I knew I should be compliant, good, and unquestioning, the way the others were. But instead I was a royal pain in the ass!" Just as she'd challenged bombast on the outside, she confronts it inside the convent, too. She defies custom and convention, sneaking cigarettes on the sly, a major taboo. She questions why her order needs to wear traditional headdresses. Aren't they symbols of an outdated notion of women that is starting to crumble everywhere else? Why should the convent remain a throwback?

"Oh my God, they were the most dysfunctional group!" Emma would eventually comment from the safer vantage point of the next decade. But back then she feels herself being sucked into an all too familiar vortex of secrecy and denial. Once a week, the nuns are supposed to be doing a kind of family therapy together. But there is a major hitch, she finds: "The other sisters don't want to reveal any secrets to newcomers." Each time they gather, the group leader asks anxiously, "Is there anything anyone feels compelled to tell us that we have to talk about?" She frames the question as if daring anyone to answer.

Like the unstated but pervasive policy of silence that maintained Emma's family's pious veneer (and forbade any discussion of that "elephant in the living room"), and the aura of secrecy at Brearley that made talking about tough topics taboo (and forbade any mention of Emma's ninth-grade suicide attempt), the hush of nervous, penitential silence at the convent obscures the nitty-gritty, gutsy real in favor of an ideal that feels to Emma as cold and irrelevant as the marble statues in the convent's sanctuary.

But following this don't-tell attitude to its extreme—the "family therapy" sessions inside the convent are almost a parody of themselves—finally forces Emma to realize that she can't live a lie. The suffocating authoritarianism, the relentless perfectionism, the stress of living up to what a good nun (or good daughter or good student) should be, all collide once again with her need to speak her own truth. The desire to live from her own heart and not cram herself into a set of edicts and expectations as constraining as her habit—this authenticity is what impassions her and turns out to be antithetical to convent life. "In trying to figure out who I was, I questioned being at the convent," Emma would recount years later.

When, at last, she confesses her doubts to her mother superior, the wise lady responds instantly. "You're not meant to be here," she counsels. Emma is out in a week.

Burrowing Inward

"In trying to be true to God, I ended up stripping away so much of my old self that I had a horrible identity crisis," Emma came to realize. "I had taken the idea of community and service too far. People were not going to die because I wasn't sacrificing." Like Pamela, who had to confront her deepest self in her late thirties, so too, after the convent's strict regimentation failed to shore her up, Emma was catapulted into a life-saving journey inward. Once the rule-bound life of the cloth began to crack and fragment, Emma, like Pam, needed to rebuild from the inside out. And as it did for Pam, this gut-wrenching, soul-searching crisis of authenticity took the form of an intense internal housekeeping.

Emma burrowed inward under the skilled guidance of a therapist she had met at the counseling center where the convent had assigned her to work. Ironically, her colleague at this convent-appointed job became her co-conspirator in getting out. Emma was no stranger to therapy. Unlike Pam, who had bravely soloed through adolescent uncertainties and the highs and lows of her twenties, too tough and independent to ask for help, Emma had maneuvered through a parade of therapists, from the time of her precocious suicide attempt, stonewalling their help even against her best interests. But the earlier therapy she'd submitted to because her parents required it. Like dieting to please a partner, it was never something she undertook for herself, so it didn't work. But now, at thirty-three, after her last-ditch effort to let God and the convent save her, she was finally ready to plumb her own resources. This time she took the journey inward for herself.

"I got down to absolutely naked soul and it was terrifying," she remembered, long after the terror had faded and the changes had been absorbed. The most liberating part was that after she reached her most vulnerable place, she "got to put back the pieces that felt authentic. I jettisoned the parts that weren't me and built what was." Emma remained in therapy for most of her thirties, and those years were a transformative time, a time she calls a "coming of age." If that is a phrase more typically linked with the transition from adolescence to the twenties, for Emma the experience was all the more powerful for being delayed. In therapy she began to learn an emotional vocabulary that had eluded her before, a language to name those things that had once held power over her for being unnameable and unspeakable.

Out went the false piety, the playing by other people's rules, the turning herself inside out to meet family expectations of perfection and godliness that she now began to see were by definition unattainable. In blew the soul-cleansing breeze of respecting her own needs, following her own star, speaking her own truth, accepting her imperfections along with her successes. In therapy she discovered the "A-minus syndrome," the never-quite-good-enough standard that her parents had been holding her to for years. Now she finally understood that not being perfect was not the same thing as being a failure. She began to enjoy what she could achieve and revel in being good enough.

Because her relationship with her family colored all her other choices, she felt she needed to confront their influence first. "I had to accept the things I couldn't change in my family," she came to realize. "I also had to accept that I could change me but not them." But as she changed, her family shifted to meet her changes. Simply being open about her own process prompted the first dramatic shift in her parents' attitude toward her. "My parents had always been fix-it people," she realized. But "fix-it" implied that something was broken and that Emma couldn't be trusted to fix it herself. But now when her father asked—sympathetically? intrusively?—"What can we do for you?" Emma had the presence to answer, "You're doing it by being supportive and listening." Her answer conveyed the message that she could handle her life changes herself, much as she valued her parents' support. That conversation was a turning point which began to alter the dynamics between them.

And gradually, subtly, as Emma became more centered, more confident, more focused on her own goals, her parents' response to her also continued to shift. "Finally, they didn't treat me as if I was broken anymore," she realized. "I started to feel extremely strong and my parents started to respect that." She was grateful that they all had some good years together before her father died, when Emma was in her early forties.

Therapy also helped Emma uncover a clearer sense of direction, and her newly sharpened focus on her talents and unfolding vocation as an editor empowered her. Her twenties and early thirties had been a volatile time of trial and error, both in love and in work. She'd had a succession of ill-fated romances and a scattering of disconnected jobs, first in education, then in writing. But now, nudging forty, she started to realize that her time and energy weren't limitless. She felt the need to narrow her choices to pursue the ones that really mattered. "The end of my thirties was a happy time. I had my own freelance business and was writing and editing professionally. I was making decent money for the first time. I had stepped away from having men in my life and the focus was on me. It was a self-empowering time."

For the first time she was fulfilling the intellectual promise of her youth, not sabotaging it. She was using her sharp mind to labor happily and productively in a field of words. Despite the two decades of challenging her family's values, she was edging closer to them than her confrontational fourteen-year-old self could ever have imagined. Like many of the freer spirits among us—Pamela, Sophia—approaching midlife, Emma felt herself mellowing. "One of the driving forces for me was the need to turn around my image as the wild child into one of the responsible, sane child," she admitted sheepishly, yet proudly, years down the road. "I discovered I was a fairly responsible person," she added. "Certain values were permanent—caring about other people, showing up on time."

By forty she was hired as a textbook editor at a venerable publishing house. Guiding writers, editing copy, supervising a small staff to get the job done, she relished her own competence, her own boosted sense of responsibility. But she also couldn't ignore the footprints of her father's workaholism on her own professional style, as she climbed the managerial ladder. Even during the emotional weekend when she returned home for her father's funeral, she caught herself fighting her brothers to get to the phone to check in with the office. She needed to prove herself indispensable even in her time of grief. Her father's legacy, which she'd resisted for so long, of intense work coupled at times with emotional denial had now caught up with her and was a contributor to her success as well as its one of its costs.

Trade-offs

Successful and fulfilling as her work life became by the close of her thirties, not so her love life. Emma had spent her teens and twenties hungry for love, puppy-dog eager, even at times desperate, to get the affection from boyfriends she really craved from her emotionally distant dad. "I was attracted to men who couldn't say, 'I love you,' and then I struggled to get them to say it," she eventually realized. Although she came to recognize the pattern—another gift of a long therapy—she couldn't seem to muster the psychic energy to change it, particularly against the background of her emerging feminism and the changing expectations that came with it. "I had a hard time finding someone who could be an equal," she explained. "Men would be attracted to me because I'm strong, but then they'd try to stamp out my strength. So the issue of power has always been major. I lose my sanity when I fall in love and then I feel powerless."

By her thirties Emma felt sick of love. She had burned out on the quest for the perfect life mate (part shining knight, part apostle, part liberated man). She had ruled out convent life as too extreme—celibacy there came with too many strings attached. But something about that purity, that intensity of focus, still attracted her. "If I wanted to define myself, I needed to be alone," she decided. It was as if to be authentic, to be true to her passions and dreams, she needed to hold herself apart. She feared she could not keep her integrity and share her life at the same time. "Then I threw myself into my work and that became a requited relationship. It paid me, too!" From the vantage point of midlife, she looked backward at her life's pattern. "It may be trite to say, but I traded love for work."

Love and work, work and love—not too many graduates of '68 turned the corner from their thirties to their forties with both in balance. They may have left home in their twenties, eyes wide with dreams of passionate love, fulfilling work—and someday a carriage full of babies. But more likely they approached midlife sobered and confounded, like Emma, by the trade-offs they'd made. They'd grown in self-awareness on their journeys inward, but that awareness also made them more sensitive to the sacrifices life had required. At eighteen they'd graduated from Brearley with limitless expectations; by forty, they realized they might not have it all.

For the seekers, especially, their purity of vision, their single-minded quest for insight and epiphany, often stood in the way of the kinds of messy compromises that juggling love, work, and family would have required. Both Emma and Pam entered their forties newly stable with self-knowledge, more comfortable with themselves than they'd ever been. But on the scales of love and work, each faced an imbalance, a benefit as well as a deficit. Emma, at forty, was settled and secure at work. Her job as a textbook editor enabled her to use her talents, be of service, and become comfortably self-supporting. She hoped to be there until she retired. Once a boy-crazy party girl, now she remained unattached. She lived on her own, comforted by her cat and a cozy circle of friends but still perplexed about why she had never married.

At forty-one, after decades of dating, one short-lived marriage, and a soul-searing journey inward, Pam met the man she's still in love with and committed to today. Matthew, Pam realized immediately, was "not in the mold." He was a gentle, compassionate television director whose first wife had left him to raise their two children on his own. He was a nurturer, and Pam felt justifiably proud of their relationship, her life's longest and most harmonious. Being able to sustain this bond was "living proof" that her therapy had helped her, she admitted and laughed at her own hard-won wisdom. But settled as she felt in this relationship, this private part of her life, she felt hesitant about her place in the wider world. Still not driven by a need to earn money, she ruled out a career that would "entrench [her] in a corporation." But what of a shaping passion, a project worthy of her intelligence and talents, a commitment beyond the personal? This she had yet to find.

Neither Emma nor Pam have had children, so they do not have the source of continuity nor the context of meaning beyond oneself that children might provide. Facing midlife and beyond, they may also need to revisit the choices they have made and confront the possibility that paths they have not chosen will yet ask to be explored.

Did all that journeying inward absorb too much energy and time for them to consider children? For some classmates the inner reckoning, the leaps of growth, came on the journey to motherhood itself, as they learned to nurture their own development along with guiding their children's.

Reluctant Mothers

W hen, at forty, my classmate Suzanne got married for the first time, her brother's wedding toast, affectionate but ribbing, voiced the family's unspoken worries and its palpable relief that their worries were unwarranted. "At her age, Suzanne had a better chance of being kidnapped by a terrorist than of getting married!" her brother declared, clinking champagne flutes with the bride. Suzanne and Ben, the happy couple, who had linked up with each other at last, laughed with the best of them. But Suzanne knew how close she'd come to falling into the statistical netherworld of the never-married and never-to-become-a-mother.

Indeed, women born in the 1950s have had fewer children than any other generation of American women. My class reflects this trend and pushes it several steps further. Whereas in their mothers' generation, fewer than one in ten remained childless, in my class's cohort—women born in the early 1950s—the statistic jumps to one in six, according to the U.S. Census Bureau. But among my classmates, almost a third have not become mothers. Suzanne had every reason to wonder whether she would be among them.

Suzanne—the Trekkie Who Came Late
to Motherhood

A brilliant and intense girl who idolized *Star Trek*'s Mr. Spock, Suzanne was caricatured to look like him in the senior yearbook. Short, dark hair cut crisp and caplike, jet-black eyebrows tilted rakishly toward her nose, she was pictured standing on a lunar landscape dressed in kneesocks and her schoolgirl uniform, as if waiting to step into her own private sci-fi drama. Instead, after Brearley graduation, she blasted off from one achievement to the next: from Radcliffe to UCLA for a Ph.D. in folklore and mythology to winning a Fulbright scholarship to Iceland for two years of research at a campus outside of Reykjavík, teaching and studying Icelandic ghost stories.

Suzanne had met Ben, a mechanical engineer, in graduate school, but they had never dated. Both put their studies and their academic goals first. Suzanne was driven, but she had known since college that she also wanted a life. "Should I go out tonight or study the Krebs cycle?" she used to ask herself at Radcliffe, where she played with the idea of going to medical school. "The Krebs cycle usually lost."

Still, when she returned to the States from Iceland in 1978, she focused single-mindedly on her dissertation. It would preoccupy her for almost a decade. In order to finish her magnum opus, she told me sheepishly, she stopped sleeping for six months. Meanwhile, she taught part-time at the college level, and when the teaching market dried up in the early eighties, she became a systems analyst at a major bank. The work was dry and repetitive, but her analytical mind could do it on autopilot. She liked the lack of grays, the unarguability of her results, when uncertainty clouded the rest of her life.

By the time she officially received her Ph.D., in 1987, she hadn't had a serious relationship in many years. As her thirties ebbed, the realization crept up on her: being married and having kids probably wasn't going to happen. She felt a cool detachment from her fate, a distance she had cultivated since adolescence. She was neither happy about it nor especially distressed. "I'd loved being single," she told me, "and I knew I'd have no problems continuing to be single."

But at thirty-nine, she ran into Ben when he came back to UCLA for a visit. He was a year younger than she was but had completed his Ph.D. in "a more timely manner" and become a professor at a big midwestern university. They went out to dinner once, and then again. After their second date, Suzanne allowed herself a tiny peek into a chamber she'd thought was forever closed. She thought to herself, I'm probably going to marry this guy. Suddenly her detachment collapsed. "I was terrified," she said.

Their marriage, at Ben's instigation, a year later, turned out to be "sort of a surprise," even to the bride. And because Ben was passionate about having children—Suzanne had convinced herself she could have been satisfied either way—she "was willing to give it my best shot." Suzanne was forty-one when Jeremy was born the next year. Despite her joy in her son and her quiet pleasure in her midlife accomplishment, she would later describe his first year or so as "sort of a blur." She was "exhausted constantly. It was wonderful, but I thought I'd never catch up—and I never have." Her eyes glazed as she remembered all that was left undone that first year—unfolded laundry, unpaid bills, unread books, unmopped floors, unreturned calls, unmet needs.

They had bought a new house and were juggling Jeremy's care with Ben's academic schedule and Suzanne's part-time office job. She hated leaving her baby and felt sorely conflicted about the job but for financial reasons hadn't wanted to turn it down. The area was overloaded with academic wives and jobs for Ph.D.s in folklore were as scarce in their snowbound midwestern college town as crocuses in February.

"The age I'm at, adjusting is a strain," she admitted when we spoke, when Jeremy was four and Suzanne forty-five. She had just driven all night through half the country to New York City

208 / Elizabeth Fishel

with her husband, Jeremy, and her eighty-six-year-old father-in-law. Given the circumstances, she seemed remarkably coherent, if a little groggy and overwhelmed, a spokeswoman in spite of herself for the joys and drawbacks of older motherhood. Groggy and overwhelmed, she allowed, have long been a familiar state. "Balance is missing," she complained. "I'm still in the toddler stage where everything feels out of balance. The process of getting through the minutes seems a frazzle." She paused to pop a pacifier in Jeremy's mouth, whispering, "Don't use it around Daddy. He's not a soft touch like Mom." Then she picked up her train of thought, like someone more than used to interruptions.

"If I get a good night's sleep, I wonder what's wrong," she continued. "Sometimes I mop the kitchen floor at midnight. I can't imagine how people feel balance in their lives unless they have an extra eight hours." A weary laugh and an indulgent look at Jeremy, who was monkeying with a lamp cord, seemed to bracket her ambivalence. "I guess there are some women who get up at five and clean the house. But I need the rest. My technique is letting it go, but I get so depressed when I look around at the mess. It seems too remote to imagine the time when Jeremy is older. Anyway, everyone tells me it gets harder!"

Jo—the Free Spirit Who Came Early to Grandmotherhood

When Jo married Chuck at twenty-four, she was as carefree and unfocused, as boundary-pushing and hungry to see the world, as Suzanne was seasoned, purposeful, and ready to settle down when she married Ben. Like Pamela and Emma, restless seekers both, Jo rode the go-with-the-flow tsunami of the sixties right through the seventies and beyond. Guitar-strumming, hoop-earringed, silver bangles dangling from her arms, Jo was as close to a hippie chick as a Brearley girl could get. In my classmates' circle of squares, she felt she was the odd girl out, always probing for the place to fit in, the route to love and acceptance. She was the dark-haired adopted daughter among a passel of blond brothers and sisters born to her parents some years after her adoption, a bright but undisciplined student among a class of higher-achieving girls, an unhappy college girl at the Vermont college a few miles from her parents' summer house—she dropped out after a year. "I just didn't know what I wanted to do with my life," she'd tell me later, admitting sadly that decades of living hit-or-miss had not made her direction much clearer.

Released from her family's orbit and unshackled from college at nineteen, she was ripe for experience in a way both specific to her own needs and of a piece with her times, her generation. She tracked experience lustily with drugs and travel and love affairs she lost count of. "Education is important," she would later reflect, "but it's also important to be out in the world." Her parents kept pushing her to settle into a responsible, professional adulthood. She pushed back just as hard. "The sixties was the revolt against all of that," she protested. She hitchhiked back and forth across the country, jumping out of a few cars when the trip got dicey, panhandled in San Francisco for spare change to see the Grateful Dead, the Jefferson Airplane. "I wasn't wild," she'd later say about that time, "just a free spirit." Chuck was another free spirit and they roamed the world together, finally settling in England. Five years later, when Jo was twenty-nine, her daughter Brianna was born, and a year and a half after that, a son she named Charlie, for his dad.

When Jo and Chuck married, his drinking seemed just a piece of their laid-back lifestyle. But as the years went on, she became painfully aware that he was an alcoholic. "He would go out with the boys and drink. He was incapable of talking with me. I just had to accept that life with him would be hard." Unchecked and unconfronted, Chuck's alcoholism careered out of control. One boozy New Year's Eve he was driving home from a party when he was

killed in a car crash. The dawning of the new year, cold and unforgiving, left Jo an unemployed widow with two toddlers to care for
and support.

To pick up the pieces of her shattered life, she left England and
moved back to the States, where her family could provide more of
a safety net. She settled with Brianna and Charlie in the annex to her
parents' summer place in Vermont. As a starry-eyed high schooler,
she'd called it the shed and hung out there with the local college
boys, playing guitar, drifting in and out of crushes, and dreaming of
the dazzling vistas that would open before her. Back then, toying
with endless possibilities, she hardly knew how unfettered she was,
and just how limited her vistas would become.

Now suddenly, in the fateful flash of her husband's premature
death, she alone would be responsible for her family's survival. Years
later when her daughter, Brianna, was at a scary crossroads in her
own life, Jo would caution her to slow down, to survey the road in
all directions. "I never would have thought that my husband would
die," she would tell Brianna. "Life is life, and you get dealt whatever
cards you get dealt. They say you never get dealt more than you can
handle, but . . ." Beneath that dot, dot, dot lay a decade of nonstop
pressures that often felt too hard to bear.

As happened to several other classmates—Alice and Sophia,
particularly—a shocking and unforeseen death in the family prompted
a sudden reexamination of self and purpose in the world. All three
of these classmates went to bed free spirits and woke up sobered,
having to shoulder overnight the awesome responsibilities of adulthood. All three stumbled through a dark time, trailing after the light
of transformation.

Settled in rural Vermont, Jo had to get down to the serious business of raising her kids single-handedly. She had weekend help from
her parents when they came up from New York, but otherwise she
was on her own. More than any of the cocooned and protected city
girls in the class of '68, Jo grew into an adulthood that turned out
to be about sheer survival. Splitting wood, covering the windows

with plastic to keep out the brutal cold and get through the winter, Jo did not have the luxury of searching out work that would fulfill her, that would draw on and develop her considerable talents, both musical and artistic.

Once Chuck was gone, Jo became her small family's sole source of financial support. A college dropout in a tight rural economy, she took the best job she could find, as a ski-lift operator at the resort an hour away. If life had been hard with Chuck, it was even harder without him. On subzero mornings she'd struggle awake at four to stoke the wood-burning stove. She'd get dressed in total darkness, so as not to disturb her kids, and be on the road to work by five-thirty. When the roads were piled shoulder-high with snow, it could take her two hours to get to the ski resort, and she couldn't risk being late. She desperately needed the job to keep her family afloat. From their earliest school years on, she'd have to leave the kids to fend for themselves. They'd get up, dress, and have breakfast alone, and be on the school bus by six-thirty. Money was simply too tight to afford a baby-sitter, and there was no extra pair of hands to help out.

As Brianna hit her teens, she started acting out more and more. Like many oldest kids—like Jo herself, in fact, who, as a troubled teen had tormented her parents by running away to the Village— being on the front line of a family under stress took its emo- tional toll. At fourteen Brianna's increasingly problematic behavior required facing a budding drug-and-alcohol problem and con- fronting it with counseling and attendance at Alcoholics Anony- mous meetings. Jo signed up the whole family—she went to Alanon and sent Charlie to Alateen—and found it a lifesaver: a place to share her troubles without being judged, to confront her need for damage control, and most important, to learn a new language of openness and honesty to counter the secrecy and denial she'd learned as a child. ("Are you sure Brianna needs AA? Is she really an alcoholic?" Jo's mother pressed her, nervous about the stigma, about what the neighbors would think, when Jo first broke the news of her daughter's troubles. "Yes," Jo finally had the gumption to retort. "Let's get it out in the open.")

But despite the new language and family attitudes that AA helped catalyze for Jo, it was not so effective for Brianna. Periods of sobriety and a tentative truce at home were shattered by heartbreaking slipups and flare-ups with Jo. Finally, one day when Jo was at work, Brianna, then seventeen, cleaned out her room and disappeared without a trace for six weeks. When she finally called home—sounding "high as a kite," Jo thought at the time—she admitted she had run away and was lying low with her boyfriend. She also admitted she was pregnant. And she was no way willing to give up her baby for adoption. So at eighteen, as a high school dropout with no visible means of support, Brianna became a mother, and made Jo, who was forty-seven, a grandmother.

Jo was not able, either financially or emotionally, to offer her daughter and grandchild shelter from the storm. Her job as a ski-lift operator was still high stress, low pay, and so backbreaking that she worried how much longer she could handle it. And her love life was equally haywire. Despite the demise of her first marriage, to a man who'd spelled trouble from the start, Jo was an incurable romantic who specialized in Mr. Wrongs: a seventeen-year-old heartthrob whom she'd fallen for when she was thirty-five; an avowedly reformed doper and dreamer she'd met in Alanon, who had ended up in jail to redress some old crimes—her passions led her into some questionable romances that usually ended badly.

Right now, poised to become a grandmother, she was embroiled in a dicey triangle that she called "wonderful and horrible." She had fallen for her boss at work, a just-divorced father of three. "I go to bed praying for help in three areas—my debts, my love affair, and my kids," she would say about this nerve-racking time, which she continued trying to patch up with support-group wisdom from Alanon and Debtors Anonymous. Despite her efforts both at work and inside her own head, she found herself admitting wearily to her expectant daughter, "I can't bail you out if you get in trouble, because I'm in too much trouble financially myself. I can't look after a new baby, because I have to work."

Trapped by her own dramas and by events that seemed untimely and out of her control, Jo felt she had failed her daughter and her daughter had failed her. "All the things you don't want your kid to do," she sighed wearily, "Brianna has done. It's hard letting go of how much she's hurt me. But it doesn't make me love her any less."

Mothers: Sooner or Later?

Suzanne, at forty-one, last in the class to become a mother, and Jo, at forty-seven, first to become a grandmother—between the extremes of their life patterns lies the story of this class and this generation and its unconventional relationship with marriage and motherhood. In their mothers' generation the timing of life-cycle events seemed almost inevitable, and the time line for adulthood was as predictable as going from bobby socks to stockings. My classmates' mothers graduated from high school and then college in straight and unquestioned succession. They married early the best catch—best provider—they could snag. And then with a possible short-lived interlude in the workforce—my mother worked in advertising and as a photographer's assistant—they had their babies one, two, three. Their families were complete by the time they were thirty or so—the age at which many of my generation were just beginning to wake up and smell the baby powder.

For baby boomers like my classmates, the women's movement, the Pill, and great strides in fertility technology had won a rainbow of choices concerning procreation. But out there on the fertility forefront, they were as often overwhelmed by their choices as liberated by them. If they did not do it their mothers' way, how would they do it? Would they marry and have children at all, and if they did, when and how and how many? Suppose they linked up and married early, as Jo did, thinking that she'd found a partner for life, only to end up single and searching for anchors later on. Or suppose they married late, like Suzanne, relishing a lengthy singlehood with its chances for solo adventure, single-minded productivity, and the necessary discovery of self-reliance—but by postponing, they might face the uncertainty of a lonely, unprotected old age.

If they became mothers in their twenties, as Jo did, their energy and spirits might be high but their patience, self-definition, and financial security much shakier. If they delayed motherhood till their forties, like Suzanne, they might have attained academic goals and greater perspective, but their energy could be waning and fatigue could become a stumbling block.

But the postponers also wondered if they'd be able to get pregnant effortlessly or if they'd find themselves up against the limits of their own fertility, unable to achieve a dream of motherhood once they'd defined it as their own. And how would they juggle their needs and obligations when children came along?

The Motherhood Crossroads

"I believed that the single most boring thing, the epitome of the middle class, was getting married and having kids," Sophia had proclaimed at twenty-one, voicing the party line for many. But biology would eventually triumph over ideology. By thirty-nine, at the eleventh hour, biologically speaking, Sophia was the radiantly happy mother of a daughter and a son. At forty-five, she surveyed her life's blessings and counted her children highest among them. "I have two wonderful kids, and I didn't expect it to happen," she declared, again speaking for many of the late-deciding wives and late-blooming mothers in the class.

Indeed, several of the women who married late in life gave their families in-laws and grandchildren in rapid succession. The decision to marry and mother, long postponed, whether because of other priorities, ambivalence, or lack of opportunity, once made, created its outcome quickly. Sophia and Judith, both marrying at thirty-six and Suzanne, at forty, all had their babies within a year.

But the decision to have children was not an easy one for most classmates, not the natural, God-given mandate it seemed to have been for their mothers. Some postponed the choice to have kids because their lives were going too well without them. Still others postponed the Baby Question because their lives were not going well enough. Or because they didn't have the right partner or the financial or emotional wherewithal to handle children. Some had an instinct they were not "kid people." Or they were afraid they had not figured out how to avoid repeating family history and might recreate the dysfunctional families they had come from.

For many, the decision to become mothers, to start families of their own, to step up the generational ladder and bind themselves ever more inextricably both to mates and to parents prompted a powerful emotional reckoning just as troubling and transforming as the crisis of authenticity for the inward-journeying seekers. Motherhood became the crucible in which much internal scrutiny took place. Becoming first-time mothers, my classmates reexamined their own childhoods' unfinished business, which raising children forced them to confront. And in doing so, they allowed their own growth to unfold along with their children's.

Childless or Child-free?

My classmates' reasons for not having children—emotional, social, and physical—were as revealing and various as their reasons for having them. For some, not becoming a mother was a decision based on reasons both conscious and underground, both emotional and practical. For others it was a choice by default, a choice that chose them, willing or no.

For Maisie sidestepping motherhood was a careful but emotionally charged decision not to re-create the disrupted family she'd grown up in. Her family had been torn apart by her parents' divorce when she was small, her mother's inability to share custody, and her stepmother's ambivalence about raising her. "My family was not a family that was good to grow up in," she said plainly. "It was very adult-centered." Her father was forty when he married his second wife, who already had a daughter from her first marriage. Although Maisie and her stepmother forged a bond later on, as a young child she didn't have the rock-solid security of knowing she was wanted and cherished.

Nor did she have a good model for motherhood. "I didn't know what a mother was like," she admitted. "Everyone has a bag of tricks they bring to motherhood. But I had no model of a nurturing, close family, because I didn't have it." Thinking about bringing up a child without dependable emotional skills may have also stirred up painful memories of loss from her own childhood. "Childhood is associated with vulnerability and dependence," speculates Maxine Harris in *The Loss That Is Forever,* and some women who've lost their own mothers "can't bear to experience such helplessness again." As children they felt powerless and panicky when divorce or death took a parent away. Now, considering becoming parents themselves, they can't bear to imagine being close to the powerlessness and the lamblike trusting innocence of childhood again.

So the one time in her twenties when Maisie got pregnant by chance, it was "at a time in my life when it didn't make sense" to have a child, and she had an abortion instead. And at forty, when she was happy and secure in her second marriage, when having a child might have made sense, she and her husband faced the question again and decided that "neither had the drive." Had either of them wanted children desperately, the "other would have come along," she speculated. But they decided that their commitments to their careers, their passions (Yoga and golf, among others), and each other came first. "So many people have marriages that don't work," Maisie reflected, "but ours does." So they opted for a child-free midlife, and Maisie had her tubes tied, so sex could be freer, and there'd be no looking back.

For Pam, the journey inward, the self-absorbing journey to

awareness and autonomy, precluded any tour of motherhood. Pam knew herself well enough to know that she simply didn't have the energy or divided focus to sustain another being. And she was honest enough to admit it even in a circle of many motherhood-choosing friends. "The need to be alone" is how she defined what she craved and what she could not give up for children. "That's the part of parenting that made it not an option." She knew she needed "some incredibly nourishing time without responsibilities" for her personal passions and pursuits, "gardening, meditating, art." "Not everyone has that need," she allowed, but admitted, "I know that about myself—it would be folly." She'd watched the round-the-clock duty of friends with their kids and accepted her own limitations. "A couple of hours, max. Then I'd go batty."

Talking to Pam about motherhood, I'm at first taken aback by her blunt confession, which another generation might have criti-cized as undue self-interest. But coming to her on her own terms as a seeker and in today's more choice-accepting atmosphere, I admire her honesty and self-awareness. She knows she'll do better as a con-tented nonmother than as a frustrated mother, torn apart by needs she can't meet.

Unlike Maisie and Pamela, who've both been pregnant once and have chosen to stay child-free, childlessness seemed to have hap-pened to Emma and Tess by default, by opportunity missed or out of reach. In their thirties Emma and Tess both put their energies into their professional lives and established secure careers in pub-lishing and in horticulture. But secure relationships did not come as readily. Emma had an early spate of lovers, followed by a long dry spell; Tess had a short-lived marriage and now a relationship that is comfortable and convenient but not long-term. And although more women of their generation have opted to become mothers-without-marriage than ever before, Emma and Tess, unconven-tional in many other ways, were uncomfortable confronting that particular convention. Neither wanted to consider having children without the umbrella of marriage and shared parenthood.

But both enjoy the company of children, and taking their aunt duties seriously has allowed them to express their nurturing sides. Emma relishes being the wild, wacky aunt for her more staid brothers' children. She's the one who'll listen to Jimi Hendrix or the latest rap music with them. She's also the sympathetic ear for their confessions. As she was a longtime, quasi-professional "bad girl," there's little she hasn't seen or done, and nothing they confide can shock her. Tess could make a second career of her aunthood—with nine brothers and sisters, she has fifteen nieces and nephews. There's always someone having a birthday. She's dispatched armloads of Mickey Mouse ears and escorted troops of enthralled young relatives around the Disney theme parks.

Being devoted aunts has let both Emma and Tess experience motherhood at one step removed; perhaps the pleasures have been diluted but so have the pains. And aunthood has brought into their lives that vital gift of "generativity," in Erik Erikson's important phrase—a concern with guiding the next generation without which, he suggests, stagnation and self-involvement threaten.

Motherhood Conflicts

Some were child-free by choice, others childless by default. Still others among my classmates were so conflicted or ambivalent about becoming mothers that they postponed the decision until it was almost too late. Would motherhood, they agonized, take the spark out of their marriages, the intensity out of their careers, the freedom out of their personal lives? And by becoming mothers would they become their own mothers, repeating everything they swore as children they would never do? For some, these doubts receded or were resolved as the twenties slipped into the thirties and their biological clocks began ticking out. But others stayed mired in ambivalence until biology almost took care of the decison for them.

Frankie felt no "biological urge" until she was thirty-four, and then it took her four years to get pregnant with her son, Jake. A renegade and committed politico who had left Brearley for the Putney School, Putney for U. C. Berkeley, and then dropped out of Berkeley for a while to work in a factory, Frankie took a long time to find her niche in the world. She married early and briefly, then went uncertainly to law school and became an activist lawyer; meanwhile she married for a second time, an older man who had a son she helped raise. She was thirty-eight by the time Jake was born. Thrilled by him and by the experience of motherhood, she admitted wistfully, "I wish I'd started earlier; I would have wanted more."

Martha's route to feeling settled in the world, to blending work and marriage with motherhood, was likewise circuitous and delayed. She was brilliant but troubled and anorexic during high school. Then her illness forced her to drop out of college and spend six months in Payne Whitney, and it continued to haunt her on and off for years. "It took me twenty years to get over the nonsense," she would say dismissively in her mid-forties, adding disturbingly, "Part of me feels I haven't gotten over anything." Finding her way into the computer world was one godsend for Martha. Computer programming took advantage of her high-level math skills, and logging on after hours to talk to other techies gave her a social network she might not have forged otherwise.

Married at thirty to a fellow computer whiz, she admitted later that she "didn't even think about kids until she was thirty-eight." She questioned her maternal instinct and thought kids would be a "drag" who would interfere with their unfettered lifestyle. By the time she changed her mind, her body—barely over one hundred pounds—would not readily cooperate. So she and her husband followed the disheartening trail of infertility—in vitro fertilization that didn't take, a promised adoption that fell through at the last minute—and then finally an adoption that brought them a beloved daughter. The following year, unplanned and unexpected, a biological daughter arrived. Motherhood has both enhanced Martha's self-worth and aroused the specter of self-criticism that has dogged her since school days. By midlife, she would say of her daughters,

"Unconditional love is so nifty," but also confess that she doesn't feel she does "a good job as a mother." "I drag others down by trying to be perfect," she would lament.

For Frankie and Martha and all the class's latecomers to motherhood, having children has opened them up to wellsprings of pleasure and vast resources of love they may not have dreamed possible. But from the moment they imagined children, through the maze of uncertainty, until children finally arrived, and then in each stage of raising them, my classmates have also opened themselves up to the unpredictability of the universe, the way things most dearly wished for often remain maddeningly out of personal control. Becoming mothers, they left behind that tightly controlled and regimented world of childhood and of Brearley, where effort was rewarded and achievement followed struggle, and gave themselves over to a different world—the real world, the adult world, a world that was not always in control, that was driven by accident and chance. Here even intelligence, money, power, and the luck of birth could not entirely guarantee the desired outcome. This randomness was also what choosing motherhood meant to my peers, and the way they coped with it reflected their own internal landscape—their sources of resilience as well as their floundering.

Making Babies, Coping with Loss

From the time Bob and I reconnect at twenty-five and marry at twenty-eight, we dream of babies. We lust after them with a shameless baby lust, making goo-goo faces at a chubby-cheeked toddler beside us in a restaurant, ogling sleeping infants on a plane. By our thirtieth birthdays—just two weeks apart, in the spring—we leapfrog over the final hurdles of our joint ambivalence and decide we are ready. I am convinced that the process will be a long haul. My maternal grandfather, after all, was a renowned infertility specialist, and his ghost still lingers in my memory, along with the ghosts of all his anxious-to-conceive patients. Besides, the media blare with scare stories of the infertility woes of older mothers.

I am not quite yet a *prima gravida,* that ominous medical term for a first-time mother over thirty-five, but in my mind I fear becoming her. My own mother was twenty-seven when she had me, and that felt old enough. The average age of first-time motherhood has been creeping up steadily ever since, and among my circle of friends, thirty still seems relatively young to start a family (my two closest Berkeley friends won't become first-time mothers till they're forty-four). Despite this social shift, my own mother's pattern casts a long shadow over my decisions. My generation is caught in the middle at every stage, between the way their mothers did things and the pattern of their peers.

Nevertheless, one month after dispensing with my diaphragm, I am pregnant. My fears seem to have proved groundless. Though cautious by nature, I am so buoyed by the excitement of this impending birth that in the next month and a half, at least in my mind, I have not only named the baby—Nate or Kate—but designed his room and outfitted her from booties to baseball cap. When I start spotting at six weeks, just before our annual summer trip back to visit family on the East Coast, my heart stops. But my obstetrician reassures me that in half of all such cases, pregnancy proceeds normally, and he encourages us to carry on with the trip.

Within a few days of our arrival in Boston, the bleeding has become dramatic. I hurry to the office of a strange obstetrician, recommended by the friend of a friend, and with my husband standing wordlessly by, we stagger beneath the news. The baby is not growing; the pregnancy is over. We weep together, astonished, as so often in grief, that this bad news is happening to us. Until now our marriage has occasioned more champagne than tears. We have celebrated first jobs, first book sale, first apartment, a funky delight with wall-to-wall shag carpeting that rattles like an earthquake each time our neighbors use their washing machine. But this earthquake we are not prepared for. With the last vestiges of my pregnancy go not only the dreams of motherhood that I have held since childhood and our shared hopes of starting a family but also a bedrock faith in the future that has been chipped away at—by the cataclysms of '68 and by Lily's death the next year—but has not shattered until now.

For several days I linger in bed, surrounded by my husband's family, anxiously checking up on me as I recuperate. But despite the comfort of their concern, the family seems to alienate me more than protect me. I so ache to be part of that precious circle of mothers which my mother-in-law, with her four strapping offspring, and my sister-in-law, with her two (eventually four) daughters, have embraced so effortlessly. Their very ease, their unquestioned confidence in mothering, remind me only of my shortcomings. I hide under the covers and sink into my own sense of failure. My body, my plans, my abortive attempt to vault myself up another rung of the ladder to adulthood—everything I've tried has failed.

For months I am in a limbo of fears and random physical symptoms that make trying to get pregnant again unthinkable. Well-meaning friends bring me stories of others' speedy bounce-back from miscarriages, as if they were bringing casseroles to the home of the newly bereft. So-and-so got pregnant a month after her miscarriage and now is jouncing a beautiful baby girl on her knee. Meant to comfort, these triumph-over-adversity tales throw me deeper into despair. Why do others have the grit to bounce back from their disappointments, while I stay mired in mine?

"Life has thrown you a curve ball," writes my mother to console and encourage me. Yes, I grumble to myself, self-criticism seething once again, and I'm not ready for it. Have things gone so smoothly for me until now that I cannot cope with adversity when it comes along? Have I not had enough failure in small doses all along to cope with this one now? Did the thirteen years of uninterrupted—unrealistic?—Brearley education prevent me from learning to adapt to life's inevitable change? Cordelia and Judith, who both entered in high school, from other crowds, other scenes, learned flexibility early, learned how to adapt to new expectations, different styles.

"What created resilience in you?" I asked Judith several lifetimes later. "The Radcliffe denial," she responded without hesitating. "It made me come to terms with failure and see that you don't always get what you want."

Now at thirty, and still at thirty-one and -two, it is my turn to confront my losses and limitations. It is my turn to forgive myself my failures and accept my lack of control. When the nine months have passed, and I grieve my way through the day that would have been our baby's birth, I am mourning not just for our lost child and the miscarried promise of motherhood but for a deeper loss as well. I have lost that childhood innocence that things will always work out for the best, that what we desire and plan will come to fruition. I have confronted my own ultimate lack of control over the events of my life and opened myself up to the chance toss of the universe.

After months of therapy and countless conversations with my kindly doctor, I come to accept that nothing I have done, thought, or eaten caused my miscarriage; it is purely a bad thing that happened to a presumably good person. For me this insight, this self-releasing from blame, turns out to be a prerequisite to moving on, a necessary readying step for considering motherhood once more.

Trying again feels like the scariest thing I've ever done, like closing my eyes, holding my nose, and jumping off a high cliff into a deep pool of uncertainty. I'm not much of a risk taker in the best of circumstances, and although statistically the odds are still in my favor—only after three (unthinkable) miscarriages do the chances of success plummet considerably—I feel I am tempting the fates. Still, if not a risk taker, I am determined and will not let my husband down easily. Becoming parents is a shared goal that has not wavered, the dreamed-for centerpiece of our marriage.

So after two years of grieving and postponing the inevitable, we try again. And again, six weeks after conceiving, I have a second miscarriage. Curiously, this time, although I am again deeply shaken and depressed, I do not feel the same cosmic gloom descend. This time I mourn the baby and the loss of our plans to jump forward into parenthood, but my grief feels more contained. I have already begun to assimilate just how chancy the universe can be, and learning the lesson yet another time is not as traumatic as the first time was, when I wore the rose-colored glasses of innocence.

This time the biological clock is tolling ever louder, and I do not take as long to recover and move on. A few months later I'm ready for the fateful plunge, thanks to my husband's steadiness, my family's support, and the confidence of a wonderful doctor. He manages to convince me that no patient he's ever had who was able to get pregnant once has ever, as he puts it, "left his office with empty arms." Perhaps it is the power of positive suggestion, but I vow I will not become the exception to his perfect record. The third time I conceive and have a positive sonogram, he beams. "This one's a keeper." And he is right. A week before I turn thirty-three—that freighted age—our first son is born, and three years later, without a hitch, our second son. Despite our struggles, our shaken confidence, our fears and near-misses, the family we have dreamed of is complete.

Like many who've postponed parenthood or who've struggled to achieve what others attain easily, we gain wisdom from our losses—patience, perspective, a deep appreciation of, even ecstasy over, what we have. Perhaps after stumbling along in the face of uncertainty we're more ready to accept the uncertainties that raising children will surely bring. Yes, we might have been more high-energy had we started in our twenties. But seasoned, reasoned, having weathered a few more of life's crises, more solid both in our lives and in our marriage, we're already primed for the balancing act that bringing up children will require.

CHAPTER 11

The Jugglers

The search for balance shapes the juggler's choices from her tentative twenties through her work-and-family-establishing thirties and then through her integrating forties, just as the pursuit of security shapes the untraditional traditionalist's choices, the drive for success shapes the unconventional career-tracker's decisions, and the quest for awareness and authenticity shapes the seeker's path.

Despite media fanfare about the Shiva-armed contemporary superwoman, fewer than half of the class of '68 turn out, by midlife, to have it all. Fewer than half are negotiating the complex, risky, head-spinning, but more often than not fulfilling juggling act of combining marriage and family and career. Another handful is balancing two out of three—either they're married and working but don't have kids or they have kids and are working but are divorced or widowed and don't have husbands.

A similar pattern was uncovered about another famously situated group of this in-between, change-straddling generation in a recent public television documentary, *Hillary's Class*—that is, First Lady Hillary Rodham Clinton's Wellesley College class of 1969, just three years ahead of mine. Among Hillary's able, highly educated classmates, many found themselves in their late forties blessed and successful in two spheres but not in all three. Both her high-powered, high-profile classmates, such as the Madeira School's headmistress, Betsy Griffith, and CBS newscaster Martha Teichner, and many competent, less well known women lamented their short-fall in one sphere despite successes in others. Teichner, for example, an easily recognizable talking head, had, by forty-six, crisscrossed the world ten times for her profession, but admitted to "crying un-controllably" when she realized after one particularly pivotal but wrenching career move that she would never stay settled long enough to have and raise children.

So having it all—creating a lasting marriage while growing a satisfying career and nurturing a family—has turned out to be a trickier high-wire act than women of my generation might have imagined. Attempting it, they've been confounded by mixed mes-sages from within and without, from their own psyches as well as from the culture. For those who were young in the fifties but came of age in the late sixties and seventies—my class, Hillary's class—the clash of cultures, the contradictory messages—traditional versus feminist—has fired imaginations with potential but left many doubting they could or should have it all. Would having it all mean solidarity with their accomplished, professional sisters or betraying their restless, nonworking mothers? Would it mean embracing a lib-erated feminism or turning their backs on their femininity? Would it create a new empowering vision or cause them to coldly reject the old? Hillary Clinton is a natural figurehead for this Janus-headed generation, and her very public dilemma over her role—devoted wife and mother or shrewd policy wonk, tea-pouring hostess or high-profile politician—magnifies and reflects the choices of most midlife boomers, my classmates among them.

Any internal doubts they might have had were compounded by the pressures from a workplace in transition, my classmates and their cohort found—unequal pay, sexual harassment, undependable ma-ternity leave, unreliable child care, and always the nonstop demands of the second shift, the extra burdens on the home front that fell unequally on women's shoulders. Many found themselves pleasing neither master—fulfilling demands at work only to shirk the family, meeting family needs only to give short shrift to the workplace. "Balance is a constant struggle," admitted one long-married classmate who juggles a demanding job as a demographer with raising two school-age children. "It's an ideal. I achieve the balance a couple of times a year. Mostly I'm teetering on the precipice, with work taking over. But I do struggle for equilibrium." If togetherness was the fifties buzzword, confrontation the sixties, the seventies, career, and the eighties me, me, me, then surely balance has become the rallying cry of the nineties, as my classmates' struggles are evidence.

Cordelia—a Juggler in Mid-Balance

The wintry Sunday afternoon I meet with Cordelia in her sturdy redbrick home in suburban Washington, D.C., is a typically jam-packed but satisfying one in the life of a family moving in many directions at once. The house's staid exterior belies the feeling of warmth and creativity that greets a guest. Inside, there's a pleasing rush of color, light, and visual treats. It's there in the living room's brilliant, coral-colored walls, the kitchen's sparkling Mexican tiles, the airiness of the family-room addition, whose floor-to-ceiling windows and folk-art decor feel more laid-back West Coast than East Coast traditional. Creative clutter spilling everywhere reflects a cooking-on-all-four-burners family style—kids' projects in mid-completion, Christmas presents to be wrapped, a tower of cards from friends all over the country. Despite the snow-covered December afternoon outdoors, inside, it's both airy and intimate, like the family feeling Cory has managed to create.

In a small, cozy music room, painted a deep ocean-blue, Cory's fourteen-year-old, Claire, is practicing her cello. The family's many instruments are scattered everywhere; often they play music together. Claire's blond Botticelli beauty suggests a more delicate version of Cory at just about the age Cory and I were when we first met, when Cory roared into our sedate city-girl class, trailing her country-girl ways. Back then she was spilling over with energy and irreverence, a big, blond girl, earthy, awkward, and lovable. Today, at forty-six, she's more trim and contained but no less full of energy, irreverence, and earthy charm. She talks fast, smokes, and laughs easily, the girl still close to the surface in the woman she's become.

Before dusk falls, her husband, Sam, will dash off to pick up their ten-year-old, Mathilda, whose Cheshire-cat grin reflects her mom's. Sam is the activist lawyer Cordelia fell in love with in Appalachia when she was a starry-eyed college girl and he ten years older and wiser. Already an entrenched idealist, Sam was fighting the Tennessee Valley Authority, and was just detaching from a rocky first marriage. When Sam and Cory married a few years later, she inherited an instant family and became a mother overnight to his school-age sons. Her twenties had faded into her thirties by the time the first two boys were raised, the terms of their marriage were renegotiated, and they felt ready to start again with a second set of children.

For a while it was impossible to imagine how they'd ever merge two families, combine two careers, and balance their own needs— separately and as a couple—with the needs of two more young children. Now they're in a comfortable family-with-school-age-kids groove. When Sam returns with Mattie, he'll have an early dinner, then excuse himself to go off to play music with friends, as he does every Sunday evening. It's one of the cherished pleasures of his week, which Cory has the good grace and good sense to indulge. On another evening Cory will have her own night off, walking or visiting with friends. Tonight Cory will have dinner with her daughters and oversee their homework while correcting her own stack of papers, going over lesson plans, and gearing up for a fast-paced, demanding week. She's an English teacher at a big suburban high school, where she passes on and also reinvents some of the lessons she learned so long ago at Brearley.

Later that evening I wonder to myself about Cory's turnaround from childhood to adulthood. Who would have thought that coming from a family fractured by divorce and instability, Cory would have ended up creating such a harmonious family life? Who would have imagined that a straight-C student whose academic confidence was shaken, not bolstered, by her own education would become a savvy and confident English teacher, encouraging and inspiring flocks of students? I wonder how the wavering self-esteem of adolescence eventually led to this secure satisfaction at midlife, this confidence that she can juggle many things at once and still hold on to her deepest self, her core values, her balance both inside and out.

The Razor's Edge

"We all walk the razor in a different way" was the image one schoolmate offered about the juggler's precarious balancing act. Without blueprints, without models, each member of '68 has had to invent from scratch a life that fits her needs, draws on her capabilities, and handles her vulnerabilities. In order to "have it all," jugglers like Cory and Judith have had to come up with some fancy and original footwork. Some have had it all—but in sequence, not at the same time. They've deferred gratification in one sphere in order to concentrate on another—accomplished early and married late, for instance—having faith that sooner or later they'll savor all life's pleasures. Others have made compromises, refined or redefined their values and ambitions, scaled back professional goals in order to concentrate on personal ones, or settled for a smaller family in order to save energy for a larger career. Still others have found themselves on one professional course and then, in midcareer, shifted courses completely, reinventing themselves and their futures when a new set of strengths or needs eclipsed the old ones. Sociologists have dubbed this the protean career, the career that constantly shifts its shape, like Proteus, and some of the most satisfied classmates have turned out to be the most protean.

Indeed, recent research suggests that women adept at juggling are also usually the happiest. Although an overloaded schedule would seem to create satisfaction-sapping pressure, the reverse is actually true. Women who balance multiple roles—that is, women who work hard at satisfying jobs and have fulfilling marriages and family lives—also feel the most overall life satisfaction, according to Wellesley College sociologist Rosalind Barnett. What pushes busyness over the line into stress-out is feeling out of control and unbalanced.

No juggler has seen her life take flight like a straight arrow (if anyone's does)—an early marriage that lasts unexamined, a single career that glides from training to gold watch, children who grow without glitches. Instead I see the jugglers' choices unfolding like a chambered nautilus, swirling in ever-widening circles with the pearly iridescence of Georgia O'Keeffe's classic image. Jugglers add a new layer only when the old layers have been revisited, reworked, and reconciled, so that evolving discoveries and newly revealed selves continue to be integrated with past revelations. Often the jugglers decipher their purpose not by defining a goal and striving forward to reach it but by looking backward at what they've done and understanding its meaning in retrospect.

What are the valuable resources that enable jugglers to find satisfaction in several spheres at once? My interviews searched out the lessons they've drawn from their education and earliest years that help them cope later on, their special sources of resilience that transform challenges into opportunities. Among all my classmates, the jugglers seem to be most gifted with these important life skills.

Learning from the Inside Out

"I see life in phases," Cordelia reflected that wintry afternoon we met, naming her life metaphor, her philosophy. "I really listen to my own soul and instincts." That trust in her instincts, that ability to listen to her own inner voice, is what empowered her—and the lack of it has sent others on the occasional wild-goose chase. For Cory, the search for authenticity was ongoing. It did not precipitate a particular crisis but rather unfolded in successive phases, shaped from within. Cory's ability to see life in cycles, to accept life's continual reworking and redefining of old themes, is a hallmark of the jugglers and of '68's best-coping women. And along with this trust in life's healing process comes an ability to alchemize challenges and disappointments into the gold of growth.

Cory's earliest phase, her childhood and years at Brearley, was full of challenges that could have broken down a less resilient girl. Her family situation was tense, shattered by her parents' bitter breakup, her father's absence, and her mother's unpredictability. Cory found herself mothering her mother as often as being mothered by her. As a ninth-grade transfer to Brearley, Cory became adept at shuttling back and forth between two lifestyles—her school-day city-slicker life of theater outings, posh dances, and Madison Avenue coffee shops and the lower-key country life at her family's weekend house of winter skiing, summer horseback riding, and smooching behind barn doors. Among her Brearley friends—and her unselfconscious charm and easy acceptance of others won her many of them—she prided herself on her country-girl smarts, like knowing "how windshield wipers worked" or "that chickens had feathers."

If Cory had social confidence and theatrical talents—she starred in many school drama productions—academically, she struggled. But the juggler's gift is to turn deficits into assets and discover the silver linings within the most threatening clouds. Surviving a troubled family and at times, parenting her own mother nourished Cory's emotional self-confidence and strengthened her belief in her own nurturing capacities. Her emotional intelligence, thus invigorated, would help her handle other tricky relationships later on and would especially prepare her to take on the challenges of stepparenting. Handling the transition between her country and city lives increased her flexibility and ease in getting along with a variety of people in a multitude of settings. Even struggling at the bottom of the academic heap turned out to have emotional rewards.

"We look back at the things that helped make us healthy," she mused decades later. "For me, I was on the bottom of the class, but I had compensating factors—being a goof, being elected president of the school; I had supporters." One of her closest friends shared similar academic struggles. "She and I would compare English papers—sixty-two or seventy?" They laughed together over their disappointments and helped keep their academic lives in perspective. Indeed, learning to fail and then bounce back has been a more important lesson for the most satisfied and adept jugglers than striving for one success after another. Not fearing failure permitted Cory to take risks and explore uncharted territory that enriched her belief in herself and deepened her empathy and her capacity for service to others.

Activist Daughter

Although many of the class's late-sixties daughters dabbled in radical politics, Cory was one of only a handful of classmates whose activism became a lifetime commitment, whose concern for the disadvantaged and disenfranchised was sustained from the fiery zeal of youth through the multiple demands of maturity. The same trust in her own instincts that let her make the most of Brearley despite academic floundering also sent her away from Sarah Lawrence to organize in Appalachia and later encouraged her to leave college for good to work for social change.

Cory's activism was her family's most positive legacy. In the late sixties, her mother had helped found a Harlem-based prep school dedicated to giving able black students the same enabling education that East Coast prep schools provided their white counterparts. And when her mother's wealthy second husband died, she created a family foundation from his estate to fund projects for social change, which Cory and her siblings would later oversee. "We were never raised to be afraid of people who dressed poor or to think we were better than they were," Cory reflected about her family's influence on her social attitudes. "I've always wanted to meet people where they were."

It was this family history, combined with Cory's natural openness—and perhaps a dash of identification with the under-dog—that enabled her to gain the trust of poor country people in Appalachia as well as inner-city kids in Washington, D.C., where, after leaving college, she worked for Mayor Marion Barry setting up summer jobs programs. As she approached her watershed thirtieth birthday, her sure instinct for her own growth and survival told her it was time to shift professional gears again. This time she chose to teach theater and use it as a tool for social awareness and change.

A Mentor's Influence

Cory's model was her Brearley drama teacher and mentor, Maggie Tucker, a warmhearted and charismatic Welsh woman who herself had combined theater, dedicated antiwar activism, and a rewarding family life. Like the most influential mentors, Maggie not only showed Cory that this kind of engaged life was possible, but also demonstrated, by her faith in Cory, that Cory could attain it, too. Maggie cast Cory as the lead in plays from Shakespeare to Brecht and gave her an opportunity to draw on her best talents and to shine. But Maggie was not just Cory's drama coach. She was also her surrogate mother during those rocky teen years when her own mother was not always accessible, her role model, comrade at arms, booster, and sympathetic ear. After rehearsals and over weekend cups of tea in her appealingly bohemian Greenwich Village apart-ment, Maggie listened attentively while Cory unburdened her struggles, acknowledged her fledgling strengths, and reached to capture her dreams. Maggie was that pivotally supportive adult out-side the family whom the best copers among my classmates man-aged to find early on. She nurtured Cory's youthful self-esteem and helped pave the way for her adult self-definition and creative focus to take shape.

And Cory would later acknowledge Maggie's influence on her in no uncertain terms. "I wanted to teach theater," Cory explained later, "because it was Maggie who recognized me for who I was." So, ready to make her break from the world of nonprofits and inner-city social programs, Cory got her M.A. from Catholic University and began teaching theater, following in her mentor's footsteps. But the context was different and considerably more intense. Rather than inspiring privileged city girls in a private school, Cory worked with troubled working-class youths, helping them put on plays in prison. "You have to give kids vehicles to express themselves," she came to believe, revisiting her own early needs. "They need a structure to be creative." As she guided her students to find their own creative structures, she also reexamined and reinforced her own creative wellsprings. This reworking of early experience, this revisiting and resolving childhood history, is yet another contributor to midlife fulfillment.

Happy on the Home Front

The most satisfied classmates were able to establish themselves not just in one sphere but in several. So Cory's twenties and thirties were not just about finding work that drew on her talents and deepened her sense of being purposeful in the world. These self-defining and emotionally intense decades were also devoted to finding a committed relationship that would grow as she grew.

Cory's relationship with Sam, passionate from the start, would go through as many shifts and redefinitions as her working life. But its strength was its elasticity; theirs was a partnership that could adapt and renew itself without snapping. Unlike Cory's dad, Sam would not walk away when things got tough; unlike her mom, Cory always felt safe enough with him to hang on tight even when their marriage hit white water. When Cory met Sam, a radical lawyer, in Tennessee in her early twenties, she was still unshaped clay, uncertain of her direction.

"Sam was on a pedestal in the beginning," Cory recalled. "He was so smart." Early on, Cory still questioned her own intellectual prowess, her self-confidence still shaken from those schoolgirl C's. In arguments she'd often accede to Sam's greater wisdom, a willing student to his willing teacher. As a stepmother to his school-age sons when they first married, she also took a back seat when the boys were young. Sam was the boys' biological father, after all; he held their trust and had had those confidence-building years of early experience. She was barely out of adolescence herself and just the boys' mother by marriage; she didn't have the emotional clout to make decisions for them. But after years of comforting their midnight ear infections, overseeing their homework, and cheering on their Little League games, she forged a bond with both boys and built more faith in her own parenting skills. By the time the boys were launched, and she yearned for children of her own, she knew the co-parenting dynamic with Sam would be very different. This second time around she dreamed they'd be equal partners, sharing parenthood from the beginning, working hard, while supporting each other's careers, basking in the glow of their marriage.

Then reality hit. Two A.M. feedings. Cranky children. Pressured deadlines. No-show baby-sitters. Working full-bore at demanding and emotionally draining careers while caring for two small babies and the two boys (who, although college-bound, still needed occasional tending) sapped their energy and took its toll on their marriage. Each felt equally beleaguered and unappreciated. Accusations flew, arguments raged, the passion that had glowed hot and sustaining for years dwindled to embers. "After the boys had left and the babies came, we almost got divorced," Cordelia remembered soberly years after the showdown had been averted.

Although Cory's family, like many of their generation, "looked down on counseling"—they believed you should solve your problems by will and self-reliance—Cory and Sam knew they needed outside help. For six months they went to a marriage counselor and "went through hell" making their marriage work "so much harder than usual." But when they emerged from the fires of criticism and self-criticism, they had saved their marriage, redefined their priorities, and rekindled their pleasure in each other. "The man I married is a loving person who loves my guts," Cory realized. Their marriage had proved flexible enough to stretch to the breaking point but adapt without coming apart.

"What kind of life do you want to live?" the counselor asked them, then asked them to ask each other. Gradually the answer unfolded: less stress, more fun, fewer demands, more balance. Together they drafted another life plan that put family in the center, work for each that would be fulfilling without requiring overdrive— and time for each other and for themselves.

Along with the reshaping of family life, Cory came to realize, this newly evolving phase would generate another career shift, another redefinition of focus. She'd switched once from organizing in the mountains to organizing in the city. Then she switched her context again, from politics to theater as a means to spread the word about social change. Now she saw she'd have to reinvent herself and redefine her purpose again. This time she'd make a lateral move, a move inside the teaching profession, where she'd come to feel so comfortable. This move would require a major switch of style and content. She'd change from outsider to insider, from bringing theater guerrilla-style to the prisons to teaching English in a large, suburban, mostly white public high school.

Teaching from the Inside Out

"My instinct took me away from theater, because I didn't want to talk to people in masks anymore" is how she explained her impulse to change. It was as if on the journey toward authenticity she had come far enough to share what she knew directly with her own voice, not through the words of characters on stage. Teaching high school also fit more comfortably with the life plan she and Sam had hammered out in the rockiest days of establishing their second family. Now her daily schedule would mirror her daughters', and when they had summers off, so would she.

But more than anything else, becoming a teacher allowed her to complete the unfinished business of her own education. Teaching high school let her circle back to those ego-deflating years at Brearley, when every essay she wrote drew the same disappointing response, when she was once suspended for a week for singing operatically in the midst of an English class on Wallace Stevens's "Peter Quince at the Clavier." "I don't know why I'm not bitter," becoming a teacher has finally allowed her to admit. "But I was genuinely interested in the ideas we shared. They couldn't squash that!" Despite the battering to her self-esteem, her passion for learning has kept on burning like a trick birthday candle that simply won't be snuffed out.

"I still have to laugh at myself for being an English teacher," she would one day confess, knowing that the kind of English teacher she's become owes much to the kind of teachers she had, yet bears her own distinctive stamp, her own struggles and style. Teaching for Cory is an organic process that unfolds from the inside out, integrating the lessons from her own education with the insights and knowledge she has struggled to make her own. "What I'm about is helping my students develop who they are from the inside and helping them make the classroom a community."

Schoolgirls Turned Teachers

I get to see Cory in action one morning when she invites me to her ninth-grade English class to speak about my own journey as a writer. Hugging each other hello, we do a double take at the way our roles have changed. Weren't we just two schoolgirls together, waiting to be enlightened by our English teacher, not standing in her shoes? "Quiet on the set," she jokes over the din of young chatter. Once she was the student actress, waiting to take direction. Now she's the director, confidently taking center stage. I stand back and admire the way she draws the class together, all those hormone-pumping teenagers in baggy jeans and oversize sweatshirts. She lassoes their wavering attention with a joke, an insight, a deft moment of confrontation. Still there's plenty of schoolgirl spilling over in Cory too—the infectious enthusiasm, the willingness to make a slight fool of herself, that goofiness she swears is what helped pull her through the hard times at home and at school.

As I wait for my turn to go on, I scope out Cory's classroom. Bulletin boards boast student-made posters for *Great Expectations* and a large sign about the writing process, boldly trumpeting the importance of revising. Side by side, there's the message I'm going to pass along—have the great expectations; always be willing to revise them. First draft, second draft, dozens of manuscript attempts scrunched up and deep-sixed in the wastebasket before the final version hits. Know that nobody gets it exactly right the first time, not in writing, not in life. There's the secret wisdom that Cory, as a juggler, has learned by trial and error as she's planned for and revised her goals, fallen down and bounced back up again, revisited the lessons of the past and woven them into the present, invented and reinvented herself, her family, her future.

Still, after six years of teaching, Cory's getting itchy to move on. Her school, though no cocoonlike Brearley, feels limiting in other ways, yet provides a structure she needs. But she finds herself missing the barricades, wanting to mix things up more directly, not from one step removed. "I'm forty-five years old," she says, as our day together ends. "I have money in the bank. So shouldn't I make a change? I want to give myself permission to do what I want to do. But I worry about structure. I'm a wild person at heart." Hugging good-bye, I know the next stage is still unfolding for Cory, the next act is yet to be revealed.

Judith—Late Bloomer

"The reason I switched so much from one path to another was that Brearley made me feel as if I could do anything," confessed Judith, settling deep into the living-room sofa in her suburban California ranch house and reflecting on her own growth as a juggler, as a two-time career-switcher, as a late-to-the-altar wife and late-blooming mother with two school-age sons. We hadn't set eyes on each other in years, not since graduation, and I was surprised, at first, to see this attractive, fit, suntanned, vibrant woman greeting me. She looked healthily, casually chic; a short sleeveless dress showed off strong, well-toned muscles. At school, she was quiet, studious, a bit plain; she didn't push herself forward. Now she had grown into herself and was glowing with health and confidence.

More than anyone I interviewed, Judith credited Brearley with fostering a confidence and nimbleness that would enhance her later flowering in work and love. Could this be the same education that shook up Cory's faith in herself and left her doubting her intellectual potential? Like two daughters of the same parents whose experience of family life is nonetheless totally different, Judith and Cory, coming out of the same school at the same time, painted opposite pictures of its impact.

It was her Brearley education, Judith said, that "gave me the confidence to switch fields from math to medicine and to be a resident at forty-four! It also encouraged me to experience motherhood and take time for that. Even with its stress on grades," she added, "at Brearley the process was the most important thing. Whatever I was doing I would be immersed in it. It gave me a joy and appreciation of reading and studying all by myself that was the most precious thing."

The seeds of this academic zeal, this fierce intellectual independence and drive were planted at Brearley, then watered and tended by Judith's family. She described her goal-driven, single-minded striving as "genetic," inherited from her father, an intellectually intense economist and the patriarch of a bookish, focused family who loved reading and studying together on weekend retreats at their country house. So Judith's academic prowess and commitment were comfortably in sync with her family's intellectual style and her parents' expectations for her, one of the traits I found linked to satisfaction and achievement later on.

But Judith was a daughter of the sixties as well and not immune to the laid-back, anti-intellectual messages of her peers. Leaving home and jockeying to get a foothold in the real world, she was as often tempted to tune in and drop out as to surge full-steam ahead for the brass ring. So as an adult, like so many classmates of '68, she followed a zigzag course. Periods of intense forward momentum were often followed by times of drifty uncertainty. Phases where she strove single-mindedly toward a goal were shadowed by times when she turned inward, times when she nurtured personal needs rather than external goals. The result was an integration of outer and inner lives and the kind of balance that marks the juggler. But Judith's appraisal of her coping style was characteristically modest. "Balance? No, I just keep falling down and getting up again."

Judith's first path after graduation was ivy-covered and checkered with advances and retreats. After doing honors work in high school—math, basketball, and Virginia Woolf's novels were her great loves—she fell into a drifting phase at Vassar. For months she seemed to be in recovery from too many high-school nights spent No-Dozing to make it through exams. For at least a semester, she holed up in her college dorm room, smoking dope and losing herself in Beethoven sonatas. But when she transferred to Princeton, her intellectual drive once again revved up, propelling her from challenging courses through graduation—in Princeton's first co-ed class—and then to Dartmouth to get her doctorate in math.

First Incarnation: Math Prof

Judith was attracted to math both for what it required and for what it didn't require. "Math was a gut major," she joked later on. "You didn't have to write any papers, and I'd do anything to avoid writing an essay!" Still, she'd liked math ever since Brearley—its complexities absorbed her the way sonatas did—and she was adept at number-crunching. If it wasn't always music to her soul, she consoled herself with her father's admonition about success: "Inspiration is only five percent; perspiration, the other ninety-five."

In graduate school, her social life, all the more compelling for its relatively late arrival, often absorbed her more than her academic one. "I was so adept I could sneak in the graduate work," she recalled, admitting she studied for two months for her qualifying exams when fellow grad students prepared for a year. Nevertheless, Ph.D. newly issued, she was appointed a math professor at Williams College; at twenty-six, she was the youngest ever to receive that honor, just barely older than her students. She parlayed her youth into an asset in the classroom, making the quest for knowledge a team effort. "I know just a little more than you do," she'd say to her bright, expectant students, "but we all know so little." She'd try to ignite them with the same "awe and wonder and joy of learning" that had been Brearley's precious gift to her.

But beyond the classroom, she found Williams "a bad place to be single." Most of the other professors, older and in the next life-stage, were knee-deep in family. Starting a family still felt as distant to Judith as retirement and Social Security. She craved excitement, the fast-paced thrill-seeking of the single life. "I was too much of a live wire for that place," she admitted. On weekends she'd blast out of Williamstown to see her boyfriend, a med student at Dartmouth. She would continue to be involved with him for seven years, the equivalent of a short marriage. But she came to realize that they were too similar, both too "strong-willed and competitive." She knew she needed someone more complementary for the long haul, a ballast to her intensity and occasional impulsiveness.

After a few years at Williams, the thrill of teaching started to wane. "Math became too isolating" was the way she later explained her disenchantment. She had "always dreamed of becoming a doctor" for, as a top-notch athlete, she was fascinated by the human body and "how it was put together." But earlier she'd been daunted by the premed courses and not sure she had the stick-to-itiveness to make it through medical school. Now nudging thirty, more seasoned and confident both at work and at play, she felt ready to take on another challenge. Encouraged by her boyfriend, she tackled the necessary premed courses while still teaching her full math load.

Second Incarnation: Medical Student

Stanford was her first choice—as well as her boyfriend's top pick for his residency. They had spent a summer taking courses there and were instantly seduced by its near-tropical warmth, its protected campus dotted by palm trees and framed by golden hills, and its academic excellence, as well as its athletic enticements. When they both found out they'd been accepted at Stanford, Judith handed in her resignation at Williams. The provost was shocked, but supportive; a mathematician himself, he confided that he, too, had wanted to be a doctor. "It was just a little quirk of timing," she called the about-face in her life plans. "I could have ended up at Williams for life."

But once in medical school, she felt convinced she had done the right thing, both by postponing her studies at first, and then by making her move. In the seven years since she had graduated from college, the face of the medical school class had changed considerably. Now almost half the class were "older" students retooling from other careers, and there were five or six women of her age. Where the younger students may have bellyached about the workload or waffled in their commitment, Judith felt focused, energized, and up to the task. The classes riveted her; the studying engrossed her. She was paid to do extra research in medical computer science, which helped her cover the not inconsiderable tuition—and she still had time to hang out in the pool every day, ride her bike, and relish the outdoorsy, easygoing California life.

Still, by thirty-four and facing the residency in anesthesiology that lay ahead, she had that nagging something-is-missing feeling. She had fulfilled her academic dreams with her Ph.D. and math professorship. Now she was just shy of accomplishing her professional ones with her medical training behind her and a new career about to open up, which would involve a major commitment of time and energy. But what about her personal life? Suddenly those dreams of marriage and a family that she'd stuffed in the background until now demanded to be noticed. In the contemplative pause between one achievement and the next, between her overachieving twenties and her nose-to-the-grindstone thirties, she tuned in to another voice. Baby fever had finally caught up with her, and she knew her live-in lover was not long-term or fatherhood material.

Next Destination: Maternity

Judith was a goal setter and not coincidentally, a long-distance biker who trained almost as intensively for races as she did for medicine. The spring when baby lust took over, she entered a two-hundred-mile bike race in Davis, the Davis Double Century. She started at six on a cool, overcast morning and, after endless-seeming miles, pushed to the breaking point but knowing she was constitutionally unable to give up, she finished at four P.M. with the heat still merciless and her spirits soaring. Exhausted, but elated, she had finished first, the champion of the women's division.

Clint, the guy who won the men's division—he finished at two—turned out to be a Stanford student as well; he was doing a post-doc in applied physics. As they got to know each other over the next weeks and months, Judith realized she had found the complementary man she had once fantasized about. Clint shared many of her interests but was "less emotional, more reflective, less impulsive and critical" than she was. Here was a potential life partner, the hoped-for father for the family she now so yearned to start. Where life decisions were concerned, she could be ruthlessly direct. Within months she had moved away from her longtime boyfriend and committed herself to Clint. Before a year was up, they were married and almost immediately, Judith became pregnant. "When you're ready, it's a timing thing" was her typically matter-of-fact explanation.

But Josh's birth, though longed for and rejoiced over, also proved "a major roadblock from which you never recover." Combining devotion to raising him, tending her still-fledgling marriage, and keeping alive her commitment to her late-breaking medical career required energy that made training for a bike marathon seem child's play. Confronting the "major roadblock" of motherhood, she quickly realized, would necessitate some fancy footwork, not a frontal assault but a deft end run, using all those "switching" tactics that Brearley had given her the confidence to develop. The next phase of her medical education became a chess game between family and career; she countered each choice that favored medicine with a move that favored and supported family life. While Josh was still little, she shoehorned in a year of internship. Then she started and soon dropped a residency in anesthesiology, both because it bored her and because she wanted to stay home with her toddler. Then, to keep her skills current, she worked part-time as an internal medicine "fill-in" at the local HMO. Then she took time off again, this time to have a second baby, another boy, Elliot; and finally she switched her specialty to dermatology.

Her mentor at medical school suggested "derm" would be a fitting choice for Judith both as a doctor and as a mother, because it combines "pathology, diagnosis, and good hours." What he didn't know was that specializing in the treatment of skin finished some leftover adolescent business for her as well. As a painfully shy teenager Judith had agonized over her own changeable skin, which was more clearly a mirror to the insecurities within than she or anyone else had the nerve to discuss. Becoming a dermatologist would give her a chance to spare others the agony and embarrassment she'd suffered silently as a teen. As she resolved her patients' medical concerns, she knew, she could also provide a sympathetic and knowing ear for issues beneath the surface.

Still, once the choice of specialty was made, more juggling was required to dovetail family life, a demanding residency, and later a practice as a dermatologist. Again, her well-developed adaptive skills came in handy. She managed her residency by sharing it with another doctor/mother who also had young children; divvying it up added an extra nine months to Judith's rotation but also gave her extra time to be home with her boys. At forty-six, with her residency finally complete and her medical boards behind her, she at last faced the decision about how she'd practice the specialty for which she'd prepared so long. Starting her own practice seemed to fit best both with her independent, self-motivated style and with her rewarding, but demanding family life.

Multiple Roles—Dermatologist, Wife, Mother, and Daughter

"I'm my own boss, master of my own fate," she acknowledges now with pleasure and relief. As a dermatologist in private practice, she can fine-tune her schedule to fit her needs and her family's: she works Monday, Tuesday, and Wednesday from nine to five-thirty and keeps Thursday and Friday for herself to work out, read, take care of household business, and then pick up her sons at school by two-thirty. She recognizes and accepts the trade-offs she has made, knowing she feels at home with her priorities. "I'm a mommy-tracker," Judith admits, as she appraises how her career has unfolded in stops and starts and sometimes taken a back seat to family life. "I didn't end up being a totally driven career woman. Now people are the most important thing to me, not a supersnazzy career."

Still, even a mommy-tracker needs a strong infrastructure to help her juggle all her demands, and Judith has created—and been blessed with—a more willing and accessible support team than many. Its linchpin is her husband, whom Judith calls something of a "daddy-tracker" himself. A researcher at a Silicon Valley computer giant, Clint works intensely and has developed three patents, but he also makes family time and obligations a major priority. Judith says his career comes first—"I'm two-thirds to his one"—but Clint has also helped make Judith's career possible, pitching in when Judith has too many pulls on her time. He sees himself as a co-parent, not an adjunct, taking the boys to school or picking them up, running them to games, checking up on their homework, comforting and encouraging them just as Judith does.

Live-in household help has also kept the wheels of family life running smoothly. But her mother's presence has been the biggest lifesaver of all. After Judith's father died, when Judith was a first-year resident, her mother moved out from the East Coast and lived with Judith and Clint for six months each year for several years. Now she lives with them full-time. So she is able to provide steady and loving backup for both Judith and Clint when demands at work preoccupy them. Years earlier, Judith's mother was a traditional housewife, bucking up her husband's career, restless for her own self-expression, devastated when her children left home, cautioning her daughter to find work of her own so she wouldn't feel similarly bereft when her kids left for college. Now she's part of Judith's support team, enabling her daughter to combine family life with a satisfying career—and feeling valued as a mother and grandmother herself.

Despite the precious balance of work, marriage, and family Judith has achieved, bolstered by a supportive mate and an unusually involved mother, there are times when that balance becomes precarious. The last time we talk, Judith's sons have been driving her up the wall. They are now a highly energetic and vocal eleven and nine, still too young to be independent but old enough to think they know everything. "I get tired of all that testosterone," she sighs. "Josh and Elliot will fight over anything, even a crack in the ceiling. For the first time I understand why my brother has only one child! Two are so much work, and there's so much fighting. I'm tired." At forty-seven, even the long-distance bike marathoner occasionally runs out of steam.

Still, most of the time she counts her blessings and values the moves and compromises she's been able to make. "I've been lucky because I've had everything," she says. "I have a part-time practice, but I've chosen a less demanding career so I can have more time for my life." Her early education was pivotal, she believes, in helping her make important choices later on and weigh the trade-offs she could most comfortably live with. "Brearley gave me the self-confidence to say I don't want that high-powered career. But I still feel very much an intellectual, because I have that rich inner life. I feel life has so many rich things to offer."

As a skilled juggler and a deft switcher, she knows she has already had and will continue to have the opportunity to savor all those rich things, maybe not all at once, but certainly piece by piece—a challenging intellectual life as well as a satisfying emotional one, a rewarding career as well as a loving family, a vital marriage as well as a sustaining relationship with her mother and sons. When she found her way to dermatology—after years of detours into academia, into math, into anesthesiology—she swore she'd "never switch again." But it's just that ability to switch that has provided her the flexibility to create the fulfilling life she has now, to respond to her "high stimulus need" as well as her need to feel settled and secure. Being comfortable and adept with switching, she says, is "the feeling you can do anything. It's a good feeling, empowering. It means you're not stuck." At forty-seven, Judith feels settled, but not stuck, knowing that many more switches, many more incarnations are still possible. Like all of the class's most satisfied members at midlife, she is a master at reinventing herself.

Sources of Resilience

Two classmates, two jugglers, two many-layered lives they've invented and reinvented to become, at midlife, settled, satisfied, and secure—what traits link them and what differences mark them and what combination of both helped set them up for success? At first their differences seem striking, for their personalities and their stances toward the world offer quite a contrast. But their common features turn out to be even stronger. Cordelia is an extrovert who attracts attention and friends in every circle. Judith is an introvert who likes to keep a lower profile; she tends to have a few core friends but not a huge social circle. Their family histories differ as well. Cordelia was a shaky student from a divorced, unsettled family. Her mother's college dreams for her were grander than what she could, at first, achieve. Yet her political commitment owed a positive debt to her mother's activist vision, and mother and daughter bonded as dedicated and visionary liberals.

By contrast, Judith was an excellent student from a steady, solid family who provided consistent support both academically and emotionally. Becoming an academic star, as Judith did after a brief interlude of resistance freshman year, fulfilled her parents' dreams for her, and her academic successes—Ph.D., early math professorship, becoming a doctor at midlife—were in sync with her family's ambitions for her.

But although personalities, family backgrounds, and academic histories differed, Cory and Judith shared influential traits that made them successful copers and helped them seek out life's satisfactions as well as handle its disappointments. Even when academic savvy occasionally faltered, their emotional intelligence—that EQ that psychologist Daniel Goleman calls the sine qua non of adult success—was well developed in both and steadied them through life's challenges. As Goleman has explained, "People with well-developed emotional skills are more likely to be content and effective; people who can't marshal some control over their emotional lives fight inner battles that sabotage their abilities for clear thought and focused work." Cory's and Judith's successes in both their personal and professional lives drew deeply on their steady emotional skills.

They also shared an optimistic attitude and buoyant temperament, an ability to bounce back that could turn failures into successes and transform closed doors into windows to new discoveries. Both, for instance, rebounded from college rejections to make something better out of their altered plans. Facing and coping with disappointment and change was an invaluable life skill for those classmates who nurtured it, and the most successful, like Judith and Cory, were also the most successful at learning from their failures.

As young girls, both practiced what psychologists call "acts of required helpfulness," particularly for their mothers. Cory helped steady her mother when her drinking unsteadied her; Judith responded sensitively to her mother's feelings of loss when she left the nest for college, and sustained a connection that remained strong for life. Such acts of compassion turned out to have emotional returns to the givers, boosting their self-esteem and the confidence that they could cope with difficulties.

Their flexibility handling adversity and change as young girls also gave Judith and Cory the confidence to reinvent themselves, to redirect their life courses when adult needs and circumstances changed. Cory switched from politics to theater to teaching, weaving in both a lively family life and a strong commitment to service and social activism unbroken since the sixties; Judith switched from academics to medicine and switched her specialty from anesthesiology to dermatology and was able to adapt her career to make room for a late-life marriage and family. Judith's sixties idealism and humanism continued to be expressed both through her practice, where she often became a counselor as well as a physician, and on the home front with her sons, where she fought "affluenza," the rampant consumerism of the nineties, and encouraged "ethical living."

But neither of them achieved their successes or created their satisfactions single-handedly. Their adaptability was bolstered by a web of supportive relationships—mentors, husbands, even children, who gave them the chance to revisit their own childhoods. Both attracted significant people to them when needed and, just as crucial, had the survival instincts to turn away from relationships that were not right for them or could have done them harm.

At Brearley, both found mentors who believed in them and modeled for them the kind of richly layered lives they, too, would one day lead. For Cory, it was a drama teacher who was also a political activist and a contented wife and mother; for Judith, it was a Latin teacher who combined a productive intellectual life with a rewarding personal one. In their groundbreaking research on women's development, Carol Gilligan and Lyn Mikel Brown pointed to the life-affirming "resonance" a mentor can provide in young girls' formative years. "To be an authority on their own experience requires another person who will acknowledge them as such," Brown has written about the impact of the mentor relationship on adolescents, "not simply an audience but a relationship in which they're taken seriously."

Judith and Cory found these pivotal relationships early on, and as their adult lives began to unfold and professional choices dangled before them, both found additional mentors at defining crossroads. For Judith, a professor in medical school helped guide her toward dermatology, a specialty that would mesh comfortably with her intellectual and personal needs. For Cory, it was her husband, Sam, who helped show her, at an impressionable turning point, that a life of activism could be possible and productive. Indeed, for both Cory and Judith, having supportive, involved husbands was another crucial ingredient in their sense of fulfillment as adults. Both wisely chose mates who shared their multiple commitments—to work, to family, to each other—and considered themselves joint partners in making this life vision possible.

That young people create opportunities for others to help them become better copers was well illustrated by the 1992 landmark longitudinal study *Overcoming the Odds*, in which public health researchers Emmy Werner and Ruth Smith followed 210 high-risk Hawaiian children and discovered that one third of them, against all apparent odds, became confident, competent, and caring adults who "loved well, worked well, played well, and expected well." These self-reliant copers, it turned out, had been adept in school at recruiting surrogate caregivers and adult mentors to give them a helping hand—teachers, coaches, even more stable adults in the families of friends. These resilient kids were able to find their way to adults who would believe in them and show them how to move forward in the adult world even if their own parents couldn't.

Besides, although not necessarily unusually academically gifted, many of the high-risk kids who became successful adults had been able to develop special hobbies or talents, like art, writing, carpentry, even hula dancing. Developing these skills bolstered their confidence and self-esteem, but also, again, helped attract influential adults outside their nuclear families.

Although the odds they faced were nowhere near so unfavorable, for Cory and Judith, too, special skills and talents proved a vibrant source of lifelong satisfaction, a cornerstone of later professional achievement, and a lure to attract life-transforming people to them. Thus, like the Hawaiian youths, they, too, were launched on what resilience researchers like to call a "positive life trajectory." For Cory it was her dramatic flair, her gift for theater, that, even though her academic record was lackluster, turned out to be a key to satisfaction and success later on. Theater gave her an outlet for self-expression and a route to professional expertise and also drew her to her first mentor, Maggie Tucker, who became pivotal in helping her shape her life dream.

Special gifts in math and science were the talents that proved invaluable for Judith, and she had the energy and adaptability to shape a life course that allowed her skills to flourish, first in math, then in medicine. Like Cory's gifts, Judith's talents also attracted mentors who could guide her self-inventions and re-inventions. And for both Cory and Judith, the careers they established by midlife also allowed them to revisit and resolve childhood concerns and adolescent uncertainties.

Finally, they have both found ways to link the old world they inherited with the new world beckoning and revealing itself to them. They have both been able to integrate the traditions of the fifties—that dream of togetherness and strong family values—with the idealism of the sixties and the feminism of the seventies. They have chosen paths of service—teaching, medicine—where their political commitment and compassion could be expressed. They have remained loyal to their own mothers while becoming independent, productive, career-minded women. But they have not let their professional goals eclipse their commitment to their husbands and children; they have struggled to keep their lives in balance but, if pushed, have put their families first. Their careers have been satisfying, their successes personal and profound. They may not be super-women poster girls, nor will their achievements necessarily be the stuff of magazine cover stories. Their lives have been lives of quiet achievement in matters of the heart and mind, which they have come to believe count the most.

Can I draw conclusions from their stories about the traits that lead toward happy and successful lives? Cory's and Judith's choices, their successes and challenges, speak not only for their own experiences but also for those of the women of their generation balancing and assessing their lives at midlife. Although their intellectual lives were jump-started by a rich and rigorous education, this academic training was not the determining factor in their later accomplishments and pleasures as professional women. Brearley breathed the love of learning into both of them, but, in Cory's case, especially, the school's academic pressures also created intellectual doubts, which were quelled only by later achievements. Nor was their privilege or affluence what set them on a course to fulfillment. To be sure, family means secured education and opportunities and gave them the confidence to network their way through the system toward their goals. But coming from affluence took my classmates only so far; in fact, for several, having too much money proved to be a disincentive more than a motivation.

Three important traits shared by Judith and Cory seem to point toward balance and satisfaction at midlife. First, having a shaping talent or passion and the ability to commit oneself to it over the long run, despite obstacles, failures, dead ends; second, the emotional skills to negotiate challenges, to bounce back from failure, recommit after loss; and third, a web of supportive, loving, and empowering relationships that help make fulfillment possible. But both Judith and Cory are independent and gutsy characters who would scoff at the notion of a formula for happiness at midlife. Each has found her own route among a multiplicity of choices, a route that suits her and speaks to her own needs, a route she's carved out once and reinvented again and again. If anything, that's their secret to success: the willingness to do it their own way and if they fail, to get up and try again.

Thirtieth Reunion

When I return to Manhattan for my class's thirtieth reunion, I'm once again struck by the surprises of the second act. F. Scott Fitzgerald may have insisted to a previous generation, "There are no second acts in American lives," but for my classmates and their choice-rich, change-savvy generation, reinvention is all. When I left the twenty-fifth reunion, the mood was dark with disappointment and doubt. Tonight, five years later, although the background buzz has grown more somber, the overall mood has improved considerably. Against the background of loss, the seeds of new possibilities are continually being planted. With an acceptance wrested from shared life passages, my classmates comfort each other on parents' recent deaths. And with an honesty that would have been unimaginable in their secretive school days, they trade heartbreaking stories of their parents' aging and growing frailer.

"What are the signs of early Alzheimer's?" one worried classmate asks another, whose mother's case is so advanced that she has had to be institutionalized. "Losing things," comes the reply. "My mother would lose her glasses a dozen times an hour and they'd turn up tucked away in drawers, fallen between the newspapers." Another classmate describes a mother in the throes of dementia who wandered from home, lost her way, and returned only half-clothed. Despite the sensitivity of these topics, classmates draw comfort from sharing them with each other and breaking the taboo of what used to be considered hush-hush. Once weighed down by the pressures of containing family secrets—a parent's drinking, a divorce, a botched suicide attempt—now, at midlife, my classmates are learning to lighten their emotional burdens by sharing them. Raised to follow in their parents' secretive footsteps, they have up-ended their history—through therapy, through spiritual quests, through the countercultural sea change; now they tell all.

And though shaken by parents' aging and dying, this group is also shifting imperceptibly into the next life stage to become their families' elders, and the shift has infused my classmates with energy. Tangled up with painful losses comes the hope of renewal and re-definition. This time the heady perfume of small changes is in-disputably in the air when the class of '68 reconvenes at another knockout apartment with another staggering art collection of an-other just recently remarried classmate. Tonight's hostess, glam-orous in a dark velvet pants suit and flowing blond tresses, has recently traded in years of single motherhood after a regrettable first marriage for this promising second marriage. Her new husband is a wealthy older man who dotes on her and her children and has gen-erously hired two butlers, who serve the sliced cold roast beef, the liqueured fruit salad and dainty sugar cookies and dote on the aging boomers all evening. While my five-years-younger sister's reunion dinner that same evening is a casual self-service event, my classmates wallow in these butlers' ministrations, for all their political incor-rectness, a perfect symbol of the traditional old world that's still seductive in its last fading gasps.

Thirty years later, my classmates, like the Janus-headed genera-tion they are part of, continue to straddle the contradictions be-tween two worlds, between the traditional, protected, moneyed, and manicured world they were raised to take over and the startling new world that opened before them at graduation, chaotic, excit-ing, rife with change and possibilities. Finding their way through these contradictions continues to define them both as a group and as a generational subculture, constantly creating models where there were none before, inventing and reinventing their own lives to keep up with the explosive breakthroughs around them.

A handful lead fairly traditional lives that seem a throwback to their mothers'—social, supported by affluent husbands, filled with volunteering and devotion to children. But these remain the exceptions. Most have leapfrogged into liberation either by desire or necessity; some are single or divorced and managing on their own, or they're married and juggling financial and child-care responsibilities with mates. A few are comfortable on the vanguard of the technological as well as the social revolution. One childhood math whiz is now a bank vice-president in charge of technology; another, artier type has developed and is trying to market her own creative computer program. But most are still quicker to phone than to E-mail. When the school sets up a reunion website, only a very brave few of the most avant-garde take advantage of it. At midlife my cohort is still pulled in contradictory directions, between mothers with monogrammed stationery and children of the electronic age; approaching the millennium, my classmates are not entirely identified with either.

Nevertheless, all evening conversations hum pleasantly with word of small improvements, enormous changes at the last minute. A chain-smoker at the twenty-fifth reunion this time fiddles only with her glass of Perrier and brags that she has given up smoking for exercise. A troubled soul who did a stint as a topless dancer has now become a preschool teacher and is settling happily into a stable third marriage. A struggling artist, whose talent hasn't always been recognized, doesn't appear but writes to the group that one of her self-portraits is being featured in a prominent local show and urges classmates to see it, to give her that acknowledgment. Two who have long been unmarried are finally aflutter with romance—one is showing off her wedding ring (a first-time bride at forty-six!) and the other has just returned from a sailing vacation with a new boyfriend. Tanned and glowing, she looks years younger and mega-watts happier than she did just one reunion earlier.

Mulling things over later that night, I'm amazed at the turn-around in mood and fortunes in the five years between this reunion and the one just past. Or is it my perspective that's changed after three years of interviewing classmates and reconnecting with them for this book? Am I like Mark Twain's famous adolescent who left home for college scorning how little his parents knew and returned home after graduation amazed at how much they had learned in four years? Has my perspective shifted along with my classmates' fates?

When I first approached the class of '68, I was still looking for world-beaters, large-scale accomplishments, painters on a big can-vas who could incorporate and synthesize the tumultuous changes of the three decades since graduation into something dazzling and new. But after my three years of interviews and observations, of shared confidences and mutual revelations, I am more attuned to the struggles and breakthroughs of the everyday. Now I've come to appreciate resources previously hidden and applaud victories I might have overlooked before. Through my altered and perhaps more narrowly focused lens I now scan the smaller-scale accomplishments that might have escaped me before. Now I value the epiphanies of the inner life as well as the successes of the wide world, the private domestic pleasures as well as the public achievements. I recognize that many of my classmates have retreated from the challenges of the wider stage for the pleasures of cultivating their own gardens. "Maybe your horizons shrink as you get older," Sophia observed, "and you think you can have power only in smaller ways—in your family and your community." Now I see how my classmates and I are all making peace with the gap between the razzle-dazzle of being special and the comforts and delights of being wonderfully ordinary.

Beyond the wavering imprint of education, opportunity, and privilege, at various times both a blessing and a curse, and beyond the gifts of resilience or the pains of its absence, lay this challenge both for my classmates and for their cohorts turning fifty with the millennium: everyone of this generation, wittingly or unwittingly, has had to become a pathbreaker. Each one has had to harvest her own happiness, plumb for her own internal wisdom, and adapt herself to a changing world, both to keep pace with the demands of history and, most important, to listen to her own heart and please herself.

Between Mourning and Renewal

Every reunion has a theme, said a wise older schoolmate celebrating her fiftieth reunion just as my class was celebrating its thirtieth. "What is wonderful is that we're almost all precisely the same age," remarked this alumna to reporter Alex Witchel, who profiled the class of '48 for *The New York Times*. "So there's the menopause reunion, the wedding and children reunion, the Social Security reunion. You know what people are talking about, and that's very reassuring."

Nudging fifty, the class of '68 has still not reached the menopause reunion and may yet experience several worklife reincarnations before its Social Security reunion. But if the theme of the twenty-fifth was mourning the gap between dreams and realities, then I would name the theme of the thirtieth overlapping transitions—parents' illness and dying, children's growing up, and my classmates' own self-inventions and renewals.

My own life is suddenly overwhelmed by watersheds, as if to illustrate my point. In the days bracketing the thirtieth reunion, on my trip back to New York, this time with my entire family in tow, I celebrate my husband's forty-eighth birthday and my parents' fiftieth wedding anniversary, have a final meeting with my editor about the manuscript for this book, and accompany my mother—who's struggling against a life-threatening illness—to the hospital. After returning home the next week, we celebrate my own birthday and our older son's turning fourteen with a basketball party and burrito bash. And the gradually unfolding purpose of this midlife phase is revealed in the overlaps between events and commitments.

"My mother's dying is rebirthing those elements in myself that are important both to me and to her," observes Cordelia, who comes to the thirtieth reunion at a crossroads in both work and family life. A few months earlier her mother died—that "person of many talents and screwups," as she calls her, lovingly and honestly—and several months after her mother's death, Cory quit her high-school teaching job at midyear. Now she's struggling to find her next path, trying to uncover a commitment that will have value both personally and socially. She's searching for something that will link her to the political ideals she shared with her mother and also assure her that the time ahead will not be wasted, for her mother's death has made her more keenly aware of how fleeting and precious time can be.

For many classmates and women facing fifty in the year 2000, the loss of parents is interlaced with other losses that are sobering but potentially revitalizing. Youthfulness is waning—hair graying, bodies sagging—but wisdom is waxing. Certain creative options feel more constrained, but other unforeseen possibilities also reveal themselves. Children's growing up and leaving home creates an emotional gap but also more time for marriages and selves. Facing losses also mobilizes my classmates to redefinition and reinvention and reminds them to savor each remaining moment. Life has become both more serious and more potentially joyful. "In turning fifty," says Tess, "I feel like I'm really an adult. It's all been a practice round until now." Card-carrying members of the postponing generation—hesitant to choose careers, late-to-the-altar brides, and reluctant mothers—my classmates have finally grown up and into themselves, revving up for that second adulthood that begins at fifty. Indeed, current life-expectancy estimates suggest that women who make it to fifty illness-free have a good chance of living till ninety-two. So many of my classmates may very well be on the cusp of the second half of their lives.

While they grapple with obligations as "the sandwich generation"—caring for aging parents alongside growing children—they also yearn to take time for themselves, to tune in to their changing needs and desires, to listen to their own hearts' desires. Sarah has just left her high-stress and ultimately unrewarding job as a children's program administrator for a less stressful and statusy but infinitely more satisfying job as a preschool teacher. "I've decided to simplify," she explains. Her own mother died several years earlier—without reaching seventy—and Sarah is conscious of making her midlife years count. "Women in our family die young," she admits, "so I want to take care of myself. My body is changing and not for the better. Until now I've never gone to a gym. But now I don't want to worry about my kids so much, and I want to worry about myself more." Seeing fifty on the horizon, my classmates see their priorities alter and shift, their values coming more clearly into focus. Knowing that loss and sadness will be inevitable, they plunge forward more hungrily for pleasure and renewed awareness of what gives their lives meaning.

The Midlife Search for Meaning

If the crossroads of their twenties was the crisis of separation—the push-pull between home, school, and family and finding a place in the wider world—and the crossroads of their thirties was the crisis of authenticity—the need to listen to their own hearts beneath the din of what-do-others-think?—then the crossroads of their forties-turning-fifties is this crisis of meaning. Now they hunger to find a context for the losses and disappointments of midlife without giving way to despair, they search purposefully for pleasure and satisfaction. As the upheavals of youth give way to the redefinitions of midlife, my classmates are trolling for what energizes their spirits, nurtures their inner lives, sustains their energy, gives a deeper dimension to their plans. Once again they're wondering how their education serves them and if they must fill in gaps they may have earlier overlooked. Now their task is to connect the selves they were at eighteen—eager, anxious, bright, uncertain, idealistic—with the women they've become at forty-eight.

Many women of '68 do not have the lives they imagined as young girls nor often the lives they were raised and educated to expect. Fleeing the nest on '68's wings of change, at each life stage, they have scurried to catch up with a culture transforming itself; without obvious models, they've had to improvise their next moves. Some classmates live more unconventional lives than they would have predicted, several, more conventional. Some found career satisfactions but not the husbands and/or families they may have dreamed of to go hand in hand with their worldly ambitions. Others discovered the pleasures of marriage and motherhood but not the professional success they might have hoped for.

Wealth and material comforts have not buffered them from the random acts of fate; the gilded cage of privilege has not protected them from emotional turmoil. Unexpected crises, unforeseen illnesses, and deaths have jackhammered their plans, called for radical redefinitions, shifts of direction. Having been programmed to expect external rewards, my classmates, like many of this questing, questioning generation, have reached midlife most satisfied with internal rewards, with the intangible wisdoms of the inner life.

Polling my classmates at the thirtieth reunion, both the unconventional and the conventional, the professional and the homemakers, the spiritual and the worldly, I find several common themes in what sustains them, what infuses their lives with meaning. Surely it is not just a coincidence that all of these resources were first discovered at the school. Nearing fifty, they've reconnected with many of the same pleasures that nourished them as young girls.

Reading and the love of books is one such pleasure that has comforted them since they curled up on the cozy window seats of Brearley's Lower School library and lost themselves in a novel or let nonfiction expand their world. Virtually everyone I interviewed about her fondest memories of the school recalled this private yet sphere-widening pleasure, and cited reading as a lifeline and psyche-charger today. For Maisie, reading was a healing and soothing childhood escape from a highly adult-centered household; now she enriches her marriage by attending a book group with her husband. Judith unwinds after a long day's juggling by reading a few pages of *Emma* before she goes to sleep (she's reread the novel at least twenty times), and Jill read every book extant on divorce to keep her sane when her own marriage came undone.

Exercise is another value first touted at our school, which some took to naturally (Judith's happiest hours were shooting baskets in the ninth-floor gym) and others resisted mightily but have come around to in sagging middle age. In the era of President Kennedy's physical fitness program, exercise was next only to godliness—and literature—at the school. In high school girls were allowed to miss almost daily gym classes only if indisposed by cramps; they'd sign a "blue slip" to signify it was "that time of month." A famous couch potato, I signed so many blue slips each month that the gym teachers would periodically call me in to make sure that nothing was physiologically amiss. And when accomplishments were listed in the senior yearbook—choral society, team captains of the reds and whites—I was honored, tongue-in-cheek, as "captain of the blue team." But like the rest of my classmates, I've come round, in middle age, to the pleasures and benefits of moving. Every day, rain or shine, I swim my laps in the pool, as much for the endorphins as for the exercise. Cordelia walks vigorously with women friends. Sarah pushes herself to the gym. Exercise has reenergized middle-aged bodies and calmed anxious souls.

So, too, are my classmates and I sustained by women friends— whether exercising, going to book groups, or turning to each other for support and laughter. This, too, is a cherished value maintained from schoolgirl days. Unquestionably every classmate I spoke with, whatever her feelings about the school itself, said in one way or another that her most powerful memory of her education was of relationships. Girls studied with girls, gossiped and smoked clandestinely with girls, ate brownies, whispered with girls about parents, and consoled each other after breakups, lost their patience with girls and eventually forgave them—my classmates were women-identified women long before the women's movement gave these friendships a label.

Thirty years later these friendships still endure. One classmate invites several others to a slumber party for her fortieth birthday; another turns up drunk and disheveled on a classmate's doorstep and is immediately taken in. After Sarah's mother dies, we spend an hour on the phone, New York to California, rehashing every shared childhood memory, between hysteria and tears. Like sisters, my classmates and I share the bitter and the sweet and continue turning to one another and to a wider circle of women friends for enlightenment, pleasure, and support.

Books, exercise, women friends—these are the common pillars I find my classmates all lean on at midlife. But each has also searched for particular wellsprings that would sustain and enrich her and offer that crucial source of midlife meaning that is necessary for a successful second half of life. So I update and close the stories of '68 by listening one last time to each of my classmates, at midlife still in the midst of her search, still struggling to balance the legacy of being young in the sixties with the requirements of being middle-aged in the new millennium. Each tells a story that is unique but also representative of the crazy quilt of choices explored by this generation, threading through contradictions without a game plan—from social activist to new conservative, from physician turned soccer mom to rebel turned corporate player, from inner-directed midlife seeker to working-class heroine, dreaming of stability. This gamut of roles, this spectrum of choices, has been history's gift to them, and their ability to invent and reinvent their roles will become their gift to the next generation.

Cordelia—Midlife Activist

"My mother married again at fifty and took on a whole new life," Cordelia observes, restless and questioning at forty-eight. "One reason I left teaching after eleven years was that it was too constricting. But I haven't yet discovered my own space." She has a strong marriage that has weathered several incarnations, thriving children and stepchildren, financial security. She has devoted the last two decades to securing this home base, and now she's ready to widen her sphere. "Now I want to give myself permission to do what I want to do."

Cory knows that whatever she does next will, of psychic necessity, draw on her political idealism, her urge toward community service, her sense of herself as "someone who would change the world." That's been a constant since, as student government president, she stood before the class at graduation, in the unnerving aftermath of Robert Kennedy's assassination, and challenged every graduate to make her mark, to leave the world better than she found it.

But the aftershocks of '68 turned even some of the more politicized in the class cynical, until they felt "a chilling break from politics," in Emma's phrase. Raised, like Cory, in a very liberal, activist family with parents who "believed in working within the system for change," Emma grew up to believe "you could demonstrate against the government." Yet in Chicago demonstrators got their heads bashed in, and after that, as Emma put it, "the cynicism that had begun to creep in really hardened." Many daughters of sixties idealism who were also shell-shocked refugees from the debacles of '68 grew to adulthood more inner-directed than focused outward, more eager to change their own heads than to change the world. If anything, they were humanitarian hippies, not hardcore radical activists. Becoming parents, many of my more politically sensitive classmates tried to rekindle the fire of sixties values in their children. Indeed, one classmate, once the group's most outspoken radical, bragged that her greatest pride in her daughter came when the girl initiated a recycling program at her school. Like much of this confrontational generation, by midlife even the more politicized classmates had largely turned away from the barricades and back toward home, their neighborhoods, and their children's schools.

But Cory was different. Where others found idealism dissipating and political commitments dissolving or taking a back seat to family life or financial pressures, Cory managed to keep her idealism alive—organizing coal miners in Appalachia and then inner-city youth in Washington, D.C., in her twenties, and then in her thirties, bringing theater to prisons and later teaching suburban teens, no less needy because they came from privilege. Now as she nears fifty—the age when her mother's second act began—she's searching for a framework within which to rediscover and redefine her own ideals.

Not surprisingly, even beyond death, Cory's mother has provided her with one such forum. She has set up a family foundation with money from her second husband's estate and deputized Cory and her four siblings to administer the foundation and give away sizable chunks of money each year to encourage grassroots activism.

The family foundation has turned out to be not only an instrument for social change—empowering groups who would otherwise be disenfranchised—but also a catalyst for subtle personal changes. The board meetings have provided Cory and her siblings a place to explore and come to terms with the privileges of class and the responsibilities of having money, as well as to hash out sibling differences and ultimately bond more tightly with one another. At midlife Cory has pushed her idealism to yet another phase, learning how to integrate it into the puzzle of life within an extended family, making the political more personal.

Family Values?

When the class of '48 was polled for their fiftieth reunion back-to-back with my class's thirtieth about their greatest source of satisfaction, '48's answer came back almost universally: family. But among my classmates that answer is not necessarily the first that comes up. Many find themselves at midlife unmarried, divorced, and/or childless, so they have sought beyond family ties for their lives' shape and meaning. And even those classmates of '68 who are married, mothers, and professional women, still voice ambivalence at midlife along with their satisfaction. They seem almost surprised to admit to the pleasures they now find in domestic life, as if betraying some intellectual mandate, some feminist promise. Surely this ambivalence is a piece of this no-role-model generation's legacy, still uncertainly caught in the middle, neither as unabashedly pro-family as the generation before nor as confident about juggling and balancing priorities as the generation after.

Judith—Soccer Mom with an M.D.

"I don't have the life I imagined," admits Judith at forty-eight, love and loyalties divided among her marriage, her school-age sons, and her dermatology practice. "I thought I'd be more of a doctor/scholar. But instead I've become more of a happy housewife type! I'm more the all-American mom with the van, driving the car pools, going to Little League games. I thought I'd have a nanny and she'd take care of the children." Finding personal and professional fulfillment in her thirties, not her twenties, Judith is no less satisfied for being a late bloomer. Indeed her medical career and her marriage-of-equals are both crucial touchstones of midlife vitality and contentment. The two sides feed and balance each other. Secure in her career, she can adjust it for marriage and family; secure in her marriage, she is free to pursue other commitments as well.

But having postponed motherhood until her late thirties in favor of academic goals and professional training, she now finds herself more of a hands-on mother than she would have predicted. And the medical career which she prepared for so single-mindedly has been "toned down," as she puts it, to accommodate the needs of family life. "I have a part-time practice," she explains simply, "so I can have more time for my life." Assessing the gap between dreams and realities, between expectations and achievements, is, for Judith, as for everyone in this age group, a necessary part of midlife reckoning. "I felt I could have gone further," she reflects. "I could have done more academics, published more, done more science. People look at me and say, 'God, how much you've achieved,' and I think, 'Yes, but not as much as I could have.' "

Yet she accepts the shortfall in achievements with equanimity, not bitterness, because her heart knows that without her family her work life would feel hollow and meaningless. "Even though I'm very goal-directed, my family comes first. I don't think I would have been motivated even to go forward in my career if I hadn't had kids. Having Josh turned my life around." Imagining facing fifty without her husband and sons, she knows she would have been "depressed and existentially bored."

Like Judith, most of the jugglers in the class of '68—many of them also late-blooming mothers—have found themselves at midlife scaling down fast-track expectations for a slower-lane, family-centered life. Cory took a time-out from the pressure-cooker of high-school teaching for self-inventory and family time; Judith chose a part-time medical practice to allow "more of a life"; I also may have written fewer articles in exchange for more time to enjoy my sons' soccer games and class field trips. But for Judith, as for most successfully juggling women of this generation, it's the pleasures of multiple roles that provide the greatest reservoir at midlife. "Your life has more meaning if you do lots of things," Judith concludes. "You have to have people in your life who matter, and then you have to be in the mainstream or you feel totally removed. I feel lucky to have balance between work and family, because it's hard to do. I definitely think you have to try a little of everything."

Sophia—Old-Fashioned Homemaker, New-Fashioned Life

As a schoolgirl Sophia imagined that by the time she hit forty she'd be doing "something of major import"—perhaps running a company on the scale of the high-profile cosmetics company that finally made her solvent in her thirties. Certainly she dreamed she'd be operating on a big stage, making big-time money, the kind that bought influence, powerful friends, and the ability to effect grand-scale change. When forty came and went—and her achievements remained more personal than multinational, her sphere the home front not the boardroom—she bristled with anger, ached with disappointment and self-criticism. But, as for many ambitious, starry-eyed boomers, nearing fifty has brought a reappraisal, an acceptance and appreciation of what she does have—the private, unpublicized achievements of everyday family life.

"I feel incredibly lucky to have made it to this point married to the same wonderful husband and have two wonderful kids. And everything about my children works! I didn't expect it to happen," she admits with joy and relief.

Sophia looks back on her childhood as a time of "divorce, difficulties, and disarray." Those early upheavals provoked a long, partying adolescence of "rebelling, not caring, doing things to get attention." Once she scribbled to me in an eighth-grade math class her party-girl credo for those years: "It's all right to be chaste—but it's more fun to be caught!" But as her twenties turned thirties, she burned out on the chase. Now at forty-eight, she admits sheepishly about her metamorphosis from enfant terrible to sweetheart of the status quo, "I'm old. I don't have the energy to be bad!"

Once her skirts were daringly short, and her shirts opened daringly low. Now, when we meet at an Upper East Side bistro for ladies who lunch, she's the model of middle-class propriety—hair just coiffed, stylish silk blouse buttoned discreetly to the neck, tailored trousers. And the whole ensemble is topped unapologetically by a fur coat. "I'm an anachronism," she admits with a Mona Lisa smile.

"I'm the only one of my mother's children who's 'doing the life,' " she says—their mother's life, that is. "After all those years of rebelling, I bought the whole thing"—the Fifth Avenue apartment with the silver and the antiques, the summer place in Southampton, the daughter at Brearley. Even that venerable alma mater, bastion of tradition and back-to-basics, seemed for a time too liberal for Sophia's reclaimed conservative standards. But she's considerably happier now that the school's new headmistress has steered the school "back to the middle ground" from its earlier swing toward what Sophia deemed too much political correctness. Middle-of-the-road veering toward conservatism is where Sophia now feels most at home. Once an untraditional traditionalist, now she's far more traditional than un-. For her the sixties are a forgotten blip on memory's radar screen, not the lifelong source of energy and idealism they've remained for Cordelia.

It's her home that centers and grounds Sophia. She works for herself as an interior decorator—that impresario of the home—and loves welcoming her kids home from school every day, providing the milk-and-cookies security and predictability that she never had. "Coming through chaos, having stability, is healing," she says. "For the girls in our class, like me, who never really had a home, we're happy to have a home now."

Maisie—Artful Self-Reinventor

"I think I'm much happier now than when I was younger," Maisie confided at forty-five during our first interview. "I've done a lot of things I wanted to do. I'm making more money than I ever thought

I'd make. I have a strong marriage. Good friends. A wonderful lifestyle." Only a small doubt clouded her glowing self-confidence. "I'm still much too busy. I have to figure out how to slow down."

Maisie has a knack for ferreting out resources for survival and a talent for reinventing herself. She sought therapy when she needed it—and blossomed from its insights; she turned around the suicidal depression following the breakup of her first marriage, and reinvented herself with a second career and second marriage that were both significantly better fits; and she found ongoing sources of spiritual and emotional nourishment in yoga and co-counseling.

But a year or two after we first spoke, Maisie had an unexpected jolt that may yet create another need for reinvention. She was diagnosed with lupus, an illness that comes with joint pain and fatigue. Although she's "not acutely sick," her illness has provoked some soul-searching. "There might be some relationship between the go-get-'em corporate lifestyle and getting sick," she conjectures, remembering how her chronic busyness was the cloud of doubt shadowing her life's accomplishments and pleasures. "I got that drive for excellence and perfectionism from Brearley, and I just don't know how to give myself a break." Even this past year, despite her illness, her bank rated her their most productive loan officer in her extensive division.

Knowing now that she may not always be able to work full-out, she's trying to think about how to adjust, how to survive on less money. But, she also admits, work has also been a crucial source of adult identity, "since I chose not to have children." Instead, she's searching for other wellsprings, other sources of meaning and connectedness. Yoga and co-counseling have continued to be anchors, although she's doing more yoga ("physical exercise is so important") and less co-counseling ("I stepped out of teaching gracefully"). She has also added a community service project offering vocational guidance for troubled teens on probation, "kids on the cusp who could go one way or another." Despite her family's wealth, her privilege, and elite education, she, too, was once a troubled teen on the cusp. Perhaps she wants to give a hand where she could once have used one.

But even with her humanitarian urges, her fantasy for the future remains home-based. "I'd love to take the summer off to read, do yoga, paint the front steps. For someone who rejected the house-wife role, keeping my own environment pleasant has become more important."

Tess—Purveyor of the Magic

"I keep plugging away, putting my passion into horticulture," says Tess, whose career has rocketed more swiftly than any classmate's, from her fledgling start at Disneyworld's tree farm to her current leadership of their entire landscaping division, six hundred employees strong. "I have friends all over the country—that's my family. It's not the way I imagined it, but so be it."

Tess's talent and passion for plants have brought her content-ment, financial security, national recognition, and a sense of be-longing. In the past year alone, not yet fifty, she's been appointed Chair of the American Horticultural Society and won two presti-gious awards—the Massachusetts Horticultural Society's highest honor, the George Robert White Medal (once awarded to Cen-tral Park's creator, Frederick Law Olmsted), and the Agricultural Alumni of the Year award from her alma mater, the University of Arizona. Returning to Arizona to accept that award tugged her heartstrings and gave her some moments of anxiety, for it was there, as an undergraduate, she had met her husband, a fellow landscaper. "I hadn't been back to Arizona since our divorce," she said, adding wistfully, "A lot of what started there with hope and excitement had changed dramatically."

Still, if her passion for horticulture didn't secure a lasting mar-riage, it has nonetheless brought her many other "satisfactions of the soul." Not the least of these has been the chance to bring a heal-ing gift to very sick children—and an opportunity to discover new meaning and connection at midlife. Recently Tess has gotten involved with a local philanthropic organization called "Give Kids the World." Its mission is to bring terminally ill children and their families to Disneyworld, for, remarkably, Tess reports, 70 percent of children who are asked to name a last wish ask to see Mickey Mouse. Something about the famous mouse's vulnerability—coupled with his magical properties—speaks to their own fears and yearnings. Visiting the theme parks, all expenses paid, these children and their families are also housed and fed in a magical Disneyesque setting. When Tess was asked to donate one of her signature topiaries to decorate this site, she hesitated at first. Away from her vigilant care, she has found, most topiaries brown and wither. But compassion overruled practicalities, and finally, she offered a fabulous sea creature, each of its humps a gracefully sculpted hedge.

One day a family brought their little girl who was dying of leukemia; she hadn't walked in months and the family had been told she had a scant two weeks to live. But when the girl saw Tess's multiple-hedged, minutely leafed, fantastical underwater creature, she shrieked and ran toward it. Her family and the other onlookers stood by in awed silence. The young girl lived for another six months. Tess calls this transformation "respecting the magic," and being its fairy godmother is one of the things—beyond money, status, reputation—that gives meaning to what she does.

Emma—Rebel Turned Corporate Player

"Never in my wildest dreams did I picture myself in a corporate role," says Emma about her midlife stability as a textbook editor at a major publishing house; it has been hard won after years of hard living. Once she was the dope-smoking, class-cutting, nose-thumbing rebel extraordinaire. Now, almost fifty, she's responsibility and respectability incarnate—she has a steady job with benefits and a pension, a condo and a cat "whom she loves more than anybody in the universe." "The scariest thing is I'm doing it, I'm advancing! My star at the company is on the rise. I used to say, 'I don't have the corporate mentality.' I thought of myself as the rebel, the person who'd say what she thought, no matter what."

But decades later, decades of playing fast and loose, of emotional upheavals including suicide attempts and hospitalizations—not to mention a brief respite in a nunnery—after all that rebelling-without-a-cause, Emma "got tired of the whole sixties thing." Eventually she felt broadsided by the "backlash to love, peace, and set-fire-to-the-flag-if-you-don't-believe-in-it." Finally, an emerging inner voice of self-care and responsibility began to whisper, "It would be nice to have some money and pay my bills." The transition from sixties rebel to panty-hosed worker bee was gradual, but once initiated, inevitable; her reversal reflects the reversals of a generation, once trashing but eventually embracing respectability. "One day I started shaving my legs," she remembers with a wry smile; the next thing she knew, "I was dating a banker."

Today she's quietly proud of her textbook-editing work, calling it "the revenge of the nerds." "All those people who could never get dates are now making textbooks for their old friends' kids!" she laughs, dragging deep on a cigarette—the one "bad" thing she still refuses to give up. Once the "hippie chick" at the center of a biker/rocker crowd, now she's happy to count her professional colleagues, those textbook-writing and -editing nerds, among her best friends. Still, even buffered by a strong circle of friends, she knows there's a romantic void in her life. "Friendships I can do," she says candidly about herself, "communing with people at work, yes. But relationships are tough. And I haven't tried much recently." Her social life has been desert dry.

Not long ago, she had coffee with an old boyfriend who's also hitting midlife unmarried. "What is it about my life that kept me from marrying?" she asked him. "It's the age, the times," he answered, and Emma found herself agreeing. "A lot does have to do with the sixties," she believes. "All that searching, that journeying, kept people like me from going the automatic route of college, marriage, a job, and children."

Now, ironically, all her searching has brought her full circle—back to the church. "The church has always been part of my life," she realizes. "I've tried to leave it, marry it, redefine it." The particular church she's found her way back to is a small, welcoming Episcopal one (her own flavor, she says, unlike her minister father's Presbyterianism), where she attends services every Sunday and is deeply involved in the church community. Listening to the liturgy and the choir singing Bach cantatas has opened her spiritual side like a sunflower opening to warmth and has been particularly healing after the hypocrisy of the convent. The God she has rediscovered at her church is not God the Father but "the goodness of core creation."

"I have to believe in something beyond humankind, which is fascinating but not comforting," she confides, "something that draws me up short when I'm not acting sensitively to other people—a tool for living." For Emma the source of midlife strength and resilience has turned out to be a giving-over to a larger, deeper, more all-encompassing purpose and presence beyond the everyday. Although she may lack certain resources that other copers draw on—a supportive mate, a mentor outside the family who believes in her and guides her—this rediscovered spirituality centers her and fills her.

Then, too, the iconoclastic minister's daughter now admits she has a crush on her minister. They've spent the last year or two getting to know each other—a few steps forward, a few back, "just like junior high school," she jokes. Now he's separated from his wife of twenty-five years, but he's also dating someone else, so Emma's relationship with him, by definition, will have to go slow. "We're becoming friends," she realizes, "and that's good, because I can do that." "What am I looking for?" she asks herself. Recently her minister friend preached a sermon "about peeling back the layers of the onion." She sat transfixed in the middle of the congregation, too shy to make eye contact, because she felt his words bore through her, touch her open heart. "We all long for closeness, yet are most afraid of it," she admits, naming her deepest longing, as yet unfulfilled.

Pamela—Vision Quester with Resources

For the fiftieth birthday of their sister, Shanti (formerly Candace before her own spiritual awakening and renaming), Pam and her four siblings hunkered down in a cozy mountain retreat and offered Shanti a gift from their hearts. Pam's offering was a line that expressed most clearly the treasures of her quest: "I live to make the world bring the seen and the unseen together."

Decades of searching had ruled out the more conventional answers—the thrills of skiing and romance, the pursuit of arts and crafts, the security of marriage and family. Years of therapy had helped her burrow down to an unshakable core, and reaching that, she had slowly begun to fill up the spiritual void that had haunted her since childhood. Now, at forty-eight, she could say unequivocally, "The most important thing in my life is the spiritual." "I lead a different life than I was raised to lead at Brearley," she confides at the thirtieth reunion gathering. "What matters to me most now is how I can have a peaceful heart. I don't want to be busy all the time. I'm much less of a go-getter and achiever than most of us." While her very private, inner-directed agenda baffles some of the more socially minded in the class, on her own terms, for her own needs, it fits right.

Together with her companion Matthew—after six years she's proud to call him her longest life partner ever—Pam leads and pursues vision quests. Modeled after a Native American custom, the quests take fellow seekers into a serene and distant spot, usually the desert, whose stillness and endless expanses ready the spirit for awakening. There they fast and soul-search and commune with nature in the hopes of gaining deeper awareness of their life purpose and receiving a mystical vision. "The things that happen on a quest are a mirror to you," observes Pam, who likens the story interpretations that conclude the quests to dissecting myths back in the Brearley classroom, looking for themes, for the meaning beneath the meaning.

While Pam's quests seek intangibles—awareness, healing visions, peace of mind—they are made possible by the very tangibles that also define and scaffold her life, the independent income from the trust fund left her by her wealthy grandfather. And where this money has unarguably bought her the chance for a lifestyle many would envy—with its opportunities for seeking, for travel, for independence and pleasure—her inheritance has also come with a price. A major piece of her midlife search for meaning has involved coming to terms with the burdens as well as the privileges of her wealth.

"Money is a real gift if it doesn't kill you," she acknowledges with a bittersweet smile, assessing both sides of the ledger. "It's nice to have extra money and not spend every minute working for it. It gives me options. I'm glad I have a nice home, and it has never crossed my mind to be with a man for his money or his security." But she also admits to the internal pressures that come with privilege, the subtle corrosion of self-esteem, the guilt and self-doubt. "I can feel I ought to be saving the world with all my free time," she says, still grappling, like most veterans of '68, with the idealistic legacy of the sixties. "I come from a family that's philanthropic, so there's a pressure to do that. I believe in being philanthropic, but I also believe in having a life which is free to just be. Instead of do, do, do." She pauses, searching for her own comfort zone. "I see people in Aspen who don't do and don't give. I'm looking for something in the middle."

Not too long ago Pam linked up with a foundation for people who grew up with family wealth. The first time she sat around the conference table with this roomful of peers, she "was almost in an altered state," so liberating was it to share the pleasures, pitfalls—and social mandate—of having money with others who didn't need explanations or apologies. Now, making collective decisions about which socially meaningful projects to fund, Pam finally has both a channel through which to share her wealth and a place to discuss the strings attached.

"I'm a big believer these days in balance," she concludes, voicing the class of '68's most common theme, the yearning of a choice-rich but sometimes over-optioned generation. "The first part of my life"—the Brearley and Vassar part—"was about the intellect. The next part has been about the emotions and the body. My life's journey has been to bring it into balance." She acknowledges the "oddball ways" she has come to integration—being a ski bum, doing psychological work, keeping a journal, going on quests. "The part I need to move into is moving out into the world."

Jo—Survivor on Horseback

The last time I speak with Jo, she has just returned from a spirit-recharging walk up Putney Mountain to watch the sunset with her little dog. "Part of keeping myself going is doing stuff like that," she tells me about her program for self-preservation. "It's important for me to take care of myself—eat well, get enough sleep, try not to abuse myself mentally or emotionally. That's easy for me to say, but not to do. When I'm depressed, I eat a lot of chocolate and spend a lot of money, and I have been quite depressed on and off lately. My life is far from perfect. I'm a compulsive debtor with more clothes than you've ever seen, and I'm still trying to pay off big debts. When things get crazy, I try to regroup and recenter."

She pauses and lets out a long, eloquent sigh, which conveys beyond words her tough lot at midlife—the backbreaking and only seasonal work as a roadwork inspector; the constant money worries ("In the summer I make great money but in the winter, I'm a pauper"); the stress of maintaining a relationship with a boyfriend who's got joint custody of three needy kids; the burdens of single parenthood as her son confronts a stormy adolescence and her nineteen-year-old daughter, now a teenage single mom, struggles to find her way in the world; her own ambivalent grandmotherhood ("Emotionally I'm still trying to feel like a grandmother, but it's so weird").

More than any other classmate, Jo's story at midlife continues to be caught up with sheer survival. And with all her awesome challenges, she lacks some of the resources that have helped the best-coping women in the class become balanced and settled at midlife—the academic confidence, the emotional steadiness, the ability to satisfy parental expectations or find a supportive adult outside the family to believe in and inspire them, the sustaining web of relationships or shaping talent or passion that leads to satisfying work and, in turn, helps create financial stability. And lacking these resources Jo has done some major-league floundering. But she also has an uncanny instinct for her own survival—how else did she bounce back from her husband's violent, untimely death and carry her family forward?—and her sources of pleasure and meaning at midlife are no less sustaining for being unusual and unconventional.

I choose to close with Jo's story because, for me, it represents the fiesty power of survival against all apparent odds. In a circle of the privileged, she remains a self-styled working-class heroine.

Horseback riding has been a lifeline since she was a horse-crazy young girl. Galloping freely with the wind at her back offered then what it continues to offer now—freedom from family constraints, intense physicality, wordless affection for and from a devoted beast. She craves these rewards more than ever now. And with a small cache of money she has managed to save for the first time ever, she has bought her own horse, a four-year-old purebred Arabian gelding. "Believe it or not!" she says, beaming, still amazed she can make her own dreams come true. She's also taking classes in "centered riding," an approach that combines body work with more traditional instruction. It has become a metaphor for what she's looking for in life—that release of tension, that willingness to go with the flow instead of fighting it, that sense of balance.

Jo has always been one to live in her body, not in her head. That physicality is part of the reason that Brearley was such an uneasy fit for her, for the school's culture valued verbal facility above all else. But now, as if to accept, even flaunt, the fact of her body power, she has covered herself with tattoos. Right around her fortieth birthday, that life-altering cusp between youth and midlife, she stumbled on a tattoo artist at a fair. She knew his name and good reputation; his specialty was Japanese-style motifs. And Jo had always fantasized about having a tattoo. He gave her her first, an exotic bird unfurling itself across her upper back, and when she appeared at the twenty-fifth reunion, she wore a sweater that dipped to a V in the back to show it off. Several tongues wagged after that. The more typical alum might show off a piece of heirloom jewelry or a new diamond ring. But tattoos? Sophia wondered nervously to her husband whether their own Brearley daughter would one day end up pierced and tattooed.

But Jo was emboldened by the splash she made. Since then she's added new tattoos whenever she's had the time, the money, or the whim. Now her body is covered with them, her legs quite black with ink—a Japanese woman on the back of one leg, a huge dragon on the other, flowers and water and fish across her chest and up and down her arms. She gets a kind of dreamy, faraway voice when she talks about the tattoos. "It's funny," she says, "but they make me feel pretty, they're so beautiful and bright." She likes to feel like "a canvas," like a work in progress. The unconventional spirit suppressed beneath all those years of schoolgirl uniforms has finally been released and taken flight.

Alanon has been yet another life-affirming, strength-giving resource for Jo. When she first took her teenage daughter to AA to confront a scary drug-and-alcohol problem, Jo sought out the network's support for herself as well. She was desperate for something to lean on, some clue about what had gone so colossally off-kilter. The weekly meetings, the sharing of similar struggles, the assistance of a supportive "sponsor," as well as the gentle nudging toward faith in a higher power—the structure of AA both introduced her to a new language and taught her to trust her own instincts, her own innate frankness. Secrecy and denial had long been her family's style, hardly unusual for that generation. Indeed, when Jo's teenage daughter, Brianna, first entered treatment, Jo's mother hid the truth behind a smoke screen. "Brianna went away," she told her friends.

But now Jo saw what a sham this practice of cover-up had been and what a wobbly reed to hold on to. "I've always been real upfront and open about stuff that's going on in my life with anybody," she admits quietly but with a newfound confidence. "I don't know whether it's a quiet revolt against the way I grew up. Or whether it's me and that's just my personality." AA gave her the courage to face, accept, and finally share the truth of what was really going on in her family, however difficult. "Well, this happened," she's comfortable saying now. "Why the hell should I be ashamed of it? You know, it's life."

"It's a constant struggle, but it's so rewarding when something goes right," says Jo about the path she's hacked through the bramble brush of her past toward her vision of balance, of honesty and integrity. She yearns to wake up in the morning and see her way clear to the next step. She dreams of living a simple life, imagines "an old house in the middle of nowhere" where she could live with her lover, her children healthy and grounded, becoming her friends. "I really have come back to the stuff I thought about a lot in the sixties," she realizes, "the spiritual stuff, being at peace with myself and the earth. Now I'm doing a lot of letting go. I'm going to spend the rest of my life trying to get back to where I was at eighteen. In a different light, with more experience."

Girls Becoming Women

"Didn't you find your classmates were everything they used to be as girls—just more so?" several friends asked me after the reunion, voicing a common preconception about personality's continuity from childhood to adult. But no, for the class of '68, change has been the only constant, and metamorphosis has been all. And the most satisfied in the group turn out to be the best reinventors of self. The happiest are those who have mended the holes of childhood and turned around its affronts. Thanks to lessons learned in the aftermath of the sixties—the recovery from the drug culture, the liberations of therapy, the insights of spirituality, personal quests, and introspection—many have remade themselves into someone new, someone linked, of course, to the girl she used to be, but kinder, gentler, and usually happier.

So Pamela has transformed herself from a bossy twelve-year-old who bullied weaker children into a contemplative and compassionate grown-up, more accepting of others' vulnerabilities and of her own. Cordelia's rambunctious energy has become the fuel for her activism, and her girlhood bluntness has matured into the honesty that grounds her. Sophia and Emma, two of the wildest and woolliest, have become almost unrecognizably staid, but also more secure than they ever were as rabble-rousing young girls.

Judith has metamorphosed from a self-conscious, self-doubting duckling into a confident and capable swan, admirably juggling responsibilities as wife, mother, daughter, and doctor. Maisie, buffeted by her parents' divorce and the chaotic upheavals of her twenties, has reinvented herself several times and created her own midlife security in a happy second marriage and as a yoga-practicing banker. And Alice has rebounded after her twin sister's shattering suicide, benefited from a circuitous journey, and now found that working as a designer can be a way to share her own vision. I, too, once timid about change and hesitant to express myself, have found that becoming a writer has helped me both face change's inevitability and learn to speak my own voice.

What have I learned from the class of '68? What wisdom can I now pass along to my sons? I've learned that it's fine to be a slow bloomer, to take a long, meandering time to grow into yourself. Some of my wildest and showiest classmates blasted out of the starting gate so early that they burned themselves out before they even touched their potential; others, who were least noticed early, matured more slowly and turned out to be the most dazzling later on. I've also learned that while training to achieve and pushing to succeed may be seductive, allowing yourself to fail and then learning to pick yourself up and move on may be the most lasting, empowering lesson of all. I've seen how success and satisfaction, if and when they do come, may not come in the shape that was once imagined but in a shape that may be a better fit for the person you've become. I've observed that being special can be a blessing or a burden, and relaxing into being ordinary can be the most delicious reward of all. I've seen how holding tight to secrets can seem, at first, the easier, self-protective course, but having the courage to speak the truth can be a more lasting liberation.

I've realized that education's most important gift can be the inspiration to find a passion and the guidance to look for it not just in the realm of the intellect but beyond—in arts, in sports, in the treasures of friendship and intimacy. I've learned that being comfortable with change is the most important skill to develop early, and once discovered becomes a lifeline to reinvention and the wisdoms of the second act. And searching for answers and conclusions, I've accepted that each of us has to find her own lessons, mine for her own happiness on her own. And though I wish to spare my sons the heartaches of their own search, I know they, too, will have to discover their paths on their own in their own good time.

A journalist, lecturer, and teacher, Elizabeth Fishel has written extensively on family issues for national magazines, including *Redbook, Child, Parents, McCall's, Ms.,* and *Cosmopolitan.* She lives in northern California with her husband and two sons. This is her fourth book.

ABOUT THE TYPE

This book was set in Galliard, a typeface designed by
Matthew Carter for the Merganthaler Linotype Company in 1978. Galliard is based on the sixteenth-century
typefaces of Robert Granjon.